The Hypnotic Investigation of Dreams

The Hypnotic Investigation of Dreams

C. Scott Moss

MENTAL HEALTH CONSULTANT
NATIONAL INSTITUTE OF MENTAL HEALTH (USPHS)

This book was written and edited by C. Scott Moss in his private capacity, and no official support or endorsement by the U. S. Public Health Service (National Institute of Mental Health) is intended or should be inferred.

John Wiley & Sons, Inc., New York · London · Sydney

Library of Congress Catalog Card Number: 66-28758
Printed in the United States of America

Preface

It would be difficult to identify two more arcane and cabalistic subjects in the whole field of present-day psychology than hypnosis and dreams. Certainly, few topics have held such a sustained fascination for most people. Ancient man, imbued with animistic conceptions of the world, tended to view dreams as direct communications from the supernatural. Dreams were often considered to possess a greater reality than conventional sensory impressions and were highly esteemed as an indisputable source of advice and guidance. It is widely accepted today that dreams can be highly revealing personal documents, although the average man continues to find them ethereal and their meaning elusive.

Hypnosis has a similar history of long and intimate association with the mystical and the mysterious, and it, too, has often been imputed preternatural if somewhat sinister powers. The fact that magic and science remain inexorably intertwined is nowhere better exemplified than by the curiously ambivalent attitudes of interest and skepticism manifested toward hypnosis in professional circles. Despite recent evidence of increased acceptance by the major societies in medicine, psychiatry, and psychology, hypnosis remains a highly controversial subject, and there is no assurance that it will not again fall into disrepute, notwithstanding the best efforts of interested professional persons to safeguard against the exaggeration and sensationalism that contributed to its demise in the past (Moss et al., 1962).

This book discusses the relation between hypnosis and dreams or, more specifically, the employment of hypnosis in the investigation of dreaming. A fundamental problem, of course, is that dreams have a mercurial quality and do not lend themselves to objective scrutiny,

v

nor does their interpretation lend itself to consensual validation. The attraction of hypnosis to investigators of the dream is that it allegedly affords one of a few select techniques whereby it may be possible to manipulate experimentally some of the more important variables involved in the production of this phenomenon.

In the professional literature of the past fifty years, there have been recurring reports of the profitable employment of hypnosis as an adjunctive technique in psychotherapy and, more germane to this book, of its use in the clinical analysis and even experimental study of dreams and other forms of unconsciously derived symbolic behaviors. Various investigators, have reported, for example, that hypnosis can facilitate recall of forgotten dream elements or encourage the completion of a prematurely terminated dream, and that some hypnotized subjects actually have the capacity to "dream" in response to suggestion or the capacity to interpret the meaning of unconsciously determined symbols. It has been claimed, in effect, that hypnosis provides access to the symbol-translating mechanism within the psyche and, as such, is of inestimable value in the exploration of both the formation and meaning of dreams. These provocative claims have not gone unchallenged; however, it is a measure of not only the complexity of studying dreams experimentally, but also of the antagonism of the psychologic community to hypnosis that such prestigious assertions have stimulated so little really rigorous research.

The first half of this book (Part One) provides a comprehensive review and critique of such studies as do exist. It focuses on two fundamental questions. What are the characteristics of hypnotic dreams and how do they compare with spontaneous night dreams? What is the mechanism of their production? Implications for future research involving hypnotic techniques in the experimental investigation of dreams are highlighted throughout the book, particularly in combination with the exciting new electrophysiological studies that are currently effecting a renaissance of scientific interest in the study of sleep, sleep mentation, and dreams. Part two of this book consists of reprints of twelve outstanding clinical and experimental studies; they are referenced into the body of the text of Part One and discussed at appropriate places. Because a considerable number of years have elapsed, in some instances, since they were written, authors of the earlier reprinted articles have provided a brief, informal commentary on their own work from the perspective provided by the passage of time.

A conscientious effort has been made to strike a balance between the skeptical, critical stance of the experimental psychologist and the clinician's ready, even enthusiastic acceptance of causal relationships. In some respects it may be scientifically premature to bring this diverse material together in view of the obvious discontinuities in existing knowledge. However, it is hoped that this book can make a substantial contribution by a sober evaluation and clarification of basic issues, while carefully refraining from prejudging evidence that is not yet available.

An anthology of this nature would be impossible without the active cooperation of many persons. I thank the investigators who contributed articles, those who provided details of present and projected studies, and those who graciously contributed their well-considered reactions to the manuscript: Joe Kamiya, Marguerite Kirsch, Gerald Levine, Perry London, Dorine Loso, and Martin Orne. Special appreciation is extended to Drs. Isidore Ziferstein and Jiří Hoskovec, and Gosaku Naruse for their contributions to the sections on dream research involving hypnosis in the Soviet Union and Japan, respectively. Finally, I wish to thank my wife, Bette, for her encouragement and support and for the conduct of correspondence as well as the editing and typing of the several drafts of this manuscript.

San Carlos, California
September 1966

C. SCOTT MOSS

Contents

PART TWO *Selected Readings*

Contents

Part One

Chapter 1

Historical Prologue and Early Experimental Studies

THE PSYCHOANALYTIC CONCEPTION OF DREAMS

In spite of thousands of years of intense interest, little progress was made toward the scientific understanding of dreams until the nineteenth century, when Sigmund Freud verified their importance as a means of access to a little-suspected, inner world of mental life. In the process he came to credit dreams as the "royal road to the unconscious", and developed free association as a technique for investigating them. In a retrospective appraisal of his life's work, Freud wrote that his monumental book, *The Interpretation of Dreams*, "contains, even according to my present-day judgment, the most valuable of all the discoveries it has been my good fortune to make. Insight such as this falls to one's lot but once in a lifetime" (Freud, 1931a, page xxxii).

Freud accorded this book such high esteem because its publication marked a turning point in the development of the psychoanalytic movement. Psychoanalysis was conceived as a system of technical procedures for the treatment of the psychoneuroses, and the analysis of dreams was first intended simply to facilitate psychotherapy. However, the concept of repression, which was originated to explain neurotic symptom formation, was extended as an explanatory concept for dreams and became recognized as the foundation for a generalized theory of unconscious mental processes. The judgment of history may well substantiate Freud's self-appraisal; certainly, no psychoanalytic writing has attracted greater attention, generated such heated discussion, or stimulated more research.

The central proposition of the psychoanalytic theory of dreams is that dream formation is an unconscious event and that the form of the dream which eventually emerges is a compromise formation be-

3

tween the demands of unexpressed sexual or hostile impulses and the resistance of moral attitudes which exercise a censorship function. According to Freud, these covert, ego-alien impulses are transformed or disguised for the purpose of evading censorship by the mechanisms of dramatization, condensation, displacement, and secondary elaboration—processes which he collectively labeled the *dream work*. Thus in psychoanalysis the dream has both a manifest content and a latent (or repressed) meaning, and the interpretation of the latter appears to be resisted by powerful forces. It was in his attempt to understand the language of the dream that Freud first differentiated between a primary and secondary mode of thinking: dreams were regarded as a distorted, perceptual-hallucinatory form of direct wish fulfillment vis-à-vis the logical, orderly manner of thinking of normal waking life.

In later formulations Freud recognized the dream as a regressive or primitive mode of thought, although he continued to maintain that the form of the dream was still a disguise as well as a language determined by the state of sleep consciousness. In his revised theory Freud also concluded that the censorship function operates almost exclusively through the mechanism of displacement or symbolization. The process of symbolization thus achieved an elevated and singular status.

In psychoanalysis, symbolism acquired a specific, restricted significance that differs from the usual literary meaning. A symbol is generally regarded as something that stands for, represents, or denotes something else. The conventional symbol, such as a word, token, or sign, is an accidental or contrived representation; however, Freud viewed the symbols that express unconscious mental content as determined by some essential physiognomic resemblance. More importantly, he differentiated between so-called true symbols and other modes of indirect representation, such as substitution, allusion, or imagery, although admitting that the distinction was often arbitrary. Two of the distinguishing characteristics attributed to the "true symbol" were, first, that it possessed a universal or constant meaning and, second, that it depicted a content outside of the subject's waking awareness. As Jones succinctly stated the case: "Only what is repressed is symbolized; only what is repressed needs to be symbolized. This conclusion is the touchstone of the psychoanalytic theory of symbolism" (Jones, 1912, p. 116). Because symbolization, as the term is used in psychoanalysis, is a process which serves not only to represent but to disguise, an interpretation of a true symbol usually evokes a reaction of surprise and incredulity on the part of the subject, since he is supposedly unfamiliar with its latent meaning.

An individual's associations to his dreams were believed absolutely necessary for a correct interpretation, except when a symbolic form of representation had been employed. Because of their constant or universal meaning, these symbols could be directly interpreted. The independence of symbol interpretation from the dreamer's associations was considered not only possible, but absolutely necessary, "because as a rule, associations fail to materialize, or if they do, they are often confused and inadequate (Freud, 1931b, p. 15). In fact, the absence of meaningful associations was accepted by Freud as evidence that a "true symbol" had been encountered. Faced with the problem of establishing the meaning of dream symbols, Freud advocated that psychoanalysis generalize from its knowledge of mythology, ethnology, and linguistics. Paradoxically, while admitting that "the symbolism occurring in these other fields I have named is by no means confined to sexual themes," Freud, nevertheless, maintained that "in dreams the symbols are almost exclusively used to represent sexual objects and relations" (Freud, 1920, p. 174). [Readers are reminded, however, that in his autobiography Freud stated emphatically, "I have never maintained the assertion which has so often been ascribed to me that dream interpretation shows that all dreams have a sexual content or are derived from sexual motive forces" (Freud, 1935, p. 84). It should also be acknowledged that within analysis considerable controversy has always existed about the interpretation of dreams without associations: most analysts today feel that this is not appropriate.]

Freud, then, did not regard symbols as exclusively or even primarily a problem of dream interpretation but as basically a problem of the understanding of unconscious or primary thought processes. The dream was only the most singular example of symbol formation. He was convinced that the person who is skilled in the technique of dream interpretation also possesses a key to the understanding of myths, fairy tales, folklore, religious rites, jokes and witticisms, neurotic symptoms, and psychotic behavior, as well as the unconscious motivations of the normal man.

Freud thus believed that the mental development of the individual parallels the evolution of society, and the terms "infantile" and "primitive" were largely synonymous. The study of dreams, folklore, and ethnology were all considered supplementary. Just as dreams were viewed as regressive manifestations of the individual, so myths were regarded as the dreams of a society. In this context, myths are not merely metaphorical expressions deliberately invented by primitive peoples, but rather the only possible expression of certain intuitive, subjective insights concerning the nature of man and the universe surrounding him, for a given state of mental development. In other words, people who speak in metaphors regard these symbols as reality and, as with the dreamer, are capable of recognizing this fact only in retrospect, from the vantage point of a more advanced level of conceptualization.

The stage had actually been set for many of Freud's most profound insights by his own early experiences with hypnosis. An interested student and translator of the work of both J. M. Charcot and A. A. Liebeault, the leading practitioners of hypnosis in that day, Freud also collaborated with another Viennese physician, Joseph Breuer, in the development of a unique "talking cure" of hysteria (Breuer and Freud, 1895). By the employment of hypnosis, Breuer and Freud convincingly demonstrated the causal connection between hysterical symptoms and unfortunate childhood experiences, which in turn led to a recognition of potent unconscious forces. The penetrating insights which evolved out of these early experiences were only gradually articulated and painfully woven in ensuing years into the rich fabric of theory advanced by psychoanalysis. Freud soon abandoned the use of hypnosis as a treatment modality, although the reasons for his aversion to this technique remain conjectural. However, there is no doubt that his rejection of the technique had the effect of discouraging the employment of hypnosis by most members of the psychoanalytic fraternity.

The revolutionary nature of the theory that Freud advanced is better appreciated when contrasted to the conception held by his medical contemporaries. They regarded dreams as the product of irregular excitations of nervous elements in a cerebral cortex largely paralyzed by sleep, and any logical components were attributed to a close anatomical or physiological relation among the cortical elements involved. There was no problem of the "meaning" of a dream for Freud's medical colleagues, because a dream was not susceptible to logical interpretation.

Freud, himself, was fully cognizant of the need to validate his speculations experimentally. In his *Revision to the Theory of Dreams* (Freud, 1931*b*) he expressed alarm at the tendency of psychoanalytic practitioners to accept uncritically his admittedly tentative formulations. He wrote, "The analysts behave as though they had nothing more to say about the dream, as though the whole subject of dream-theory were finished and done with" (p. 16). Freud recognized that the psychoanalytic system must inevitably outgrow his incomplete formulations and that its ultimate value could not be judged by the faith of the many who became zealous converts to its doctrine. In the face of a complex and uncertain subject matter, there was evident appeal to many in the "closure" provided by the comprehensive scope of analytic theory. A legion of papers by psychoanalysts on the topic of dreams and their analysis discloses a tendency toward clever, dogmatic speculations, far removed from objective, behavioral observations.

It is not this author's intent to promulgate the psychoanalytic theory of dreams in any detail or to review again the many existing theories of dreams. It is evident that, whatever the limitations of Freud's conceptualizations, they had a great germinal effect, energizing a vast amount of study and activity in the field. As Rapoport (1965, p. 104) stated it, "Freud's contribution to the psychology of the future remains immense and will remain so even if every one of his conjectures turns out to be false, because he brought man's symbolic life so clearly into focus."

Experimental psychology, which has often indulged in caustic criticism of psychoanalytic theory, has also tended to neglect the study of symbolic behavior, particularly spontaneous forms of preverbal expression. As a result, there is even today no generally accepted definition of symbolism. The sharp distinction made by many authors between sign, signal, and symbol, between discursive and nondiscursive (socially agreed-upon versus idiosyncratic) or conscious and unconscious symbols, and the like, are dichotomies advanced more for purposes of illustration and discussion rather than as valid depictions of man's actual symbolic behavior. Hacker (1965, p. 731) captured the attitude of many authorities on an essential point when he wrote that "regardless of fine subtleties of definition, symbolism is a basic attribute of human behavior and not an archaic, frustrated, repressed, regressive, primitive, pathological, or defective form of behavior."

Man is quite obviously the symbol-producing and utilizing creature par excellence, and the process of symbolization is precisely that which distinguishes human from subhuman mental operations. A persuasive case has been advanced by psychoanalysis for studying the full spectrum of symbolic behaviors, with special emphasis on dreams, daydreams, and marginal states of awareness as a means of retaining contact with the collective wisdom of the human race as expressed in the myth and of keeping in touch with the deeper layers of the individual personality. In view of the resurgence of scientific interest in sleep and dreams, the time would appear propitious for a thorough appraisal of hypnosis as a possible avenue to the understanding of the nighttime fantasy and other preverbal symbolic manifestations of human behavior.

EARLY EXPERIMENTAL INVESTIGATIONS

Karl Schroetter is credited with the first published report (1911) of the use of hypnosis as a technique in the experimental investigation of dreams. In an early revision of *The Interpretation of Dreams* Freud noted that Schroetter had already experimentally confirmed the occurrence of sexual symbolism in dreams. Three reputedly unsophisticated subjects in "deep hypnotic sleep" were induced by Schroetter to dream about certain prescribed content, including tabooed or sexual activities. The suggested dreams gave many evidences of the mechanisms of displacement, condensation and secondary elaboration, as well as a striking use of symbols. Dream suggestions ranged from isolated words, sometimes combined with real or suggested bodily stimuli, to designated areas of circumscribed or general behavior.

Schroetter considered the product quite similar to nocturnal dreams, and the symbols utilized as consistent with those being advanced at the time by psychoanalysis. Sometimes symbolization in the reported dreams seemed a spontaneous act and at other times it was evidently the result of specific suggestion. Schroetter was mainly interested in the manner of translation of a suggested content into a symbolic representation, and he had little interest in his subjects' personal wishes, needs, and experiences. The importance of the hypnotically induced dream to him was that the experimenter assumedly knew the meaning in advance, thus obviating the need for analysis. Schroetter's failure to obtain detailed associative material from his subjects prohibits any accurate reconstruction of their dreams, but he did recognize that the phenomenon of transference was involved and that the hypnotist sometimes played a role in a suggested dream. Unfortunately, the investigator committed suicide soon after his preliminary report, and there is no evidence that he and Freud conducted any personal communication on the subject.

In an extended series of experiments, Roffenstein (1924) and others failed in an effort to replicate Schroetter's results—subjects either did not dream or, contrary to the expectations bred by psychoanalytic theory, reported frank sexual activities without distortion, even when symbolic representation was directly suggested. Roffenstein suspected that Schroetter's subjects may have been familiar with Freudian dream theory after all, but finally he found "complete proof" of the correctness of the original report and of the validity of sexual dream symbolism with one naïve subject, although it was necessary to direct her to distort the suggested content.

More sophisticated experiments were performed by Nachmansohn

(1925) who was interested in how the suggestion was shaped by the personality of the subject in his dream. Whereas preceding investigators were interested primarily in the mode of symbolic representation and made their interpretations only in accordance with knowledge of the dream stimulus, Nachmansohn took into account the subject's personality, background experiences, and free associations. Identical themes (for example, intercourse and pregnancy) were suggested to several subjects or the same subject was presented with one theme in different forms. Nachmansohn observed that the extent of distortion seemed proportional to the complexity of the personality.

In a test of the fundamental Freudian hypothesis that the function of dream distortions is to protect sleep, Nachmansohn gave the same subject dream contents for both direct and disguised dream representations. It was observed that anxiety accompanied direct representations with much greater frequency, and Nachmansohn concluded, "We can assert that censorship, with the aid of distortions, endeavors to maintain sleep." Nachmansohn also introduced the first effort to establish a control group: he found that waking subjects, given unlimited time, were unable to invent dreams comparable to those produced almost immediately in hypnosis. It was further recommended that hypnotic dreams might expedite psychoanalysis through the revelation of repressed needs, wishes, and fears.

It is unfortunate that these first imaginative studies were not actively pursued, because the investigators displayed remarkable ingenuity in anticipating many basic issues involved in this type of research. It is clear from these reports that many variables interact to determine the outcome: the personality of the subject, the nature of the hypnotic relationship, the manner in which the specific suggestion is administered, and the type of the content suggested. Above all, it was clearly established that the hypnotic subject is not a mere symbolizing automaton. Dreams tend to range far beyond the original stimulus and are commandeered as a vehicle for the expression of highly personalized wishes and conflicts. The more general the dream suggestion, the greater the possibilities for personal contribution to the dream. [Rapaport has provided an impressive critique of these early studies (1951, pp. 234–287).]

In the period 1925–1943 very few experimental studies involving the hypnotic investigation of dreams merit mention. Klein (1930) described the influence of discrete physical stimuli (for example, the smell of creosote and the sound of a tuning fork) on the "imaginal associations" or dreams of hypnotized subjects. Characteristically of Klein's results, one subject who was pinched on the hand invariably dreamed of a black rat, whereas another subject whose hand was touched with cotton dreamed: "A cow licked my hand." In a startlingly direct attempt to elicit Freudian (sexual) symbolism, subjects were subjected to a gentle stimulation of the genital region or were asked to fondle a candle or a cotton-covered cardboard triangle. Further reinforcement was provided by the olfactory stimulation of perfume, kissing of the neck and forehead, stroking the hair, and whispered amorous words. Klein stated that "We could find no evidence for the psychoanalytic view of distortions" and, in a conclusion based solely on inspection of the manifest content, estimated "that the chances are not over 10 per cent of dreams are sexual."

In an investigation of the representation of space and time in dreams, Welch (1936) instructed hypnotized subjects to respond to six highly structured dream stimuli, such as walking a specified distance along a familiar road or watching a clock for a prescribed period of time. The resultant dreams never exceeded two minutes in duration, although wide individual differences obtained in the average time required for the assigned tasks and in the number and detail of reported visual images. The only constant element was an adherence to the suggested logical sequence. Welch also noted that, in the absence of a specified content, subjects sometimes dreamed until awakened.

A major study, reminiscent of the first promising investigations, was finally reported by Farber and Fisher (1943). They successfully repeated the earlier experiments in which hypnotic subjects were trained in the production of dreams and concluded that "Dreams obtained by hypnosis or by posthypnotic suggestion have all the characteristics of spontaneous dreams, and the subjects do not make a distinction between them." An important innovation introduced by these investigators was an exploration of the capacity of the hypnotized subject to translate the "dream language." Presented with a wide range of symbolic phenomena, such as dreams, myths, and psychotic productions, a few subjects demonstrated an apparent ability to interpret such content. There was, in some instances, a high degree of intersubject agreement. As an additional control, subjects were questioned about the dream before and after hypnosis, and in no case provided comments comparable to those obtained under hypnosis. *This study retains a position of prominence in the field and has been reprinted on page 115.*

Chapter 2
Clinical Studies of Hypnosis and Dreams

EARLY CLINICAL APPLICATIONS

The tantalizing possibility that hypnosis may yet provide a means of appreciably reducing the often extended duration of psychotherapy has always been a main attraction to clinicians. Advocates of hypnotherapy claim to have successfully treated all forms of psychopathology from the neuroses and psychoses to addictions, psychosomatic disorders, and even organic conditions. There is general agreement, however, that, viewed in its proper perspective, hypnosis is an auxiliary technique and in no way substitutes for sound psychotherapeutic experience and skill. An impressive array of specialized hypnotic techniques are available to the psychotherapist, many of which involve some manner of memorial revivification, imaginal activity, or other forms of fantasy involvement.

A psychiatrist, Milton Erickson, was among the first to make extensive therapeutic application of specialized hypnotic techniques, which he skillfully tailored to the unique needs of his individual patients. It is not surprising to find that he also pioneered the clinical applications of hypnosis in the exploration of dreams and symbolism. An early study by Huston, Shakow, and Erickson (1934) used hypnosis to induce artificial complexes by the implantation of two equally obligatory but mutually exclusive suggestions. The induction of a temporary neurosis provides a method for studying the relations between the nature of the implanted conflict, the resulting symptom picture or "choice of neuroses," and the unique psychodynamic personality structures of different patients. A variation of this technique was devised by Erickson (1935) in the presentation to a patient of a *symbolic formulation* of an actual deep-seated personal problem.

The procedure employed was that of fabricating a story that would parallel and symbolize the patient's neurosis in terms of an ordinary and credible, but unpleasant instance of social behavior. This story was then told to him while he was deeply hypnotized in such a fashion that he would believe it to be a true account of an actual past experience, one which he had repressed completely. In the case of a patient suffering *ejaculatio praecox*, Erickson formulated a fantasied incident in which the patient was encouraged in a clumsy effort to deposit his cigarette ashes in an ashtray belonging to an attractive girl. There appeared to be an identification of the induced conflict with the original neurosis in the mind of the patient so that when he had relived, abreacted, and gained insight into the suggested conflict, he made a spontaneous clinical recovery from his original symptom. Erickson wrote a second article (1944) to explicate the method, and McDowell (1948–49) employed this technique in the successful treatment of a second patient suffering from premature ejaculation.

The first thorough discussion of the use of induced dreams in psychotherapy was by Wolberg (1945), who proposed that the hypnotic instigation and interpretation of dreams can play a vital part in hypnoanalysis. He stated that dreaming under hypnosis can bring about the recovery of forgotten memories and experiences, aid in the knowledge of transference reactions and the dissolution of resistances, and help in the recapture of nocturnal dreams that have been repressed or distorted by secondary elaboration. Wolberg reported: "Dreams may be artificially stimulated on command during hypnosis or they may be posthypnotically suggested to appear later during spontaneous sleep. Hypnotically produced dreams have all the characteristics of spontaneous dreams" (p. 184). He also cautioned that the ability to dream in response to a hypnotic suggestion must be developed slowly through a training process and at least a medium or deep trance is required.

F. I. Regardie and J. M. Schneck were among the first to report hypnotherapy cases involving use of hypnotic dreams. Regardie (1949) described the brief, successful treatment of a male homosexual in which the decisive tactic was the patient's interpretation of his own hypnotic dreams. Regardie comments: "It was soon discovered that he could be made to dream of any topic, about any conflict, or any person in his background—dreams that were far more dynamic, direct, and clear than any nocturnal dreams" (p. 6). These induced dreams were coupled with age regression under hypnosis, allowing study of the chronological development of crucial problems and relations. In a second paper, Regardie (1950) reaffirmed his belief in the efficacy of age regression in combination with hypnotic dreams as a method of tracing the development of a conflict and thereby measurably reducing the time and expense of psychotherapy.

In a series of reports, each based on the single patient-subject, Schneck first provided an account of the role of dream analysis with hypnosis which resulted in the relief of a troublesome symptom (1947); next reported an investigation of the psychoanalytic tenet that all dreams occurring the same night are dynamically related (1952); and finally concluded from the inspection of the nocturnal, hypnotic, and autosuggested dreams of a woman undergoing hypnotherapy that no differences existed between these products with respect to the extent of embellishment and the nature of symbolization (1954).

An innovative approach, originally described by Moreno and Enneis (1948) and elaborated by Krojanker (1962), combines the techniques of hypnosis and psychodrama in a therapeutic reenactment of a disturbing dream. The dreamer or so-called protagonist reenacts the original dream. He is next encouraged to enter hypnosis and to redream a "corrective version," more acceptable solutions to the issues represented in the dream being suggested either by the dreamer or the therapist, such as a happy ending in lieu of a distressing one. The protagonist is then asked to thoroughly rehearse the modified dream through hypnodrama with the assistance of "auxiliary egos" who portray the other characters populating the dream.

This approach derives from the premise that it is possible to change even unconscious expectations and behavior by the employment of action-oriented psychodramatic techniques and that the symbolic correction of fantasied or dream conflicts is facilitated by the diminished consciousness and lowered resistance to therapeutic suggestion produced by hypnosis. Advocates argue that the skillful combination of hypnosis and psychodrama results in a highly realistic simulation of actual problem situations—a corrective experience that is therapeutically far superior to mere verbal discussion of a problem.

THE HYPNOTIC INTERPRETATION OF DREAMS

In studies clearly foreshadowing the investigation by Farber and Fisher, Erickson collaborated with L. S. Kubie in the report of two separate case studies which demonstrate the exceptional ability of hypnotized subjects to understand and interpret symbolic modes of thought. The first case (1938) involved the treatment of a young female patient who suffered from an acute depressive reaction. She manifested several bizarre symptoms, one of which was an encapsulated obsessional drive toward repetitive "doodling" of a geometric design involving cylinders, triangles, looping spirals, and straight lines slanting in all directions. In response to the hypnotically implanted suggestion that her "unconscious" would inform her of the meaning of her scribbling, she soon revealed that these drawings were a symbolic representation of a repressed conflict. Her interpretation was objectively verifiable, proved to be correct, and contributed to an early resolution of the problem.

In the second study (1940), Erickson and Kubie provided another impressive account of the ability of hypnotized subjects to intuit the meaning of unconscious and symbolic modes of expression. Detailed observations of the manner in which one hypnotized subject was able to interpret the complex, cryptic, automatic writing of another, were provided by a series of autohypnotic episodes, each of which resulted in new and spontaneous insights. Although neither subject could decipher the writings in the waking state, both of them eventually arrived independently at identical interpretations. Because automatic writing suffers from many of the same types of distortion found in dreams, an implication of both of these studies is that hypnosis can provide a reliable means of translating the dream language. *A reprint of this informative article begins on page 101 of this book.*

It is rather astonishing that experimental psychologists have paid so little attention to the allegation that at least some hypnotized subjects have an exceptional talent for the analysis and interpretation of symbolic content—as if the contention did not deserve serious consideration or had already been negated. The type of clinical evidence that many hypnotherapists have found convincing is well illustrated in the following sequence, which represents one patient's facility for interpreting his own spontaneous nocturnal dreams.

DREAM. The patient found himself in a room in which a long box covered one whole wall. It had a dozen square holes in it, several feet off the floor and in a straight line. These holes were filled with water. Atop the machine and over the holes were tubes filled with water of various hues. Someone stated that each tube represented "a different location in the world and the color of the water, its calmness. If the water is very dark there was a bad storm." One of the tubes was extremely dark and the man said that a ship in that area was in extreme danger. The patient then heard a voice calling for help. "I rushed over to one of the holes and told a fellow to hold my left arm while I plunged in my right. I fished around until I found something that seemed to be caught and I pulled on it. Some strong force seemed to push me away and I slipped and fell on my face, but not before huge quantities of wreckage from a ship came out of the hole." The scene suddenly shifted and the patient found himself on a tropical island, talking to a blond girl. "She said that even if I did deserve this vacation that she was still going out with the other fellow—that he had better looks and money. Then she reached into a car, took out a candy bar and started eating it."

Waking associations. To the *box* the patient associated a feeling of dislike for any type of complicated machinery. The general scene reminded him of a story he had watched on television the previous evening in which there had been a room housing two big dynamoes; a bad storm had caused one of them to fail, with the result that the hero had to climb inside to fix it. He also had a strong sensation of water boiling and bubbling. The memory of the finger-catching episode brought associations of various objects that had been stuck—an icetray, a drawer, a window latch, etc. The patient also recalled that the force pushing him away had made him fearful that he would fall on his back—a thought that aroused anxiety and apprehension and reminded him of a time when he had slipped on ice. At this point he remarked that his eyes had begun to water and additional associations failed to materialize. Hypnosis was quickly induced by a preestablished signal.

Hypnotic associations. The central meaning of the dream as revealed by the patient's further associations was as follows: The *generator* represents his mind and the holes are hidden recesses therein. The fact that there were a dozen holes depicts the element of time (twelve hours in a day and twelve months in a year) and emphasizes the long duration and continuing nature of his conflicts. The stormy *water* symbolizes his inner turbulence or hostile emotions. The activity throughout is symbolic of the therapy process and of his dawning awareness of the intense and pervasive hostility felt for his wife and father—a knowledge that he found overwhelming. He had allowed only occasional, very limited, and controlled expressions of hostility heretofore (the small *tubes* over each hole). With the therapist's encouragement (the "fellow" who held his arm) he had boldly plunged into this area. The *wreckage* represented his fear of the havoc that his hostility could cause, including the possible dissolution of the therapy relationship itself.

The patient's hypnotic associations to the brief, final dream fragment are presented verbatim in order to capture the full flavor of how these interpretations developed.

"It seems that I'm trying to reach her with words more than with action or by attempting to do anything. Whatever it is that I'm trying to do she is refusing it . . . . It looks like my wife but she has light hair and is somewhat taller and thinner, but there is a definite facial resemblance. . . . My mouth is moving and I seem to be talking but I'm not really saying anything. But evidently she can hear because she is shaking her head 'No.' . . . It was suggested to the patient that he could now hear his voice. I'm saying, 'I love you, please talk to me, let's argue this thing out, aren't you getting enough affection?' She shakes her head, 'No.' That means, 'No, I'm not' to my question, but it also means 'No,

I don't love you.' She then goes over to the car, gets in, starts eating a candy bar and then drives away." . . . *Candy bar:* "She likes the candy bar more than she likes me. I think of affection, something substantial or solid, but also that maybe it is something that is here now but later will be gone. The candy bar means her devious ways of getting affection, material things, even though they are satisfactions that won't last." *Blond hair:* "No, not blond, but light that is, grey hair makes me think of my mother. The girl is also my mother in some way or another . . . . [It was suggested to the patient that upon a signal the "mask" of the character would drop away and he would see clearly who it was.] . . . Why, it's myself that I'm looking at—as if I had on a wig or a mask. It seems like me, but it isn't. That is, it looks like me but it is still my wife. Actually it is both of us, both Ellen and myself. We both have the same problem; neither of us can show affection or feeling for the other, we can't talk out or discuss our problems . . . . I can see a scene that took place several years ago, the time I had a fight with my wife and her mother and how we almost broke up and got a divorce . . . . I feel that it should have warned me that Ellen was a mother's baby. When I think of it, I think that I was a fool for marrying her. But then again, maybe if I had been more considerate and showed her some affection then she wouldn't be like she is. I always felt that I had to win her from her mother. Even to this day she is afraid to offend her, has to call her every day so that she won't become angry. But it is the same thing with me, I guess, she with her mother and me with Dad!" Here the parallel nature of these relationships was discussed. It became clear that his inability to cope with the wife's relationship to her mother reflected his inability to cope adequately with his father; and that because of the latter relationship he found the former extremely irritating and threatening. The displacement of repressed hostility from his father to her mother was clearly depicted; the displacement of hatred of self to wife was also delineated. The patient continued: "If I can't like myself, I can't like anyone else, especially Ellen who is so much like me. Seeing both Ellen and myself as the same person in the dream shows me this—I'm trying to reach Ellen and at the same time I'm trying to get to myself as well." . . . [The "light hair" represents the close identification of the wife and her mother, the domination of the daughter by the mother, and the need to win her away; it also reflects certain aspects of the patient's own mother.] "When I think of light hair, I think of how grey Mother has gotten from her mistreatment by Dad. Living with a man like that for 26 years would be enough to make any woman grey. In the dream I also feel that I am trying to reach my own mother as well as to Ellen, to show her that I love her, too. But I can't. In this way it is a situation parallel to that with Ellen. So actually the girl in the dream is three people: Ellen, my mother, and myself. It also represents the idea that much of my difficulty is my own fault, that if I had treated them differently, they would be different. It makes me feel bad. I feel that like Mother, Ellen could get grey hair from living 26 years with me. It's like a jigsaw puzzle, all of the pieces are dropping in place." . . . *Car:* "It is a big convertible—the kind of car which in my opinion is unsafe. It is a means of escape, but an unsafe means. It stands for childishly keeping things inside, as I have always done, of getting away from things." . . . *Beach:* "Makes me think of water, something that I have always been afraid of. It, too, represents the past, my fear of saying or doing things, an unsafe means of escape—as on an island, my inability to escape or get away."

"I come back always to thinking that Ellen, my mother, and I are alike in that all three of us have always tended to withhold our emotions and thoughts, that each of us was dominated by someone of whom we were afraid . . . . I think again of last Saturday evening and Ellen's hesitancy in talking with me. She had to force herself because she was afraid of my reaction, of a rebuff . . . that she does these things which I consider irrational because it forces my attention upon her, but more than that, it is her way of showing freedom from my domination. It is so much my own fault. I've never been an easy person to talk to. Seeing her relationship with me as I do now, it is like a mirror; in it I see myself, and that's why it is so difficult to help her or to do anything about the situation because her problem is my problem. I feel ashamed because I allowed this to happen but I also feel that now that I can see what is taking place, perhaps I can do something about it." At this point, tears were rolling down the patient's cheeks. He identified these as a "good sign" because he had always been ashamed to show any emotion.

A virtue of this approach is that the arbitrariness of therapist-imposed interpretations is markedly reduced by a patient's enhanced accessibility to the latent meaning inherent in his dreams. At the same time, an uncritical acceptance of the view that hypnosis somehow permits the rapid penetration of all defenses, resulting in a direct revelation of repressed or unconscious content, would be a culpably naïve position, as if the hypnotized subject was rendered incapable of distortion or fabrication.

Farber and Fisher cautioned that the form of the dream translation can vary, depending on interpersonal considerations at the time of report. The following vignette shows that the translation is also influenced by the nature of the changing relationship with the hypnotist. The subject in this instance was a young nurse in a psychiatric hospital, engaged to a resident (J.), who came to the author with the request that she be hypnotized in order to facilitate the understanding of a recent, distressing nightdream.

DREAM. "All the attendants were sick, so I was on duty in the female adolescent ward. Everything was quiet so J. left. The patients got ready for bed and then everybody got real wild—fighting, yelling, screaming, engaging in vulgar and sexy dancing. I tried to quiet them and maintain order but they ignored me, so I went and sat in a corner on the floor and watched them. The noise got louder and louder. J. came and everyone jumped in bed and was real quiet. I ran and threw my arms around him and said how glad I was to see him. He went and sat on the edge of a patient's bed and laughed and talked with them. I kept trying to get his attention but he ignored me. I felt let down and exhausted. Finally, I tried to attract his attention with a sexy dance, and then I started growing smaller and smaller and I turned into a snake, though not exactly."

Hypnotic interpretation. "Lenora [a second nurse whom the subject was now able to identify as the patient in her dream on whose bed J. had sat] was a witch because she did terrible things and talked about people all the time. She was never good to her husband's relatives and said terrible things about them. We told her that we were going to burn her at the stake. I had to tell everything I knew she had done wrong. Instead of doing a war dance, J. and I were going to do a snake dance. We were going to put snakes all over her and to tell her that she was a snake in the grass because she always knew everything that everyone does. A snake is a slimy, curved, quick creature, and this is the way she distorts things and decorates them. Since I had to work with her I had to do the dance. J. was supposed to put the snakes on her first but wouldn't do it, so somebody else had to. Then because I couldn't, I felt terrible because I had disappointed him, but instead of running away or apologizing, I just grew smaller and smaller. I was never permitted to go back to the hospital."

This interpretation of the dream left both parties dissatisfied, but the subject was obviously reluctant to delve further into its significance. In the ensuing weeks there was opportunity to cultivate the rapport, at which time the subject acquiesced to another attempt to divine the meaning of her dream.

Second hypnotic interpretation. "The main impression was that of being locked up with a lot of wild people, who were just like animals. I was supposed to control them, but I was in the cage with them and was overpowered. These kids are mean and vicious and don't have any moral or ethical standards. And for the moment I became like them. I tried to regain control but I couldn't and I felt beaten. J. came and I thought everything was OK but he just ignored me. He knew I had lost control and he tried to punish me by sitting on that bed. I got jealous and started a sexy dance, like they had been doing. Then I began to change and I felt myself getting smaller and smaller.

In one way the dream is concerned with my hate for Lenora, just as I told you before. I've talked these feelings over with J., even threatened to quit, but he told me to control them and I can't! I'm trapped with her and my feelings about her. I was afraid he was disappointed with me. But there is another side to the dream that concerns my feelings for J. It is all mixed up with the first set of feelings, and I guess I knew it [at the first hypnotic session] but didn't want to face up to it. I am ashamed to admit it now, but after we got engaged we began an affair. I didn't want it, that is, I did and I didn't, and I was afraid of what it was doing to me. I tried to control my sexual feelings but I couldn't, and I finally gave up. And J. wouldn't help me with them. One thing that made it hard not to was my jealousy of J. and his relationship with all those delinquent girls. I had to keep his attention! But when I let go to those feelings, I felt myself changing. I lost respect for myself and got lower and lower. I felt miscast, like a snakecharmer. I remember how, as a little girl, I was sometimes made to sit in a corner as punishment. The feeling about the snake also ties this back to Lenora. I've been afraid that she suspected and would gossip about it, the way she does about everyone. I hated her and feared she might catch us. Her tongue was like a snake, and I was afraid her gossip might reduce my character around town. In the olden days they used to torture and kill witches, and this town reminds me of something medieval."

The competent psychologist or psychiatrist is, of course, quite aware that he must guard against making dogmatic interpretations, but the dramatic results elicited by hypnosis have been known to dilute this natural caution. An instructive article in this regard is that by Watkins (1946) who employed hypnosis in the search for a misplaced library book. Watkins utilized a variety of clever and imaginative techniques to uncover memory traces of the lost object, including the interpretation of several symbolisms, until he eventually encountered a conflict area in his psychiatrist-subject that seemed to explain the loss of memory, although it did not result in recovery of the memory of the misplaced article. Special attention is directed to a final footnote, appended after submission of the article for publication, which reveals that the book had turned up in an unexpected and prosaic location. The author is to be commended for his honesty! Too frequently only the successful and exceptional cases are reported in the literature.

A recent paper featuring a specialized technique for the interpretation of symbols by hypnotized therapy patients is that written by Klemperer (1961). She advocates visual rather than verbal associations as the more direct line of communication with ego-alien content. Patients are simply instructed to allow a self-produced symbol to change gradually, through a series of visual images, to what it really means or represents. Klemperer claims that this method is therapeutically more effective than the word association method employed in traditional psychoanalysis.

Figure 1. Projected desymbolization of a dream symbol. (Reproduced courtesy *Intern. J. Clin. Exp. Hypnosis.*)

In *The Case of Alice M.*, Moss et al. (1962) present an instructive example of this procedure. A hypnotized patient who had been led to reexperience a recurrent, terrifying childhood dream in which she slammed a door on a small, white dog, was provided with a pencil and paper, was told that, on opening her eyes, she would actually "see" the little dog clearly etched on the paper, and was asked to carefully trace over its outline. After successful compliance with these instructions, she was told that, when she opened her eyes again, she would see a second image representing the central meaning of the little dog, and again she was to "trace these lines exactly as they appear there on the paper." She responded with a body in a coffin (Figure 1).

When she perceived what she had drawn, the patient immediately recognized the relation between the two images and found herself suddenly confronted with the full significance of her childhood dream—a sense of abandonment associated with the death of her beloved grandfather when she was six. Analysis of this experience in turn led to an increased understanding of a lifelong and inexplicable fear of death, a fuller comprehension of her distorted relationships with all men, and insight into the manner in which her mind had learned to "close the door" on events of a nature distressing to her.

Psychoanalysis has long advocated that the therapist attend to his own dreams and fantasies in order to clarify the marginal reactions evoked by his patients. An interesting variation on this theme is for the therapist to provide the patient with his own nocturnal dreams or to deliberately generate daydreams during the therapy session itself, which are then shared with the patient on the assumption that such fantasy material will effectively communicate with the "unconscious" of the patient. A further innovation, completely unvalidated experimentally, of course, is for the therapist to utilize autohypnosis as a technique for increasing his intuitive or empathic understanding of unconsciously determined verbalizations of the patient, such as his dream reports. Self-hypnosis has actually been used on occasion to stimulate fantasies or dreams that supposedly capture important dynamics, or nuances, of the relationship, either during or subsequent to a therapy session.

The proper conclusion must be that much work remains to be done to demonstrate that a hypnotized individual is indeed more capable of interpreting imaginal productions than the nonhypnotized individual, but this hypothesis is not as resistant to empirical test as the dearth of experimental evidence would indicate. It is entirely possible that the hypnotic dream could fail to resemble the night dream in any essential respect and yet be useful as a therapeutic tool. It is even possible that the hypnotic subject is in no way able to interpret dreams more accurately than the unhypnotized subject; nevertheless, this could still be a therapeutically viable technique, as will be seen in the next section.

THE DREAM AS A PROJECTIVE METHOD

Psychologists have repeatedly observed that, because of minimal commitments to reality, dreams constitute a relatively pure form of projection. Schafer (1954, pp. 94–110) has compared the formation of dreams with the Rorschach test response process. In the projective test situation the subject is asked to structure a relatively ambiguous stimulus, such as a blot of ink, whereas the dream utilizes recent, usually innocuous, content drawn from experiences of the preceding day. In both instances, subjects project onto these stimuli their conscious and not so conscious wishes, fears, and anxieties. The test situation is generally characterized by a greater degree of self-conscious control and there is much less evidence of regressive or primary thought processes, except in instances of extreme psychopathology. In either case, a subsequent inference must be made by the clinician from the projected fantasy material to the underlying personality of the respondent. Theoretically, the hypnotic dream should be intermediate between the nocturnal dream and the projective test, because it requires elaboration of a more or less specific stimulus and, although providing great latitude for response, it does occur in the context of an immediate interpersonal relationship and, therefore, has a communication aspect.

An infrequently quoted early study was conducted by Earl (1941) in relation to an actual projective device, the Rorschach inkblot test. He hypothesized that responses indicative of a fantasy process (characterized by determinants of *M, FM, m*) or of an inner disturbance (*K, FK, KF*) would be relatively rich in symbolic significance, whereas pure-form (*F*) responses would be devoid of symbolic meaning. Earl administered the Rorschach to a group of unstable, borderline mentally defective boys (ages 13 to 15) and then had them free-associate to their own responses and those of the other boys while hypnotized. He found that all *m* (inanimate movement) responses had symbolic significance, as did half of the human movement (*M*) responses. The number of *FM* or animal movement responses were too few for inference, whereas vista (*K*) and pure-form responses elicited little evidence of symbolism. Earl also observed that intersubject interpretative agreement was low and provided no evidence for common or universal symbolisms.

Acting on the conviction that dreams are "The most sensitive of the projection tests," McCord (1946) undertook to assess the possibility of using hypnotically induced dreams in explorations of personality. He advocated that subjects be given a mere schematic outline of a dream—a minimal stimulus or dream "blank"—which could serve as the basis for a dream in much the same manner that an ambiguously structured projective test could be used to solicit responses. His one subject reacted with highly personalized and embellished nonsymbolic "dreams," which McCord interpreted as verification for his very positive expectations.

The use of the hypnoprojective fantasy in psychotherapy—a manner of investigation and treatment that combines tactics drawn from psychoanalytic dream interpretation, hypnosis, and projective methods of personality appraisal—was developed by Watkins (1956). The hypnotized patient is stimulated to initiate a dreamlike, self-directed fantasy and then to respond to his own productions with a continuing projective self-structuring, so that he becomes progressively more immersed in an increasingly realistic fantasy experience. Considerable covert dynamic content is projected in the process. The following vignette is illustrative of this approach and graphically depicts the degree to which hypnotized individuals can become preoccupied with their own psychological state and subjective experiences. (Source: Moss, courtesy *Intern. J. Clin. Exp. Hypn.*, 1957c, pp. 61–63.)

Asked to free-associate to a recent, distressing experience, the patient reported that, in characteristic fashion, a "heavy dark cloud" had appeared in his mind and he was unable to think. "It seemed that a wall shut my mind off, and I got a dull cloud in my head." The patient was then rapidly inducted into hypnosis and instructed that he was sitting in a movie theater looking at a blank screen. It was suggested that he would next see the "dark cloud" projected on the screen. When he reported a clear visual hallucination, he was told that substitute pictures would appear which had for him the same meaning as the cloud. In rapid succession he reported seeing a "lock," "curtain," "wall," and a "door." He spontaneously remarked, "Put together, they seem to represent a barrier that is locking something in or out."

At this point, the suggestion was made that the door up on the screen had become tridimensional and that the patient would walk through the door and describe what he saw. He replied, "There is bright sunlight and people walking back and forth. One of them, over there, is my wife. She is holding her arms out to me." The patient tried to walk towards her but his feet seem "glued to the ground." It took considerable effort, but he finally reached her, put his arms around her and kissed her. When asked the meaning of this situation, the patient replied, "The sunlight means freedom, I think, and the whole thing seems to represent the future to me."

It was suggested that the patient again open the door and re-enter the present. He did so and immediately reported sight of a "black cloudy mixture." The patient's efforts to entice his wife to enter were to no avail. "She says that she can't come. She is shaking her head and crying. She says that she is afraid. When I walk back through the door, I will have to leave her." The patient and the therapist then re-entered the darkness. The patient reported, "a heaviness swirling about me. Through it I can see figures in black cloaks. I don't understand what is happening." The therapist then instructed the patient to grab hold of one of the figures. With considerable emotional involvement, the patient stated that he had hold of one of the figures, but that it was struggling, and that now it had gotten away, leaving the cloak in his hands. The therapist's immediate response was that the creature had not escaped; that the patient still had firm hold of it. Even so, the patient stated that it was too dark to identify it. "He seems to emit a feeling of uneasiness." It was suggested that the patient drag the creature to the doorway, but he responded that he did not have sufficient strength. The therapist then stated that he would take the other arm of the creature and between them, they could force it into the light. When they arrived at the door, however, the patient reported that it was stuck. It was finally opened only when the therapist again lent his strength to the task.

In the sunlight the creature held its hands up over its face. "It seems to want to hide its identity," remarked the patient. He was instructed to pull away the hands and finally succeeded after a considerable struggle, only to report that the creature wore a "skull face." The therapist's immediate response was that this was a mask and, as he snapped his fingers, it would pop off. The patient blanched and reported that he saw two faces before him alternating back and forth, those of his brother and his father. "My brother seems to have a devilish grin on his face." The patient was told to ask his brother what he was doing in there, and the brother replied, "I'm hiding; I like it in there because I can torment you." Asked why he was hiding, he replied, "Because I've got something that I don't want anyone else to find out about." The brother adamantly refused to tell the patient what he was hiding, however.

The patient was told to walk some distance away, and the suggestion was then given that the patient's right arm would become disassociated and engage in automatic writing as a direct means of communication with the brother. The "brother" was asked to confide to the therapist what he is hiding. The arm wrote, "I am totally unreliable," and then refused further elaboration. The patient was called back and instructed to ask his brother what the haze represented. The brother replied through the patient, "It is like a smoke screen and protects one from letting people know what I am really like. I am ashamed to let people know what I am because then people would laugh at me." By this time the patient appeared emotionally exhausted and it was suggested that he and the therapist return through the door and into the movie theater.

In the discussion which followed while the patient was still in the hypnotic state, he volunteered that he had spontaneously obtained insight into the meaning of a dream he had reported earlier in the session. He identified an unknown assailant as his brother and the dream theme as his inability to retaliate against the brother's aggressive behavior in spite of the support he had experienced from the therapy sessions. He then added reflectively, "You know, I get a puzzling feeling of familiarity about this character (in the fantasy) who represents my brother. At times it seems as if I am talking about myself, too." Continued discussion elicited that while the patient was concerned with his brother's aggressivity, the dream and the fantasy also depicted fear of losing control over his own hostile impulses.

The hypnoprojective technique is reminiscent of the forced fantasy approach employed by Ferenczi (1926) as a catalytic agent in psychoanalysis. When resistances prevented the productive utilization of free association, patients were strongly encouraged to fabricate fantasy material. More often than not Ferenczi provided the theme and even dictated details of the content to be fantasied. He reported that, as in the preceding instance, patients would lose their objective detachment and the fantasy would "transfix" them. Although the form of the elicited fantasies ordinarily had few points of similarity with the usual night dream, they were apparently a rich source of projective content.

The hypnoprojective fantasy technique bears a closer resemblance to the method of the *rêve éveillé dirigé* or guided waking dream perfected and promoted these past 40 years by Robert Desoille (1945, 1961) but little known outside France. The patient is invited to recline, relax, concentrate on some somatic process such as respiration or heartbeat, and to become receptive to his innermost fantasies. In contrast to psychoanalysis, care is taken not to direct the patient to look introspectively into the past; instead, it is suggested that he "prepare for imaginary trips into the realms of creative imagination." Sessions often begin with the request that the patient focus on a particular image. This image may be designated by the patient, but Desoille has found a remarkable constancy in the occurrence of certain images that he now exploits.

The psychotherapist may present some imaginary object, such as a sword to a male or a vase to a female patient. The next question might be, "What are you going to do with it?" The patient is then encouraged to embark upon fantasized journeys in a vertical direction (rising or descending), depending on whether positive and constructive or negative aspects of personality are to be explored. The therapist may suggest threatening or protective images. The patient could be requested to descend into a grotto at the bottom of an ocean, where he will encounter a sorcerer or sorceress. Once a general theme is established, the patient is allowed considerable latitude in its subsequent development.

Most of the literature on the subject of the guided waking dream is in French; fortunately, however, an article by Van den Berg (1962) is available in English and has adequately captured the essence of this procedure. According to Van den Berg, the patient experiences a series of imaginative happenings, and the element of the unexpected remains the typical feature. The psychotherapist does not play the role of a passive spectator, but instead accompanies the patient as his "traveling companion." Van den Berg goes on to state that whereas psychiatrically sound persons are easily persuaded to cooperate in these symbolic ascensions and descensions, neurotics always encounter hindrances "regularly embodied in a person, an animal, a figure, or in any case a living being that expressly forbids any advance—*the keeper of the threshold*." The psychotherapist frequently intervenes in the case of a barrier, suggesting symbolic means of circumventing the obstacle.

In all these cases it is necessary for the psychotherapist not to waver, but to choose the means quickly, adequately, *ad rem*. It becomes harder to assist when a keeper of the threshold has taken up this station. A choice has to be made then between entering into a contract, the clever mollifying of the dangerous guard, or a life-and-death struggle. The psychotherapist gives the patient the necessary weapons, magic weapons, such as an efficacious charm or an annihilating ray from a sparkling diamond, real arms, such as swords, lances, revolvers, rifles, atomic bombs also, if you will. Should the struggle appear to be taking an unfavorable turn, then the psychotherapist himself enters the fray; if necessary he rushes up armies of well-trained and well-equipped soldiers with tanks or planes. For the battle must be won (Van den Berg, 1962, p. 15).

The remarkable coincidence between this report and the brief excerpt reported by Moss is particularly impressive in view of his total ignorance of Desoille's work at the time; an imaginary journey beginning with a vertical or "staircase" method of hypnotic induction, the encounter with a *keeper of the gate*, and the ensuing struggle necessitating the therapist's active intervention are all common elements. One difference is that the symbols encountered by Desoille are not usually interpreted, at least not in any objective sense, although the method itself largely obviates the need to do so.

Desoille takes issue with the Freudian psychoarcheological emphasis on the dream as a means of access to developmentally early sources of trauma and conflict and the consequent employment of a *linear*-type free association designed to reveal the infantile substructure. Instead, he has been highly influenced by Jung who believed that dreams are valuable in their own right and advocated a *prospective* understanding of them. Dream images in this framework are accepted as valid reflections of important internal psychic processes, and the objective of a *radial* association approach is to amplify the immediate meaning of each dream element. The content of the directed waking dream is not ordinarily related to external situations and persons, although in later phases of treatment a patient is encouraged to make the transition from an imaginary to the real world.

Those familiar with analytical psychology will recognize the relationship to Jung's technique of "active imagination" (concisely described by G. Adler, 1948). The root conception of analytical psychology is the absolute seriousness with which it accepts the reality of the unconscious and its contents as the really potent and creative layer of the psyche. Active imagination entails cultivation of an attitude of contemplation or meditation of the images emerging from the unconscious. These images have an impressive autonomy and convey a convincing sense of being independent of one's ego. "It is not unlike watching a film . . . the only difference being that in active imagination the 'film' is being unrolled inside." Like Jung, Desoille believes that when a patient can relate himself to the archetypes of the "Collective Unconscious," he has attained an appropriate basis for resolving the problems of life.[1]

Van den Berg applies an existential interpretation to the experiences and results obtained by the method of the guided waking dream. Regarding the patients' frequent fantasied encounter with barriers and obstacles, he comments: "The explanation of this remarkable thing is only too obvious. The patient is looking for help because important territories of his existence got lost or were closed. We may assume that he himself repeatedly attempted to reopen these territories and review his possession of them. He failed in these attempts . . . (the therapeutic relationship) gives him the strength to enter territories which, if he were alone, would be inaccessible to him, or even would not be there at all" (Van den Berg, 1962, pp. 30–31).

Somewhat surprisingly, Desoille has come to favor a Pavlovian interpretation of the guided waking dream, attributing the results to a hypnoidal state in which the consciousness of the patient is pegged at a point intermediate between "true hypnosis" (with subsequent amnesia) and a pure sleep-dream stage. In this hypnagogic state the primary signal system is freed from the constraint of the secondary or socialized signal system or, in other words, the imagination, accompanied by imagery of a hallucinatory intensity, is dissociated from the critical faculties.

Another derivative of Jung's technique of active imagination was the meditative psychotherapy of Carl Happich (1932, 1939) based on contact with the "symbolic consciousness" as a means of release for creativity and its therapeutic potentialities. A recent innovation is the Initiated Symbol Projection method developed by Hanskarl Leuner in West Germany. Although the term "hypnosis" is again avoided the patient is encouraged to relax and to relinquish contact with the outer world, and then to visualize a series of symbolic situations, such as strolling through a meadow, gazing into a pool of water, or glancing through an old picture book. The goal is to initiate a projective dreamlike fantasy or hallucination leading to a "symbolic catharsis" rather than to the recovery of suppressed early memories.

The Initiated Symbol Projection method can be used as both a psychodiagnostic and psychotherapeutic technique, and Swartley (1965) comments that it is truly remarkable that such widespread use has been made of symbols in psychotherapy, yet so few methods have

[1] In 1963 a Clinic and Research Institute for Jungian Psychology was established at Dolderstrasse 107, 8032, Zurich. The Institute research program places priority on dream studies employing electrophysiological techniques.

applied symbols during the diagnostic procedure. He points out that a diagnosis obtained in symbolic terms has immediate applicability to therapy conducted on the symbolic level, requiring no intermediary analysis or interpretation.

CONCLUSIONS

Schneck summarizes the affirmative position for the hypnotic manipulation of dreams in psychotherapy thus:

Hypnotic dreams may bear such close structural resemblance to nocturnal dreams as to be essentially indistinguishable from them. They may be simple or complex, in accordance with the manner in which the patient tends to express himself in this fashion, and in keeping often with the form and content of his spontaneous nocturnal dreams. The variety of dream mechanisms employed in the latter are evident in the former, and the analysis of hypnotic dreams is often therapeutically beneficial. Hypnotic dreaming may occur spontaneously or on suggestion. Hypnotic suggestions may influence subsequent nocturnal dreams. Scene visualizations and hypnotic dreams may form a continuum for any one patient. Problems may be depicted, explored, and analyzed in a series of such visualizations and dreams. Scenes and dreams may emerge in some patients with greater freedom, initially, if suggestions tend to structure the settings and content. Some patients, immediately, and other patients, in time, visualize hypnotic scenes and dream freely without such assistance. Symbolizations, condensations, displacements, and substitutions, representations by the opposite and a broader array of mechanisms are readily discernible. Scenes and dreams reflect resistances and transference relations in abundance, and are subject to analysis within the hypnotic setting or subsequent to the hypnosis sessions, as is deemed clinically expedient. In hypnosis, forgotten dreams may be retrieved, new dreams stimulated, and previous nocturnal dreams continued in some new fashion or concluded in a new way.[2]

In sharp rebuttal, two papers by Kanzer (1945, 1953) specifically concerned with the hypnotic dream, typify the disillusionment of many psychotherapists as a consequence of their experience with hypnosis. In the first paper Kanzer affirmed that "Hypnotically-induced dreams provide the psychiatrist with unusual opportunities for direct intervention in the unconscious of the patient, and offer a field for the experimental study of the dream process" (p. 333). In the second paper, Kanzer recanted, leveling the charge that not only does the hypnotic dream fail to provide access to unconscious material but it is usually

[2] From Schneck, J. M., *Hypnosis in Modern Medicine*, 1963, pp. 184–185. Courtesy of Charles C Thomas, Publisher, Springfield, Ill.

briefer, shows a lack of associations, and actually provokes defences that may be even more difficult to penetrate than during normal consciousness. He argued further that dreams induced under hypnosis show evidence of a *greater* censorship than do spontaneous nocturnal dreams. The important point was also advanced that the content of hypnotically induced dreams are interpretable mainly in terms of the immediate therapeutic relationship.

It is noteworthy how often clinicians have conceived imaginative hypnotic techniques to meet the exigencies of a particular case. It is an equally interesting commentary that so many of these inventive and promising techniques receive only a transitory attention and then pass into oblivion. A majority of psychotherapists, to be sure, have been reluctant to employ hypnosis in any form, maintaining that the complications involved far outweigh any possible virtues. At the same time, our restricted knowledge of the process and outcome of the therapeutic enterprise forces recognition that militant advocation of the superiority of any particular form of therapy is emotionally based and theoretically biased, because there exists little convincing evidence that any one system is more effective than another. Numerous legitimate questions may be raised, of course, about the employment of hypnosis in psychotherapy, many of them referable to the nature of the phenomenon itself, about which far too little is known. Much work needs to be done to demonstrate convincingly that the hypnotic dream represents a useful, therapeutic modality, but even this brief, focused excursion should indicate the seemingly inexhaustible armamentarium of hypnotic techniques, limited only by the creative adaptiveness of the therapist, which some practitioners have found attractive.

Chapter 3
Recent Experimental Studies
of Hypnosis and Dreams

THE COMPARISON OF NOCTURNAL AND HYPNOTIC DREAMS

If it could be established that hypnotized subjects possess an uncommon ability to replicate spontaneous night dreams in any essential respect or to make valid interpretations of symbolic content, it would unquestionably represent a monumental advance over the highly arbitrary and subjective methods of dream study and analysis still employed by clinicians today. How fortunate, indeed, if such a complex and difficult problem should have such a simple solution! However, a strong note of caution is introduced by the reminder that throughout history man has felt compelled to attribute supernormal and even supernatural abilities to the somnambulist. In the early nineteenth century, for example, hypnotic subjects were believed to have remarkable powers of clairvoyance, and it was not an uncommon practice to employ trance subjects to diagnose ailments, prescribe remedies, and predict the date of recovery. There remains even today a widespread belief that hypnosis endows its subjects with abilities that they do not ordinarily possess in the normal waking state, such as enhanced muscular prowess, increased sensory acuity, and improved memory.

A quotation from Brenman (1949, p. 455) addresses itself to the problem of experimenter attitude in the following way.

There has been a good deal of glib talk regarding the power of hypnosis to create dreams which, according to most researchers on this problem, are in all ways like spontaneous night dreams . . . . It is curious that investigators appear to have taken it for granted that the hypnotic suggestion "to dream" actually issues in a dream. It is as if the belief in the magic powers of hypnosis overwhelms the investigator as well as the subject and thus, when the subject responds with a production which often resembles a night dream, it is assumed without further question that there is no difference between the two.

Brenman, *in an article reprinted in this book* (*p. 127*), questions the assumption that the hypnotic dream duplicates, either in structure or function, the nocturnal dream. She suggests that there is a wide variation of response to the hypnotic suggestion "to dream," ranging from "embellished reminiscences" of an actual event and "static pictorial images" to "quasi-allegories," resembling the conscious daydream but including some elements of unconscious symbolism, and "quasi-dreams" that can hardly be distinguished from the usual ones. The average hypnotic production, according to Brennan, has a structure intermediate between the daydream and the regular nocturnal dream, in that the primary processes are more evident than in waking thought but less than in the typical night dream. She also states that whereas the basic function of the nocturnal dream is to preserve sleep, the motive power of the hypnotic dream is to safeguard the relationship through compliance with the expressed wishes of the hypnotist.

It is astonishing how little has been done, by way of any objective comparison of the hypnotically induced and nocturnal dream. The only experimental studies reported in the literature which undertake to compare and contrast empirically the manifest content of hypnotic and spontaneous night dreams have been conducted by Mixer (1961) and Tart (1964*a*). Mixer used subjects hypnotized to a "deep trance state," and two hypnotic and two nocturnal dreams were collected from each subject in an *ABBA* order, a night dream being collected first in all cases. The productions were analyzed into units consisting of one complete thought or action. Three experienced clinicians were asked to rate independently the degree of reality orientation expressed in each unit as either "impossible," "improbable," or "probable." Mixer interpreted the absence of significant differences between the two sets of data as confirming his hypothesis that "there is no difference in the degree of realism shown in hypnotic and nocturnal dreams of the same subjects, when their hypnotic dreams occur in a deep trance under conditions which duplicate night dreaming as closely as possible."

Tart trained subjects to achieve a deep-level hypnosis and then asked them to respond to two detailed and affectively loaded dream stimuli, one immediately while still hypnotized and the other that night while asleep. A rating system for objectively assessing the extent to which each dream had been affected by the specific stimulus was devised, based on the number of "action units" of the suggested narrative which were clearly present in the reported dream. Ten dreams obtained in the hypnotic state were contrasted with 38 posthypnotic dreams. For nine of the ten subjects the hypnotic dream showed a greater compliance with the suggestion than did the night dream. It was also the investigator's impression that none of the dreams seemed disguised although no associations were obtained from the subjects. In view of the confused and contradictory nature of the evidence in this whole area, it should come as no surprise that, contrary to Mixer's results, Tart concludes that the equation of dreams occurring in hypnosis with those occurring in sleep is open to serious question. These two studies represent the total reported effort to date to effect a systematic, quantitative comparison of the content of nocturnal and hypnotic dreams.

It is encouraging that in the past decade an increasing number of reports in the hypnosis area have evidenced concern with quantification and methodological rigor. Mazer (1951) employed the hypnotic dream to study the symbolic representation of emotions, the self-concept, and interpersonal attitudes. In 333 experimentally induced dreams he found that common or universal symbols were rare and selection is influenced by such factors as education and social background. Parts of the body were usually symbolized by objects or similar forms, emotions by activities and natural phenomena, and so forth. An important observation was that although a dreamer might use different symbols for the same function, person, or emotion on different occasions, his attitude toward the "latent" content showed remarkable consistency. It was also Mazer's impression that many of the attitudes displayed in these dreams were outside the subject's waking awareness. Another observation was that the ability to dream symbolically was related to the depth of hypnosis. *This study is reprinted in this book beginning on page 137.*

It will be noted that Mazer takes sharp issue with Brenman. In an affirmation of the essential identity of hypnotic and spontaneous dreams, Mazer argues that the hypnotic dream typically possesses all of the qualities characteristic of the regular night dream, and he asserts that a dream should be defined by the nature of the manifest content, not by the circumstances of its occurrence.

TESTS OF THE DISGUISE FUNCTION OF DREAMS

The psychoanalytic tenet that dream symbols have a disguise function, allowing expression of repressed impulses in disguised form, has intrigued investigators for many years. In an interesting test of this belief, Sweetland and Quay (1952) trained 16 psychologically naïve college students to dream under hypnosis and then presented each with 50 dream stimuli of an assumedly ego-alien, ego-syntonic, or neutral nature. The positive or negative emotional tone of the stimulus seemed to have no effect on reaction time, duration of dreaming, degree of symbolization, or stimulus rejection (refusal to dream). Instead, differences were found to correlate with social-emotional and intellectual characteristics of the subjects. It was observed, for example, that, contrary to expectations, the best adjusted subjects, according to a battery of psychological tests, displayed the greatest distortion in their dreams. Intelligence was also slightly correlated with the degree of symbolization. Similarly, waking recall of one's dreams seemed determined by the factor of recency and was independent of whether the dream stimulus had been ego-enhancing or detracting (*see reprinted article by Sweetland and Quay, p. 167*).

The investigation made by Sweetland and Quay was largely qualitative in nature. In a follow-up study by Quay (1952), a random sample of 405 dreams from among those procured in the first investigation provided the data to test several additional hypotheses concerning the emotional attitude of the central dream character. Dreams were judged on a frustration scale a la Rosenzweig (1934), featuring, "extrapunitive," "impunitive," and "intropunitive" categories. When dreams involved flattering or enhancing situations, three allegedly complimentary "praise" categories were substituted. Results were interpreted as lending support to the conclusions of the earlier study: (1) The connotative tone of the hypnotic dream had little relationship to the suggested stimulus tone, because of the substantial personal contribution of the dreamer. (2) The emotional adjustment of the dreamer, rather than the character of the stimulus, seemed the primary determinant of the feeling tone of the dream. (3) Well-adjusted subjects produced dreams in which there was considerable alteration and a minimum of emotion, whereas the more maladjusted subjects tended to produce dreams in which emotional attitudes were readily evident, but not always consistent with the originally suggested theme. Quay concluded that a person's dreams are a repetition, in principle, of the way he meets conscious situations.[1]

As previously recognized, a major impediment to the scientific investigation of dreams is the extremely loose manner in which psychoanalytic and related theories have been formulated. In recognition of the need for a redefinition of terms and a statement of hypotheses

---

[1] One measure of adjustment in these studies was the MMPI. The K score, often interpreted as indicative of "test-taking attitude," correlated highest of the various scales with dream symbolization (72). The investigators were sufficiently impressed with this finding to write a paper on a possible reinterpretation of the K score (1953). In this paper they characterize the person who symbolized his hypnotic dreams as "comfortable in his social contacts, above average in intelligence, and little bothered with doubts and indecisions."

in testable form, Moss (1962) translated Freudian concepts into C. E. Osgood's mediation learning theory. Osgood (1957) asserted that meaning and its objective measurement is the central issue in contemporary psychology. He defined "meaning" as a "representational mediation process." It is *representational* because it is part of the same behavior produced by the significate itself, and it is *mediational* because the resulting self-stimulation can become associated with a variety of instrumental acts.

It was posited by Moss that selection of a dream symbol would arise from (*a*) a drive toward expression of some affect-laden content and (*b*) an aspect of similarity between the mediational processes of the symbol and the object (significate) for which it substitutes. Ordinarily, symbols should be chosen on the basis of mediational similarity, the more direct, adequate representation being preferred. Freud, of course, postulated that dream symbolism also serves the purpose of censorship, rendering a dream incomprehensible through the representation of a prohibited impulse in a disguised form. In conformance with the laws of stimulus generalization, then, the greater the anxiety associated with a given object or latent content, the wider the generalization of anxiety to similar objects; that is, the higher the anxiety, the more distant the symbol chosen to represent it and ipso facto the greater the degree of disguise. Apparently, this is the mechanism responsible for the clinical phenomena of displacement, of which dream symbolization is the prime example.

In contrast to psychoanalysis, the mediation learning theory would predict no difference in the selection of symbols under conditions of anxiety and nonanxiety, because anxiety resulting in prolonged repression should cause an increasing drive for expression; the effect would be to raise this gradient, counteracting the inhibitory effect of anxiety and resulting in the selection of symbols that are semantically as close to the latent content as under nonanxiety conditions. Moss actually found in several experiments (1957*b*, 1960*a*) that anxiety associated with the latent content did not apparently determine the semantic distance between the ordinary meaning of the sign selected as a symbol and the meaning of the thing being symbolized. These studies were summarized and elaborated on in a further *paper by Moss (1961) which is reprinted in this book on pages 185–197.*

RELATIONSHIP BETWEEN DREAMING AND HYPNOTIC DEPTH

Several investigators have observed an apparent relationship between the depth of hypnosis achieved by a subject and his ability to respond productively to the suggestion to dream. In the one systematic study of this relationship, Tart (1966a) found a significant positive correlation between the vividness of the experience and his subjects' tested capacity on two measures of hypnotic responsiveness or depth. However, the occurrence of vivid and dreamlike responses was apparently not dependent on whether subjects had actually undergone an immediately preceding hypnotic induction procedure; this observation will be elaborted elsewhere (p. 68).

An experiment by Wiseman and Reyher (1962) reversed the relationship because it involved the use of the hypnotic dream in deepening the trance state. Subjects were first trained to dream while hypnotized, and it is noteworthy that most of the 60 subjects were able to comply readily with the suggestion. They were then told that experiments had conclusively demonstrated that dreams always preceded the onset of deeper levels of ordinary sleep, and in this instance, as they dreamed, they would gradually enter a deeper hypnotic sleep than ever before. Using amnesia as a criterion of depth, it was found that significantly more subjects experienced complete amnesia under these conditions than when other conventional methods were employed, but with the important qualification that an enhanced amnesic reaction occurred only where this tendency was already present; it did not decrease the number of subjects failing to experience any amnesia.

TEMPORALITY IN THE HYPNOTIC DREAM

One of the most intriguing clinical and experimental applications of hypnosis is its alleged ability to manipulate and control the factor of psychological time. It is always startling to witness a subject being regressed in age back along the time continuum so that he reacquires discarded patterns of childish and even infantile behavior and reexperiences long-forgotten events in considerable detail, often accompanied by intense abreactions. The dramatic way in which subjects relive their past experiences is not proof of the validity of this phenomenon, of course, and the genuineness of hypnotically induced age regression is open to serious question. Less well known is the fact that subjects can also be induced to live out events of a future date or age with equal verisimilitude to their accounts of the past (Rubenstein and Newman, 1954). The widely publicized *Search for Bridey Murphy* (Bernstein, 1956) is a dramatic instance of *time regression*.

As mentioned earlier, hypnosis has been used in psychotherapy to recapture forgotten dreams or to carry a prematurely terminated dream to completion; it has also been used on occasion to extend the duration of a dream so that essential details can be examined in slow motion as-it-were (Moss, 1958). Regardie combined hypnotic dream induction with age regression in order to study the chronological development of a neurotic complex. The investigation by Welch of the representation of space and time in dreams has also been described. Apparently unaware of the last study, Schjelderup (1960) reported on time relations in hypnotically induced dreams, and results support the notion that experiences corresponding to long spans of objective time may be represented in dreams of very short duration.

In a book entitled *Symbol Formation* (1963), Werner and Kaplan advanced an "organismic-developmental" approach to the study of the symbolization process. A major aspect of linguistic systems of symbolization is the use of an abstract time dimension as a receptacle within which events can be localized, and one objective of the book was to examine ways in which the temporal locus of an action is represented and referred to in the medium of visual imagery. Results of a hitherto unpublished research carried out by Erle (1958) on the representation of time of action in hypnotically induced dreams was analyzed at length.

The procedure was to confront hypnotized subjects with groups of four sentences containing the same verb but varying the tenses; for example:

Simple present: He fights
Progressive present: He is fighting
Past: He fought
Future: He will fight

Subjects were instructed to represent the meaning of each sentence in visual images or pictures. A typical response to the stimulus "He fights" was as follows: "A person sort of looking around for a fight as though he wanted a fight, a sort of anxious look on his face. I guess he was a fighter, someone who likes to fight. He had a blue shirt and green pants. I think his shirt was ripped and he was very masculine, his chest was very strong. I remember his standing sort of in a doorway; it was all wood and it was very weathered wood."

In their examination of the products of this experiment, Werner and Kaplan were impressed by the high degree of elaboration and circumstantiality of the dreams and the extreme individualization of expression of the depicted actions. It was also noted that the element of time or time differentiation generally is not directly represented in the image medium. On occasion temporality could be inferred from the context of the dream, and temporal locus was sometimes expressed through variations in depictions of the principal agent, situational elements, phasing of an event, and so forth. Multiple expressions of time were frequently used in the same dream. In most instances the meaning attributed to either the total dream or to its image components was so personalized that an observer not privy to the idiosyncratic attitudes, states, and past experiences of the symbolizer would have had extreme difficulty interpreting the often subtle and tangential references to temporality, even though they were almost always present.[2]

THE ROLE OF PHYSICAL STIMULI

It is a popular belief that physical stimuli play a major role in the formation of dreams. Freud never denied that external sensory and internal somatic stimuli can initiate dreaming; he simply raised the possibility that there was a psychic contribution to the content of the dream. "We may take our choice. We admit that the laws of dream-formation cannot really be traced any further, and so refrain from asking whether or not the interpretation of the illusion evoked by the sensory impression depends upon still further conditions, or we may assume that the objective sensory stimulus encroaching upon sleep plays only a modest role as a dream source, and that other factors determine the choice of the memory-image to be evoked" (Freud, 1931, p. 29).

The precise effect of physical stimulation on the dream remains a matter for speculation; however, a number of studies on the subject exist. An imaginative, early, nonhypnotic investigation, for example, was conducted by Cubberly (1947). He sought to determine the influence of external stimuli on spontaneous night dreams by dissecting the skin surface of his subjects into three-inch squares and systematically applying a two-centimeter piece of gummed paper to each center, thus making a generally complete survey of the body surface for its "tension associations." Results were interpreted by Cubberly as

---

[2] In a private communication Erle reported work on a doctoral dissertation investigating the expression of connectives, namely, "because," "but," and "if" in a pictorial medium. "However, instead of having used hypnosis, I merely requested the subjects to close their eyes and to transform the verbal statements into images. Interestingly enough, with graduate students in psychology who are comparatively introspective, the images were actually similar to what probably would have been obtained under hypnosis. Also the images obtained in the study on time were not of real dramatic dreamlike substance [which I did not want for a good analysis would have been very difficult with respect to the particular problems] but were more of the quality of the perceptualization of thought."

indicating that dreams are "largely caused by immediate physical stimuli and recent, minor day residuals, a type of stimuli which can be studied without going beyond the safe limits of experimental control." Readers were introduced earlier to Klein's (1939) study of the effect of discrete physical stimuli on the dreams of hypnotized subjects.

Beigel (1959) asked hypnotized subjects to report a recent natural dream and then instructed them to reexperience it five different times while a series of physical stimuli were introduced: (*a*) whistling sound, (*b*) perfume, (*c*) a bright light, (*d*) air from a fan, and (*e*) a cushion placed on the lap. In certain instances the stimuli acted to inhibit the continuation of the dream, in others the stimulus was ignored, but 79 per cent of the dream versions reflected clearly the nature of the intrusive stimuli. In some cases the stimulus was directly incorporated into the dream in a manner consistent with the preformulated pattern of the original dream. In a number of instances the stimulus altered minor and sometimes even major aspects of the mood or content of the dream or even initiated a new dream sequence. The experimenter was impressed with evidence of mental processes at work which led from an initial groping for perception of more or less vague impressions to a meaningful organization of sensations, feelings, and thoughts that fed on memories of reality experiences, past problems, and acute emotional states.

Freud recognized that much of the manifest content of the dream is drawn from memory images of the preceding day. He also observed that dreams have a peculiar affinity for incidental and indifferent perceptual stimuli and that these "day residues" are utilized as the tools of expression out of which the dream is fashioned. In an investigation of the role of day residues in the process of dream formation, Poetzl (1917) conducted an experiment involving the tachistoscopic presentation of highly complex pictures. He claimed that many aspects of the pictures apparently not consciously perceived by his subjects appeared in the manifest content of their dreams the following night. Interest in the relationship between subliminal stimuli and the manifest content of dreams and images was revived by the work of Fisher (1954*a*, 1954*b*, 1957, 1959, 1960). He observed that "In many of the experiments every single detail of the visual structure of the dream could be traced to preconscious visual percepts of the day before" (Fisher, 1954*b*, p. 422). The tentative conclusion was advanced that the dreamwork cannot compose an entirely new visual structure any more than (as Freud had maintained) it can create new speech, although in his later studies Fisher came to recognize that Poetzl's contention that only subliminal percepts are used in the construction of a dream was far too narrow.

It was hypothesized by Lesser (1961) that if external stimuli can be registered without essential awareness, then hypnosis, conceptualized as an altered state of consciousness, should enhance recovery of the subliminal stimuli. Perceptual thresholds were carefully determined for 16 subjects, and the experimental stimulus was presented below the briefest exposure at which a subject could correctly "guess" whether a stimulus was even shown. Following presentation of either a figured (clocklike) stimulus or a blank, three images were obtained from each subject in the hypnotic and in the waking condition. Each subject was next requested to experience a hypnotic dream and also to report dreams from the night following the experimental session. Although judges could not detect the influence of the subliminal stimulation either in the images or among the reported night dreams, effects were clearly observable on hypnotic dreams. That is, judges were able to distinguish between dreams following exposure of the figured stimulus as contrasted with those occurring after the blank (control) experience.

On the assumption that recent perceptual images are literally "drawn into the unconscious," becoming the symbolic vehicles of unconscious wishes, it was hypothesized by Wiseman (1962) that if the Rorschach inkblots could be used as stimuli for hypnotically induced dreams, the postdreaming Rorschach protocols would capture a residual effect in the form of an increased proportion of responses indicative of primary process thinking. The Rorschach inkblots were considered uniquely suitable stimuli for such an experiment, because their ambiguous nature should lend itself to the emergence of primary process activity.

The feasibility of using the Rorschach inkblots as stimuli for induced dreams was quickly established—the "Rorschach dreams" seemed to cover the entire range from a true dream experience to a normal Rorschach response. Considerable support was found for the hypothesis that such an experience would significantly heighten the intrusion of the primary mode of thought in Rorschach protocols (when compared with earlier records). The Rorschach responses elicited after the hypnotic dream experience contained a significantly higher proportion of primary manifestations, both with respect to formal mechanisms of thought (for example, autistic logic, condensation, and symbolization) and content aspects (for example, libidinal and/or aggressive content).

When the experimental group was compared with yet another control group consisting of subjects who simulated hypnosis and faked dreams to the cards, the results were in essential agreement with the previous findings but not as clear-cut, that is, the total amount of primary process thinking remained significantly higher for the experimental group; however, the faking control group was more similar than had been the nondreaming control groups. It was concluded that results were consistent with Freud's theory of the Dream Work and specifically supported that aspect of the theory which contends that anxiety-provoking, unconscious impulses find expression in the dream by utilizing "recent impressions" of the day.

PSYCHOSOMATIC EFFECTS AND THE HYPNOTIC DREAM

A very large number of studies have been conducted on the bodily alterations deriving from the hypnotic state itself, the direct suggestion of changes, and physiologic concomitants of hypnotically induced emotions, hallucinations, and other phenomena. Investigators have testified that hypnosis provides remarkable opportunity for the study of psychosomatic interrelationships in the laboratory; however, findings are more often than not contradictory and inconclusive and open to differing interpretations. (Several survey articles are recommended: Gorton, 1949; Crasilneck and Hall, 1959; and Barber, 1961a.) Only three studies have dealt even superficially with the influence of the hypnotic dream on physiological functions. No studies of record have attempted to employ hypnosis in the manipulation of physiological events as endogenous stimuli to the dream.

Scantlebury et al. (1942) investigated the effect of naturally occurring and hypnotically induced dreams on gastric motility and found that both can have a similar inhibitory action, the duration of the effect depending on the point at which the dream occurs in the hunger cycle. In a comparison of the hostility expressed in verbal productions of hypertensive and nonhypertensive patients, Kaplan et al. (1961) found support for the hypothesis that essential hypertension accompanies inhibited hostile-aggressive impulses. Induced dreams were obtained from one subject on 25 occasions, and each dream and the patient's hypnotic associations thereto were scored on a simple hostility count scale. It was found that the diastolic blood pressure correlated significantly with hostility scores, whereas the relationship with systolic blood pressure just failed of significance. No attempt was made to direct the content of suggested dreams; however, most of them concerned the psychotherapeutic situation and relationships. Weiss (1962) reported on hypnotic dream production in a patient suffering migraine headaches.

DREAM INTERPRETATION THROUGH HYPNOSIS

In the single recent effort to examine experimentally the proposition that hypnotized subjects have an enhanced ability to intuit the meaning of unconsciously derived symbols, Moss and Stachowiak (1963) presented a series of rather detailed symbolic test items to 5 subjects for interpretation, first in the waking and then in the hypnotic state. No confirmatory evidence was forthcoming. A control group of 22 seemingly well-motivated waking subjects similarly failed to provide any evidence of valid interpretive ability. The most positive finding was that hypnosis had the effect of loosening the associational process, with the result that subjects presented rich and meaningful personal projections. *This study is reproduced on pages 198–205.* In the absence of satisfactory objective criterion, Moss and Stachowiak conclude that it is a moot point as to what any unconsciously determined symbol *really* means. The fact that the act of symbol interpretation under hypnosis provokes meaningful projective responses, makes it a valuable clinical tool in diagnosis or psychotherapy; however, this is scant consolation for the investigator interested in developing a more objective means of studying the meaning of dream symbolism.

INVOLVEMENT OF ACADEMIA IN STUDIES
OF THE HYPNOTIC DREAM

It is unfortunate that those who are best prepared by temperament and training to develop sophisticated, objective, definitive studies in this area have been reluctant to become involved. In an article on the present status of university-based research and training activities related to hypnosis Moss et al. (1962) concluded on the basis of questionnaires received from 54 (out of 55) psychology departments with APA approved training programs and 39 (out of 85) AMA approved medical schools that, although hypnosis is no longer a tabooed subject, there has been no ground swell of interest in hypnosis in academic centers comparable to the interest manifested by the more clinically oriented professional person since World War II. In the past decade, the faculty of only 18 psychology departments have participated in research studies with hypnosis, whereas only 9 departments have had MA theses and 13 have had PhD dissertations. The level of research activity in medical schools during this period was even less impressive—a total of 14 studies (a "best estimate" for all 85 schools might be 28 or 30). The prudent graduate student is well advised, of course, to avoid the complications inherent in experiments on the topic, if only out of deference to the still generally negative attitudes of faculty members. Nevertheless, in the past ten years there have been occasional studies of real merit conducted at the graduate level, such as those by Mixer, Tart, Lesser, and Wiseman.

Despite the limited involvement of university student and faculty in this general problem area, some satisfaction may be found in the fact that both the quantity and quality of research productivity have perceptibly increased in recent years. The growth rate of activity generally in this field has been little short of phenomenal. The article by Moss reveals that between 1950 to 1959 there were 502 entries in the *Psychological Abstracts* pertaining to hypnosis. Unfortunately, many of these studies were blatantly clinical in nature or only quasi-experimental. Deckert and West (1963) performed a qualitative analysis of 175 studies comprising the total published literature on hypnosis in the area of experimental psychopathology (which included studies on the hypnotic dream), and although they found that only 11 of these papers met reasonable standards of scientific rigor, they made the encouraging point that most of these had appeared since 1959. This is probably an accurate reflection of the still exceedingly limited but slowly increasing competence of researchers in this field.

Chapter 4
Experimental Advances in Related Areas

Electrophysiological Studies of Sleep and Dreams

BACKGROUND AND DEVELOPMENT

The wide variability of response stimulated by the hypnotic suggestion "to dream" has a parallel, it appears, in the spontaneous dream, which also varies greatly in terms of structure, content, and types of distortion. As Brenman states the issue, "it is probably a meaningless formulation to ask whether hypnotic dreams are the same as spontaneous night dreams, as if *all* hypnotic dreams have certain formal qualities in common which distinguish them as a group from *all* night dreams" (Brenman, 1949, p. 457). At this stage in our knowledge we cannot identify the typical or average hypnotic or night dream nor do we possess any explicit data regarding the wide range of mentation encompassed under either category. Any determination of the comparability of the hypnotic with the natural dream must await greatly expanded information concerning the nocturnal dream.

The development in recent years of elegant electrophysiological techniques for the study of sleep and dreams at last promises a breakthrough and the means of resolving some of the classical issues in dream theory. The observation that dreaming is a universal human phenomenon that occurs nightly in all individuals in a highly predictable fashion has excited great scientific interest. The biological phenomena associated with dreaming sleep are so truly remarkable that many investigators have become preoccupied with the study of the physiological, pharmacological, biochemical, and neuroanatomical vicissitudes of sleep and associated complex technical problems of methodology and instrumentation. A cardinal feature of these studies is not only their departure from the more traditional concern with the analysis of dream content, but a diverting of attention from a simple comparison of the neurophysiological concomitants of the waking and sleep

43

states to a concern with the extensive variability displayed within the sleep period itself.

Although the revitalized study of sleep and dreams is barely a decade old, the electrophysiological techniques involved appear applicable not only to the study of the dreams of normal sleep, but to a careful scrutiny of the hallucinatory mechanism as it is manifest in a wide variety of situations and conditions. An extended series of interrelated investigations is already contributing to the rapid growth of an inchoate body of knowledge. This exciting turn of events was initiated in the early 1950's with the observation by Aserinsky and Kleitman (1953, 1955) that cycles of rapid conjugate eye movements (REMs) appearing during sleep are reliable indicators of dream occurrence. Dement and Kleitman (1955, 1957a) by the simple expedient of continuous, all-night electroencephalographic recordings discovered further that these eye movements occurred in stage 1 sleep when the brain wave configuration most resembled the waking pattern.

The many psychophysiological dream studies now underway generally utilize a basic experimental model. Briefly stated, subjects are studied with full-night, continuous EEG recording from parietal, frontal, and occipital scalp leads. Electrodes are also placed about the eyes, providing an electrooculogram (EOG) which is a record of the changes in potential between the cornea and retina that occur when the eyeball moves, a highly reliable technique of recording the occurrence and direction of REMs. Resting muscle tone, pulse rate, and respirations, all of which show higher levels of activity and greater variability during REM periods, are also recorded simultaneously via the electroencephalograph. As many as five consecutive nights of uninterrupted sleep may be observed in order to provide a person's baseline patterning of sleep periods. Dream research is arduous and difficult, and the number of subjects in any one study has been limited by the necessity of monitoring subjects for many days and nights in succession.

The characteristic sleep cycle of the young adult evidences four EEG stages, repeated three to seven times each night. Discrete bursts of REMs and associated dreams are invariably accompanied throughout their duration by a low-voltage, fast-frequency, nonspindling EEG pattern—variously called the stage 1, REM, D state, activated or paradoxical sleep stage—whereas the other three stages or non-REM periods (NREMPs) show generally higher-voltage, slow-frequency, and sleep spindles. The term REMP is actually a misnomer because both slow and rapid eye movements occur with greatest frequency during this period; more accurately it might be called an ocular activity stage.

Typically, when a normal adult goes to sleep, he moves rapidly down to sleep stage 4, remains there for an hour or so, then moves back upward through stages 3 and 2 to stage 1. Then he has his first real dream period, usually a short one averaging perhaps ten minutes. He next drifts back to stage 4 for another comparatively long stay and rises again to stage 1 and another dream period. As the night progresses, the sleeper sinks only to stages 3 or 2, and when he moves upward again, he spends more time in stage 1. Later dream periods may last half an hour. However, the time of the cycle—the 90 or 100 minutes from the end of one dream period to the end of the next—remains constant. Although there are wide individual differences in the percentage of time spent in each stage, there is a consistency in the pattern of individual subjects. It has been reliably determined that adults spend approximately 20 to 25 per cent of their sleep in these REM periods. Each stage 1-REM period consists of several dreams, accounting for 10 to 20 separate dream episodes in a night.

The exact relationship between dreaming and rapid eye movements is only now being investigated. There is considerable anecdotal evidence that the REMs are correlated with alternations in the dreamer's subjective gaze, that is, they are a physical representation of what the dreamer is "watching" in the dream scene. The evidence on this point is circumstantial, of course, and a number of possibilities exist: there is no relationship between the REMs and the imagery experienced, there is a correlation, or the relationship is causal, that is, the imagery determines the REMs or vice versa. At the moment there are conflicting opinions held by equally eminent authorities. Illustrative of the contradictory findings in this area, Gross et al. (1965) studied eye movements in the congenitally blind and concluded that "the eye movement mechanism pre-prepared at birth persists in subjects with life long blindness in the absence of visual imagery and presumably visual dreaming. It does not disprove the possibility that when visual dreaming is present the eye movements can be taken over for purposes of visual scanning."

In their early comparisons of REM and NREM periods, Dement and Kleitman reported dream recall in 70 to 80 per cent of REM period awakenings and only 10 per cent or less of NREM period awakenings. However, other investigators have reported mentation upon awakening subjects from other stages of sleep, although such content in quantitatively less and qualitatively different from that obtained in stage 1. When awakened during NREM periods, subjects often report a fairly logical preoccupation with recent events, that is, the ideation is relatively bland and innocuous, there is less distortion, many pure memories are related to recent activities, and the subject himself labels the experiences as "thoughts," not "dreams" (Foulkes, 1962). A dramatic shift in cognitive functioning occurs in REM or stage 1 periods of sleep—there is a transformation that results in processes akin to those that Freud called the "dreamwork." Thus there appears to be some manner of mental activity present in all stages of sleep, although it is the mentation present during REMPs that is most consonant with the conventional definition of dreaming.

Studies of the dream-sleep pattern in neonates, infants, children, and adults show the characteristic cyclic alternations in all subjects from one day old to 70 years of age. Changes in the proportion of REM sleep to total sleep time was noted to vary with ages of subjects, with highest percentage of REM sleep in the newborn and least in the aged. The sleep patterns of all mammals thus far studied are similar to that of humans in exhibiting stage 1-REM periods alternating with higher-voltage, slow-wave (NREM) periods. The fact that infants are born with a sleep cycle suggests that these periods are generated subcortically, and studies of decorticated animals indicate that the REM state is indeed triggered in the brain stem, probably in the caudal pontine nucleus of the reticular formation (Jouvet, 1960).

Investigations have already been instigated concerning the relation of the sleep-dream cycle to the following:

The effects of internal somatic drives, such as hunger and thirst, and external physical stimuli (water, sound, pain, temperature, odors).

The relation of NREM content to the dream process.

Sleep patterns in psychosis and other pathological conditions, for example, narcolepsy, congenital nystagmus, enuresis, and suicide.

The results of intermittent and continuous, partial, total, and selective sleep and dream deprivation.

Color in dreams.

Maturational effects on percentage of REM time.

Autonomic response patterns during sleep.

Telepathic perception.

Dosages of tranquilizers, sedatives, LSD, alcohol, and other drugs.

Content and process during REM and NREM sleep.

Experimental brain lesions.

The electrical activity of different brain areas, such as the discharge patterns of the lateral geniculate neurons.

Brain temperature changes during the sleep stages in infrahuman species.

REMs during sleep in dark-reared kittens, as a consequence of deprivation of patterned vision in monkeys and in congenitally blind humans.

The differences between good and poor sleepers and between dream recallers and nonrecallers.

Somnambulists or sleepwalkers and sleep talkers.

Oxygen consumption as a measure of metabolic fluctuations.

A cycle of penile erection synchronous with REM sleep.

Cross-cultural studies, including one of sleep patterns in the polar regions.

This list is representative rather than exhaustive, but does accurately mirror the exceedingly wide range of studies now in progress.

Several very excellent reviews of the mushrooming literature in this area of the psychophysiological studies of sleep and dreams are available (Dement, 1965; Trillin, 1965; *U.S. Public Health Serv. Publ.* **1389**, 1965).

SOME IMPLICATIONS OF EEG STUDIES FOR THE HYPNOTIC DREAM

Early investigators generally regarded hypnosis as a form of artificially induced sleep, and it would certainly buttress the position of those who contend that an essential identity exists between hypnotic and spontaneous night dreams if it could be proved that hypnosis is physiologically akin to sleep. However, Kleitman, in his book *Sleep and Wakefulness* (1963), depicts hypnosis as something other than sleep, and most authorities in the past two decades have concluded that hypnosis is physiologically analogous to the waking state. The literature on EEG patterns associated with hypnosis actually divides rather equally between studies reporting patterns similar to different stages of normal sleep and those reporting waking EEG activity. Still it can be stated almost categorically that there is at this time no really solid evidence to be had about the neurophysiological similarity of these two types of dreams.

At the same time, the evidence can no longer be considered quite so firm that the nocturnal and hypnotic states in which dreaming occurs can always be clearly differentiated. Recent facts arising out of the electroencephalographic studies illuminate the complexity of the issues involved. An undoubted complication is posed by the marked resemblance of the irregular, low-voltage, rapidly changing brain wave pattern during dreaming sleep to that of the alert, waking brain, highlighting the fact that the distinguishing characteristics of the various stages of sleep are at best somewhat arbitrary, and the issue of what EEG criteria are to be used in differentiating between REM sleep, wakefulness, drowsiness, and hypnosis remains debatable (O'Connell et al., 1965). Furthermore, evoked cortical potentials during the waking state are quite comparable to those evoked in REM sleep, and if the accompanying EEG patterns are not identical, they are certainly very similar. A rapidly growing cohort of studies reflects a striking correspondence between brain responses in waking and dreaming. Nevertheless, although the REM EEG indicates a vigorous level of cortical excitation, the generalized suppression of motor and reflex activity also indicates distinctive differences in the functional organization of the brain.[1]

In a valuable recent book reviewing the experimental evidence on daydreaming, Singer (1966) emphasizes the continuous activity of the brain and the fact that in an ongoing stream of mental activity dreams and daydreams represent different points along a continuum. Under ordinary circumstances responsiveness to external stimulus sources have priority. Attention to waking fantasy develops under conditions similar to those conducive to night dreaming, that is, under greatly reduced or monotonous external conditions, such as those shortly before sleep when the person is in bed. Gross physical activity, a rapidly changing external stimulus field, or even the emergence of vivid inner imagery at sleep onset may act to maintain arousal even when sleep is desired. Growing drowsiness is accompanied by an increase in task-irrelevant thinking and visual imagery; at a certain point a striking break in content occurs between waking thoughts or daydreams and the sleeping dream, and the person experiences a rapid transition into deeper sleep accompanied by hypnagogic imagery. "There exists a certain amount of fairly continuous preconscious associative activity which comes 'conscious' as soon as sleep begins" (Singer, 1966, p. 50). Visual imagery is the predominant modality for both waking fantasy and night dreaming, but symbolism plays a limited role in the former; as drowsiness passes into sleep, the allegorical or metaphorical quality of thought characterizing nocturnal dreaming begins.

Silberer (1909) was among the first to make systematic investigation of what he referred to at the time as the "autosymbolic phenomenon,"

---

[1] It is the gross loss of muscle tonus that allows perpetuation of behavioral sleep, and this is the ostensible reason why the REM period escaped attention for so long. Two interesting exceptions to the generalized motor paralysis in dreaming sleep are the presence of large numbers of fine-finger movements and a cycle of penile erection synchronous with dreaming sleep (Fisher et al., 1965).

a form of mental activity, predominately visual in quality, associated with sleep onset. He determined that in a state intermediate between waking and sleep the effort to think conceptually would produce an automatic visual symbolization of what had a moment before been an abstract idea represented in conventional symbols. Barber's attempt (pp. 221–222) to distinguish between the so-called autosymbolic phenomenon and hypnagogic imagery on the basis that the latter is less apparently contiguous with preceding thought, must be tempered by the recognition that both are products of sleep onset and, if not identical, they are certainly fraternal forms of the hypnagogic reverie.

Dement *loc cit.* posed the rhetorical question as to whether hypnagogic imagery should be considered dreaming, and his negative answer, based on the allegation that hypnagogic images are not regarded by subjects as "real," reflects his strict definition of what constitutes "dreaming." It may be countered that hypnagogic images, like dreams, do occur in extreme drowsiness or sleep onset, the transition from the waking state is a sudden one, they are divorced from conscious control, they terminate with the experience of awakening, and many subjects do experience them as real visual hallucinations, although of limited duration (Sperling, 1961).

In an experiment designed to discover the precise point during sleep onset at which involuntary, symbolic imagery appears, Roffwarg et al. (1965) made the determination that REMs commence at the moment of alpha dropout. (Alpha is the 9–12 cycles/second rhythm that appears during a relaxed waking state, but not when a person is tense or thinking about a problem, or even when he is drowsy and about to fall asleep. Alpha suppression is, therefore, directly related to the vividness of visual imagery and to the inhibition of verbal-conceptual thinking.) The data are not yet complete, but the findings suggest that "during alpha activity the subject is generally controlling his thoughts and is aware of being awake. With the fragmentation and disappearance of alpha, there is a loss of contact with the surroundings and a sensation of drift. The thinking is described as having become involuntary and looser. In many cases of awakening from this state, vivid and immediate imagery is recalled." In a related study Vogel et al. (1965) report that "The usual, though not invariable, sequence of events during sleep onset is as follows: during alpha EEG reality testing and thought content are intact; during descending stage 1 there is a loss of both functions; and during descending stage 2 reality testing is completely lost but thought content is no longer regressed."

The EEG in the hypnotic state is most often characterized by a sustained alpha rhythm, which would appear to refute a sleeplike state;

however, again the evidence is not clear-cut. EEG records of REM period sleep in many individuals display a clearly visible, if somewhat reduced alpha wave (one cycle/second slower). The presence of an alpha rhythm during REM sleep should be considered another indicator of a relatively aroused level, and it is the reverse of the normal waking state in which attention-demanding tasks give rise to a disruption of the alpha rhythm. It is also a reminder that individual variability is so extensive that EEG discrimination between sleep stages or sleeping and waking is a relative matter and subjects are best used as their own control.

Since the first recognition of REM sleep, a distinction has been made between descending and emergent stage 1. The former, occurring at sleep onset, has been described as extremely brief, accompanied by slow eye movements rather than REMs, and having a much lower arousal threshold than stage 1-REM. The possibility exists that some "dreams" experienced during hypnosis may be the product of a transitory descending stage 1 state. This speculation remains to be experimentally validated, but could account for the relative brevity and the less dramatic character of dreams produced during hypnosis (as distinct from the situation in which a dream is posthypnotically suggested to occur subsequently during the night and the resulting product of which may sound very much like a true dream).

Evidence on this point is suggestive only. Foulkes and Vogel (1965) have reported that dreamlike, hallucinatory episodes not dissimilar to REM reports occur with considerable frequency during both descending EEG stages 1 and 2, and also that these brief periods are accompanied by an absence of rapid eye movements and a perceptible alpha rhythm. The contention of Dement and his collaborators that dreaming occurs only during REM periods would also appear to be contradicted by the common experiences of many persons who have noted that they dream immediately upon falling asleep, as during afternoon catnaps. Consider, for example, Singer's report based on a careful introspective self-study:

> The occurrence of moderately extended dreams with rich symbolic personal content emphasizes my observation that the dreams I have noted immediately after falling asleep do not have the qualities ascribed to hypnagogic phenomena but represent genuine dreams. Except for being somewhat shorter, they seem quite representative of the general pattern of my own dreams and, for that matter, comparable in structural qualities to the dreams reported in psychoanalytic literature. In the instances where I have had an opportunity to be wired up for EEG study during afternoon naps, I have had dreams with no EEG evidence of rapid eye movements (Singer, 1966, p. 49).

It has been frequently reported that if left alone hypnotized subjects will often drift into natural sleep (or, conversely, that natural sleep can be transformed into hypnosis). It is curious that apparently no investigator has undertaken to induce hypnotic dreams by deliberately trading upon the possibility of persuading a hypnotic subject to natural sleep in the session itself before producing a dream.

A paper which presents an interesting speculation has been written by Domhoff (1964) with special reference to electroencephalographic studies of hypnosis and sleep (*refer to pp. 206–213, this volume*). Domhoff argues that it is quite possible that EEG differences reported in relation to the hypnotic dream may be a function of the method of induction, that is, techniques involving specifically suggested symptoms of sleep (Barker and Burgiven, 1948, 1949), individual differences among subjects (so-called active versus passive), or the vicissitudes of the hypnotist-subject relationship. Until such variables are carefully controlled and their influence partialed out, it is Domhoff's contention that the equivalence of the EEG patterns of the hypnotic trance, particularly those associated with induced dreams, to the dream stage of natural sleep cannot be ruled out.

EYE MOVEMENTS AND THE HYPNOTIC DREAM

Another avenue of exploration into the involved relationship between hypnotic and nocturnal dreams is through the sensitive EOG (eye movement) index. Hypnosis provides a method for the control and manipulation of both dream content and eye movement, and several investigators are already pursuing this approach. The relationship between EEG patterns, eye movements, and type of activity in the dream was first investigated by Schiff, Bunney, and Freedman (1961) through the dreams of one hypnotized subject. The EEG patterns of both trance and posthypnotic dreams were deemed essentially those of the waking state; however, eye movements similar to those in natural dreams occurred, and the frequency and amplitude were clearly re lated to the amount of activity in the dream. It was concluded that although trance states cannot be equated physiologically with normal sleep, hypnotic dreams produce the same phenomenal experience of dreaming. Suggested variations in the amount of activity within the dream and the dreamer's relation to her dream (as participant or observer) demonstrated that hypnosis could be used to study the finer nuances of the relationship between eye movement and dream content. Inhibition of eye movements by direct suggestion in order to study the intrinsic relationship of ocular movements to the occurrence or content of the dream proved most difficult for the subject. She reported a feeling of uneasiness and seemed compelled to scan and orient herself in relation to the visual field of her dreams.

In a study of the relationship of eye movements to attentive activities, Amadeo and Shagass (1963) speculated that REM rate increases as a nonspecific concomitant of attention, rather than as a consequence of the dreamer's scanning of his visual images. The major aim of the study was to test the hypothesis that fundamental changes in attentive functioning characterize the hypnotic state. Results obtained from 20 subjects indicated a consistent reduction of rapid eye movement rates during hypnosis. The hypnotic effect was demonstrated to be even greater than that produced by a waking, voluntary effort to hold the eyes immobile, and was interpreted to mean that hypnotic induction produces a reduction of overall attentive activity. These results are compatible with the characteristic sleeplike appearance and failure to respond to external stimuli of the hypnotized subject. The intrusion of various mental tasks resulted in an increased REM rate, consistent with the interpretation that REM rate increases with attentive activity. Although it was not the intent of his experiment to compare EOG patterns in the dreaming phases of hypnosis and sleep, the authors report that preliminary observations with three subjects suggest that the REM rate during the stage 1 sleep was about the same as during hypnosis (considerably lower than that found during active attending in the waking state).

In a study of the eye movements accompanying fantasy activity in waking and hypnosis, Deckert (1964) found that subjects instructed to imagine a beating pendulum develop smooth pursuit-tracking eye movements of a frequency comparable to that of a previously visualized real pendulum under both conditions when their eyes were closed, whereas saccadic (rapid shift) movements were characteristic of the eyes-open-imagining conditions in either state. Hypnotic dreaming and hallucinating were also accompanied by saccadic eye movements. Deckert suggests that the appearance of pursuit movements in the eyes-closed-imagining condition supports an "outflow" theory for central control of eye movement, that is, an appropriate *cerebral* image is the only necessary prerequisite for the elaboration of pursuit eye movements.

It is unclear why pursuit eye movements occurred in hypnotic imagining but not in hypnotic dreaming. It also remains to be demonstrated that pursuit eye movements would occur in natural dreams in relation to a similar imaginal stimulus. However, the results do suggest an objective technique for differentiating reactions to visual hallucinations in spontaneous and hypnotic dreams. It is reasonable to anticipate, for example, that slowly moving imagery in either day or night dreaming would correlate with smooth pursuit eye movements, whereas slow gazing in hypnotic dreams would be accompanied by disconnected, saccadic deflections. Such results could be interpreted to mean that the hallucinations of dreaming sleep have a different neurophysiological basis than those associated with hypnosis. The cause-and-effect relationship between eye movements and the act of dreaming has yet to be established and a totally unexplored approach to date has been the determination of whether posthypnotic manipulation of eye movements could influence the content or possibly even evoke a dream during regular sleep.

The available electrooculographic evidence regarding the hypnotic dream suggested and experienced during hypnosis is quite preliminary. Ocular motility is apparently a concomitant of hypnotic dreaming, but it may vary in essential respects from that accompanying normal dreaming, and it could be an artifact referable to the nature of the hypnotic state rather than directly attributable to the act of dreaming in hypnosis, although the same distinction could be applied to dreaming in natural sleep as well.

If the eye movements correlated with the hypnotic dream are not precisely the same as those associated with nocturnal dreaming, neither is there evidence that waking daydreaming and the hypnotic dream are identical in terms of associated eye movements. Daydreaming is associated with minimal eye movement (Antrobus, Antrobus, and Singer, 1964). An interesting related observation is that the deliberate suppression of an ongoing private fantasy provokes considerable rapid eye movement, a finding consistent with an experiment by Antrobus (1963) which found that habitual nonrecallers of dreams actually show more eye movement during REM sleep than do persistent recallers. Singer and Antrobus (1965) further report that engagement in even vigorous daytime fantasying involves relatively little eye movement. Clearly, the exact relationship between daydreams, night dreams, and hypnotic dreams in terms of EOG data remains to be explicated.

A PROTOTYPICAL STUDY OF THE POSTHYPNOTIC DREAM

The most ambitious and well-controlled study to date involving the use of the post hypnotically suggested dream in conjunction with electrophysiological measures was reported by Stoyva (1965). Utilizing 16 subjects, he undertook to answer such questions as: When during the night does the subject dream about the suggested topic? How is the implanted content contextually related to the remainder of the dream? *This study is reprinted on pages 255–268.*

Briefly, Stoyva confirmed again that some hypnotized subjects will respond to a posthypnotic suggestion to dream about a specified topic. They differ in degree of responsiveness from total compliance to minimal or no reference to the implanted topic. In each instance the suggested dream elements were embedded or woven into a sequential episode. The most surprising finding was that the posthypnotic suggestion influenced not only the content of the dreams but reduced the total amount of dreaming as well, particularly for subjects who repeatedly dreamed in accordance with the suggested topic. This is the first experimental demonstration of a psychological variable influencing the physiological concomitants of dreaming.

What mechanism accounts for the reduction of stage 1-REM time? Are the extensive individual differences in compliance with suggested topics a function of the fact that analysis was restricted to the manifest content of the reported dreams? Does the length or complexity of the hypnotic suggestion influence the amount of time spent in dreaming? Stoyva deliberately restricted his investigation to dreams occurring in the first 210 minutes of sleep. Because it seems established that dreams early in the night are preoccupied with minor details of the day's events whereas later dreams are much more personal and memorial, would the effect be sustained throughout the whole night? Awakening a subject at successive intervals throughout the night might also show how a suggested theme was gradually elaborated and changed. It would be surprising if the effect of a hypnotic suggestion were restricted only to REM periods; hence, does the hypnotic suggestion reduce dreaming by increasing other forms of ideation during the remaining stages of sleep?

The assertion by Schiff et al. that posthypnotic dreams actually occur in a brief interval of wakefulness is not dealt with by Stoyva, and the possibility remains that the reduction in REM time may be attributable to a transitory interruption of the sleep cycle. The observation that there is a spontaneous reactivation of the hypnotic state at the moment a subject begins to carry out an implanted suggestion at a later time has been well documented by Erickson and Erickson (1941). An impressive demonstration of this fact is the ease with which the hypnotic relationship can be reinstated at that moment; it would be of considerable interest to determine whether the same susceptibility prevails at the point of initiation of a posthypnotically suggested dream.

Tart (1966*c*) studied two highly hypnotizable subjects in order to assess the feasibility of controlling various aspects of their stage 1 dreaming via posthypnotic suggestion. The efficacy of posthypnotic suggestion in effecting stage 1 dream content was confirmed. Posthypnotic suggestion was also effective in producing awakenings at the beginnings and ends of stage 1 dream periods, although the mechanism of the discrimination and arousal processes remains unclear. The effect of the experimental procedure in extending and in curtailing stage 1 dream time was limited and, if present, was rather small.

THE PROBLEM OF RECALL

A main virtue of the REM technique is that it allows identification of periods of dreaming, hence immediate recall and an assumed veridicality of the dream report. In the last analysis, despite impressive methodological refinements, the investigator remains dependent on a verbal report based on an introspective process; that is, we are still restricted to the study of dream recall rather than dreams themselves. Psychologists have long known that dream reports were of limited validity, subject to distortion by faulty recall and other factors that influence memory. Recent findings have confirmed the soundness of this skeptical attitude. It has been demonstrated, for example, that the memory traces for dreams are short-lived. If a subject is awakened during an REMP, he can be expected to recall a dream four times out of five, and often the wealth of detail is extraordinary. But in most instances the amount of detail fades rapidly and within a few minutes after the cessation of the telltale REMs memory for the dream may have disappeared entirely. To illustrate the point, Kahn et al. (1962) found that a large majority of dreams contain color, but the memory for this element apparently fades much more rapidly than the memory for form, thus suggesting that the usual "black-and-white" dream is probably an artifact of recall. It is obvious that only a small fraction of the night's dreams are available to later recall, and retrospective recall obtained in morning reports is vulnerable to great distortion.

There are people who typically recall at least a proportion of their dreams and there are those who do not. It is now known that even habitual "nondreamers" manifest sleep cycles with the same proportion of REMPs and that it is in relation to the factor of recall that people actually differ. The results reported by Antrobus et al. (1964), as well as others, suggest personality differences along a sensitization-repression continuum. People also differ in their receptivity to the suggestion to increase waking recall of their dreams.

An unexpected finding by Shapiro et al. (1964) was that subjects sometimes report, when awakened from REMPs, that they were "thinking" rather than "dreaming." This led to the speculation that the memory of a dream may be replaced by thoughtlike experiences even as the subject awakens (hypnopompic phenomena). It was observed that these reports of "thinking" were more frequent after gradual awakenings than after abrupt ones. Further findings by Shapiro et al. (1965) suggest that the effect of the method of awakening is more pronounced among habitual nonreporters than among subjects who usually recall dreaming. The effect is also greater during late REM periods of the night, whereas occasional no-content reports tend to occur early in the night after REM period awakenings with relatively high arousal threshold (Goodenough et al., 1965a, 1965b).

It is widely recognized that the high degree of vigilance characteristic of alert wakefulness is antithetical to the observation of unconsciously determined mentation and, conversely, that relaxation and drowsiness aid and abet introspection. It is commonly assumed that hypnosis reduces vigilance and facilitates the free flow of associations, placing the subject in much closer contact with covert ideational processes. In a study still in progress, Arkin et al. (1964) have undertaken to capitalize on the fact that sleep talking throughout the night is a common occurrence and that it changes in tone, growing more expressive and emotional during REM periods. Hypnotizable subjects who also have a history of active sleep talking, are trained in somniloquy or talking without awakening. It is hoped in this manner to study ideational processes in all stages of sleep with minimal arousal, perhaps even to capture descriptions of dreams in progress. Preliminary results with one carefully studied subject indicate that the posthypnotic suggestion (PHS) to report dreams while they are ongoing had several striking effects:

1. A marked increase in the frequency of sleep speeches.
2. A shift in the concentration of speeches from the first to the second half of the night.
3. A shift of speeches from NREMPs to initiation during or in immediate association with REMPs.
4. Awakenings after REMP sleep-speeches resulted in recall of closely corresponding dreams, whereas the proportion of direct correspondences obtainable by morning recall was much less.
5. Administration of a presleep hypnotic trance *with or without* PHS seems to be followed by an increase in REMP time.

The technique of encouraging subjects to describe their dreams without awakening thus appears promising. Certainly, the PHS has widespread consequences in terms of the sleep-dream cycle, although the mechanism involved is far from clear.

Examination of the hypothesis that a subject momentarily reverts to the hypnotic state when carrying out a posthypnotic suggestion to dream produced equivocal results. EEG and EOG data suggest that the sleep-speech episode is an admixture of sleep and the post-hypnotic state. On the one hand, the presence of unusually large amounts of alpha frequencies and muscle tension artifacts suggests a greater degree of arousal than is usually found in natural REMP sleep. On the other hand, there was an uncharacteristic lack of continuity, such that sleep-speeches were not usually recoverable even with hypnosis the following morning. Furthermore, despite extended practice in dream reporting, it became evident in the final phase of the experiment that the subject still had to learn to "dream" during the hypnotic state. At the same time, the EEG accompanying these hypnotic dreams resembled the drowsy (but still awake) state and, other reports to the contrary, no REMs were observed despite the fact that the dreams often involved extreme activity. The hypnotic dreams also differed from natural dreams, according to the subject, in being less "deep" and in his inability to forget the presence of the experimenter as an expectant audience. Another major phase of the project will assess and compare the recall of dreams in the waking state the next morning and during hypnosis involving an attempted reinstatement of the earlier natural dream.

MENTAL HEALTH IMPLICATIONS

Psychoanalytic theory postulates that dreaming is a safety valve and that failure of this outlet can result in a compulsion to dream (hallucinate) in the waking state. Fenichel (1945, p. 422) aptly represents the psychoanalytic viewpoint that because the unconscious has become conscious, the psychotic is dominated by archaic modes of thinking. He writes: "The schizophrenic shows an intuitive understanding of symbolism. Interpretation of symbols, for instance, which neurotics find so difficult to accept in analysis, are made spontaneously and as a matter of course by the schizophrenic." Fenichel goes on to say that the schizophrenic often expresses ideas that are deeply repressed in others, so that the verbalizations of the schizophrenic are similar to the unconscious, repressed thoughts of the normal or neurotic. Symbolic thinking for them is not merely a method of defensive distortion; it is an archaic pictorial mode of thinking that occurs in all regressive states.[2]

Dement conjectured that much might be learned about the function of dreams if he could temporarily disrupt or prevent dreaming sleep. In a much heralded study he reported that deprivation of stage 1-REM sleep by repeated awakenings at the inception of these periods produces an intense compensatory pressure to dream (Dement, 1960). Preliminary evidence indicated that the frequency and duration of REM periods increased in direct proportion to the degree of deprivation. After several consecutive nights of dream deprivation it became literally impossible to deprive a subject of his dreams without depriving him of all sleep. Control studies showed that loss of total sleep time and awakenings from other sleep stages do not result in any compensatory rise, although NREM sleep tends to take precedence over REM sleep when there has been deprivation of all stages. In other words, there seems to be a mechanism that demands a certain nightly amount of REM sleep.

Disordered sleep is well known as a precursor of many mental and physical illnesses, and it seems plausible that dreaming could contribute to adaptive functioning and its disruption to maladjustment. Subjective and behavioral changes were noted by Dement and his co-workers in subjects deprived of stage 1 sleep; they became increasingly anxious, irritable, unable to concentrate, susceptible to an increase in hunger and sex drives, and some even developed paranoid or psychotic-like symptoms. Studies are being initiated to determine whether any link exists between the "waking dreams" of the psychotic and the nocturnal "hallucinations" of normal persons. Fisher and Dement (1963) found that when psychotic patients are deprived of sleep, and thus of dreams, they react with intensified psychotic symptoms.

---

[2] It is generally agreed that, although dreaming is one form of hallucinatory behavior, not all hallucinations are dreams; however, Rosen (1953) literally equated schizophrenia with dreaming. He thought enough of the schizophrenics' facility in understanding the symbolic aspects of psychotic behavior to employ patients-in-remission to advise him in the conduct of psychotherapy. Alerted to this possibility, Moss (1957a) employed selected schizophrenic patients in Rorschach content analysis. Although content analysis is freely practiced today, Rorschach's original disparagement of this approach has retarded full development of a dynamic theory of content analysis. Moss found that despite the absence of any formal training in symbol interpretation, some schizophrenic patients possess an unusual capacity for interpreting Rorschach protocols. While the study was basically of a clinical nature, results were sufficiently promising to suggest that this talent should be tested in relation to dream content.

Agreement about the normal sleep configuration allows for studies of the aberrant sleep-dream patterns associated with acute mental and emotional disturbances, evaluation of the effects of different types of treatment on the sleep-dream pattern, and investigation of the effect of experimental manipulation of sleep schedules. The possibility that increased dreaming might provide a useful therapy in the treatment of the mentally ill is now being explored. It is tempting to speculate that it might be possible to treat by carefully prescribed "dream dosages." If this were so, it would become all the more important to determine whether precisely controlled hypnotic hallucinations could substitute for the REM type of dream? Results of a recent study by Fiss et al. (1966) strongly suggest that the distinguishing mentation of the dreaming sleep stage is not "switched off" following awakening but may persist into the waking state, and whatever the function of a dream that a fantasy may serve a similar, substitutive purpose. In this regard, if hypnotic dreams possess any essential comparability to nocturnal dreams, it might be expected that they could counteract the compensatory effect associated with dream deprivation.

The literature indicates that the act of daydreaming, like the night dream, services important adaptive functions, although there is limited agreement about the nature of these functions. Singer (1966) suggests that fantasy deprivation, too, might well be accompanied by unpleasant effects, particularly among frequent daydreamers. He also posits that the antisocial, hyperactive, and delinquent child may suffer from an insufficiency of fantasy skills and that there could be definite advantage in training such impulse-dominated children in an enhanced imaginative capacity.

The studies relating to recall in the preceding section suggest one further innovation—a variation of the dream deprivation technique in which hypnosis would be used to effect recall deprivation. Psychoanalysis has consistently emphasized the value of remembering, understanding, and being guided by one's dreams. What consequences, if any, would ensue from the expedient of employing posthypnotic suggestion to eradicate systematically any memory for dreams in those persons who ordinarily recall and value them?

It needs to be borne in mind that the relation between mental illness and the amount of dreaming (or fantasy) time is far from clear. Several recent studies have found that the deleterious psychological consequences of even prolonged REMP deprivation were quite minimal. The point is that at the moment the psychotic hallucination has no more been proved equivalent to the normal night time fantasy than has the hypnotic dream.

Additional Experimental Advances

QUANTITATIVE STUDIES OF DREAM CONTENT

Discovery of objective neurophysiological indicators of dreaming has led to a very appreciable increment in research concerning the frequency, regularity, and duration of dreaming and its biological concomitants; however, there has been a relative neglect of interest in the content characteristics of dreams. Calvin Hall and his associates at the Institute of Dream Research in Santa Cruz, California (formerly Miami, Florida), represent an effort in opposition to this trend through a broadly based program of research focused on the quantitative, systematic study of the content of dreams and the relationship between content and personality.

Hall has been active in this phase of dream research for the past 15 years and his basic datum now consists of over 30,000 dreams collected from males and females of all age groups throughout the world. Experience gleaned from this material has allowed the staff to prepare a series of technical manuals to facilitate the content analysis of dreams. These comprehensive schedules permit classification and quantification of practically every important element in the dream narrative, from characters, settings, and objects to activities and emotions (Hall and Van de Castle, 1966).

The staff of the Institute have either completed or are currently conducting a variety of investigations, such as content changes associated with age and sex, interrelations between dream and personality variables, comparative studies of the dreams of different ethnic and nationality groups, measures of ego strength in dreams, the relation of conscious attitudes to feelings expressed in dreams, and the frequency and stability of certain categories of manifest content in an extended dream series. Long-range plans call for studies of the dreams of deviant populations such as the mentally ill, further studies of the relationship of dream to waking behavior, and detailed studies of dream symbols.

These studies are all predicated on the importance of developing reliable units of content analysis as a basis for inter- and intraindividual comparisons. They bring into sharp focus the confounding factor of wide individual differences in the accuracy of recall. A special investigation now being conducted at the Institute involves the collection of dreams from throughout the night using electrophysiological indicators of dreaming, the objective of which is to compare and contrast the content of dreams in the various stages and sequences of the sleep cycle. Another important aim is to compare the dreams obtained throughout the night with those reported in the morning.

The classification schedules and methods of investigation developed to date at the Institute are largely applicable to the study of manifest content—the more objective and quantifiable aspect of the dream report. A fair representation of Hall's position might be that although inferences can be made from the manifest dream content to the underlying meaning, as one does with Rorschach responses, this is a rather hazardous business, because who is to say what a symbol really means? Hall and his group have evidenced interest in comparisons between dream variables and responses evoked by projective tests, on the assumption that both reflect unconscious impulses. It has further been maintained that the content schedules can be applied to associative material supplied by a subject in relation to his dreams: however, this would appear to be a complex procedure.

In compatible fashion, Hartmann, Kris, Rapaport, and other psychoanalytic investigators engaged in the development of ego psychology have maintained that it is quite erroneous to equate "latent" with "depth" and "manifest" with "surface" (or "triviality") in dream interpretation, and that the manifest dream content is of equal scientific value to the latent content for what it can tell us about the meaning of the dream and the personality of the dreamer. Erikson (1954) has shown that the manifest content may be as revealing as the latent one, and readers are referred to Jones' monograph on the epigenetic method of dream analysis (1962).

An obvious application of Hall's techniques would be in the comparison of spontaneous night dreams with those stimulated by hypnotic suggestion, and the reprinted article by Domhoff elaborates upon this possibility.

PHARMACOLOGICAL STUDIES

One other research approach merits especial mention. Pharmacological agents are widely used to induce and sustain sleep, although there is at present only limited information available regarding the effects of drugs on the sleep cycle. In general, drugs that either increase sleep (hypnotic or hypnosedative agents) or increase wakefulness (amphetamines,, barbiturates, and other stimulants) act to depress dreaming time. A night of increased REM time can be achieved pharmacologically by administering for a time and then withdrawing phenothrazines, alcohol, or dextramphetamine (Hartmann, 1965). One of the few drugs identified thus far which directly increases the amount of dreaming sleep in humans is d-lysergic acid diethylamide (LSD-25). Toyoda (1964) reported an increase in total REM time in a single subject, as did Green (1965). Dream periods in the latter study were distinguished by a marked delay in emergent stage 1 sleep, increased vocalization and gross body movements, and heightened galvanic skin responses.

Muzio, Roffwarg, and Kaufman (1964) also report that small doses administered in conjunction with sleep will moderately increase the total dreaming time by lengthening the REMP occurring at the height of the drug's action. In a still unpublished study (1966) these investigators found that LSD stimulates arousal or REM sleep depending on the dosage. In order to study the effect on the sleep cycle, it was necessary to utilize low dosages to minimize the possibility of sleep interruption; however, they still observed an appreciable extension of either the first or second REM periods in the majority of subjects (ranging from a 20 per cent to 245 per cent increase). LSD did not interfere with the identifying EEG characteristics of any sleep stage, but it did promote alterations in the sleep EEG configuration. The usual pattern of brief early REM periods and longer subsequent ones was in effect reversed, and there was an interposition of REM bursts during NREM intervals. The potentiating effect of LSD on REM sleep supports the possibility of a shared hallucinatory mechanism, possibly of a neurohumoral nature.

There is need for assessment of the subjective experiences during LSD prolongations of REM sleep; that is, were subjects experiencing typical dreaming or some other hallucinatory activity? Work in this area is of importance because of the apparent similarities between psychodelic, hypnotic, and dream states of consciousness. Although there are wide individual variations in reaction to LSD, influenced by the personality and mood of the subject, environmental setting, and absorption rate, laboratory and clinical accounts are in agreement that the drug induces pronounced perceptual changes, illusions, pseudohallucinations, alterations in affect and ideation, depersonalization, and modifications in the relationship between the subject and his environment. Subjectively, there are reports of greater perceptual flexibility, enhanced imagery and fantasy activity, and a decreased reliance on verbal-associative thinking. Consistent with the dominance of visual imagery in thinking, there have been reports (not altogether uniform) that the LSD state is characterized by a significant degree of alpha suppression.

Gubel (1962) reported that many of the experiential features of the drug-induced hallucinogenic experience seem to be remarkably similar to experiences reported by hypnotized subjects. Halpern (1962) argued that no essential qualitative differences exist between hypnotically induced visual percepts and toxicogenic hallucinations. About the same time, Aldous Huxley (1961) recognized similarities in the two states and suggested that hypnosis might be used to control the LSD reaction; the next year Fogel and Hoffer reported the successful use of hypnotic suggestion in the termination of an LSD experience in one patient. The degree to which the LSD experience is susceptible to direction by psychosocial factors is not generally recognized even today.

Since 1950 there have been many reports on the use of LSD as an adjunct in the treatment of psychopathology, and improvement has been reported throughout the entire spectrum of neurotic, psychosomatic, and character disorders. Clinicians have attributed the beneficial effects of the drug to a reduction in defensiveness, the reliving of early traumatic experiences, increased awareness of unconscious content, and greater freedom to engage in ventilation and catharsis. Downing (1964) speculated on similarities in the relation existing between researcher and subject in the hypnotic and drug situations, but it remained for Levine and Ludwig (1965a, 1965b) to employ hypnosis in the direct manipulation of an LSD experience for therapeutic purposes.

The "hypnodelic" treatment method (a contraction of the terms "hypnosis" and "psychedelic") devised by Levine and Ludwig involves the use of hypnosis to control, modify, and direct the LSD experience while it is in progress. It was first used in the treatment of narcotic addicts. After the simultaneous induction of hypnosis and the administration of the drug, the therapist conducts intensive psychotherapy. The investigators attributed the startling improvement exhibited by many patients to an altered state of consciousness in which thoughts and feelings achieved an exaggerated sense of importance and significance and in which there was a marked increase in receptivity to new ideas, that is, therapist interpretations. Hypnosis was particularly effective in keeping the patient's attention focused on his problem and in assisting him in assimilating the unexpected, irrational, and novel quality of his experiences.

Most discussions of altered states of consciousness in the psychotherapeutic setting are dependent on clinical judgments; however, Ludwig and Levine employed a revised questionnaire developed by Linton and Langs (1964) to quantify subjective changes experienced by subjects exposed to the hypnodelic treatment method. The data indicated that the combination of hypnosis and lysergic acid diethylamide produced a more profound alteration in consciousness than was achieved by either agent alone; that is, subjects admitted to a much greater loss of voluntary control, body image changes, distortions in time sense, altered thinking, and somatic changes under the condition of dual administration. As a matter of fact, however, the effect of LSD could not be statistically differentiated from that of hypnosis, lending support to the assertion that the hallucinogenic qualities of the drug-induced state are similar to those experienced in hypnosis. Both the drug and hypnotic conditions, taken individually or together, were readily differentiable from the reactions of a control group who experienced conventional psychotherapy.

Chapter 5
Critique of Experimental Studies

This author's critical assessment of the many studies that have been reported in connection with the hypnotic dream has been assisted greatly by the existence of two excellent evaluative reviews of the literature, one by Barber (1962a) and the other by Tart (1965), *both of which are reprinted in Part Two of this book (pp. 214 and 236, respectively)*. It would be redundant to paraphrase their keen analytical observations; instead, the aim will be to critique the critiques, as it were, and then to extend the discussion, building upon the foundation laid by this procedure.

Barber has occupied a position of prominence this past decade through his repeated demonstration that all of the more dramatic hypnotic phenomena—anesthesia, amnesia, hallucinations, and posthypnotic behavior—can be induced by direct suggestion in at least some waking subjects. He charges that theories of hypnosis are cluttered with vague concepts, and he takes sharp issue with the traditional view that hypnosis is a state that a subject enters, goes deeper into, and comes out of by the application of special hypnotic induction techniques. Barber believes that whether or not subjects cooperate depends on the careful selection of people who possess a natural suggestibility, whether in "hypnosis" or out. In short, resistance or acquiescence is a problem of personality and not the establishment of a distinctive or altered state of consciousness that is somehow different from the subject's normal waking state. Unfortunately, Barber shares in the frustrations of those who have attempted to identify the personality attributes of the "good" hypnotic subject.

As would be anticipated, Barber's evaluation of the literature on the hypnotic dream is completely consistent with his well-publicized point of view. Succinctly stated, his position on the hypnotic dream

is that the typical product is prosaic and mundane; very similar responses can be obtained via waking suggestion; hypnotic dreams,
whether rendered immediately or at night, are quite likely to be purposefully contrived or "made up"; and dream interpretations obtained
from "hypnotized" subjects are no more meaningful than those of
waking subjects. Thus Barber completely discredits the genuineness
of the hypnotic dream and lightly dismisses the question of whether
hypnosis can enhance the interpretation of dreams, for only one experimental study supports this contention.

Barber states that the only distinction between waking and hypnotic
suggestibility is whether the application of suggestion is preceded by
the administration of a "trance induction" and that the behaviors
elicited in either case are substantially the same. It is a revealing commentary that so many investigators have disregarded such a fundamental consideration of methodological rigor as a waking control
group. Several studies by Charles Fisher, will convincingly document
the importance of the point in relation to the hypnotic dream.

Fisher in his studies of the influence of day residues on dream formation found himself confronted with the question of why the dreams
reported by his experimental subjects were structured principally
about the tachistoscopically exposed pictures, when these constituted
only one brief visual fragment among the many millions registered
in any given day. His plausible explanation was that the instruction
to subjects to record any dreams occurring the night following the
experiment was in effect a command to dream about the picture
(Fisher, 1954, p. 391). Fisher attributed the potency of this suggestion
to the "transference" relationship that exists between any experimenter
and his subjects.

Fisher also discovered that the usual process of free association was
incapable of recovering or identifying the tachistoscopically implanted
visual precepts which formed the basis for the dream, and he developed
the method of having subjects relax, close their eyes, and then describe
and make drawings of any images that might emerge. This free
imagery technique was effective in revealing the connection between
the exposed picture and the subsequent dream or fantasy image. Fisher
further observed that the process of distortion in dreams may begin
at the moment of perceptual registration, because these images possessed the same types of transformation that are characteristic of
dreams, that is, fragmentation, special dislocation, condensation, symbolic transformation, spatial reversals, and rotations. In still another
study (1953) Fisher demonstrated that dreams can be successfully

suggested to patients in analysis and even to normal subjects in a classroom situation.[1]

Most authorities would concede that it is possible to find subjects who are equally amenable to suggestion in either the waking or hypnotic states. The fundamental question is whether a hypnotic induction procedure effects any difference in the performance of even some subjects. Notable increases in responsiveness have been demonstrated following induction in a carefully controlled study by Weitzenhoffer and Sjoberg (1961). Even Barber (Glass and Barber, 1961) admits that hypnotic induction can make a difference, although he qualifies the statement with the admonition that a placebo administered under the guise of a "powerful hypnotic drug" can cause the same increment in performance.

Numerous studies have reported changes of one type or another associated with the induction procedure, of course. That "something" happens is strongly indicated by a study such as reported by Stachowiak and Moss (1965). They focused on the interaction between the hypnotist and subject and found that one effect of induction was an immediate elevation in status of the former, which would seem to account for the increased potency of his suggestions. An effort to influence positively the subjects' social attitudes and values (about Negroes) proved at least temporarily effective, but at the price of a subsequent deevaluation of the source of the communication, the hypnotist. Studies such as this suggest the importance of the interpersonal relationship in determining subject susceptibility.

Tart's position on the hypnotic dream is less well known. His paper concerns itself initially with a definition of terms which reveals basic convictions developed in his analysis of the literature and from the experience acquired through his own studies. The "dream" is defined as a vivid hallucinatory experience, experienced at the time as subjectively real, and accompanied by stage 1 physiological concomitants. "Hypnosis" is conceptualized as a psychological state brought about

[1] Reyher has reported on the employment of "free imagery" promoted in the waking state as a useful adjunct in psychotherapy. "We have found that eyes-closed free association, with an emphasis upon visual images, also is a powerful technique. If this procedure is utilized properly, most clients can be brought to experience vivid visual fantasies that are dominated by primary process and which manifest clearly the mechanisms of the 'dreamwork.' At times these fantasies become so well organized that they differ from dreams only in that they are less disguised, and they are valuable because they often lead to the uncovering of repressed material with intense abreactions and regressive behavior" (1963, p. 454).

by conventional induction techniques, characterized by hypersuggestibility, and a waking EEG pattern throughout. The "hypnotic dream"
is conceived of as quite simply an experience in hypnosis elicited by
the suggestion "to dream." Tart reemphasizes the point that the re-
ponse to the suggestion "to dream" may range from thinking, fantasy,
and vivid imagery to a hallucinatory experience of some intensity,
but he expresses doubt regarding the comparability of hypnotically
induced and spontaneous nocturnal dreams. He also makes two
novel points: (*a*) the variability of subject response may reflect real
individual differences in the experience of dreaming and (*b*) Barber's
success with waking suggestion may result from spontaneous, transitory autohypnosis.

Elsewhere, Tart (1966) has found a significant, positive relationship
between the extent to which subjects' rated hypnotically induced
dreams as vivid and dreamlike and two measures of hypnotic depth,
but the variable of actual hypnotic induction did not discriminate
among types of response. In other words, as Barber has maintained,
persons who score high on tests of susceptibility possess the capacity
for dreamlike experiences, whether or not this behavior is preceded
by a formal hypnotic induction procedure.

In another unpublished study on the relationship between waking
and hypnotic suggestibility, Hilgard and Tart (1966) conclude that
subjects fall into three categories: those who are incapable of experiencing the altered state of mind called hypnosis, those who do equally
well on suggestibility tests whether or not they receive a hypnotic
induction, and those who require a hypnotic induction in order to
achieve the requisite suggestibility. Sharp exception is taken to Barber's
operational definition of hypnosis—it cannot be assumed that, because
a subject has been exposed to a hypnotic induction procedure, he
is "hypnotized" and, conversely, that the absence of such a procedure
guarantees that a subject is unhypnotized. When so-called waking
subjects successfully comply with a suggestion "to dream," the possibility remains that these are people capable of drifting into hypnosis
spontaneously when a task demands it. This study found that the
degree to which a person felt himself to be hypnotized, whether or
not he had submitted to a formalized induction procedure, was highly
predictive of the dreamlike character of the fantasy produced.

Probably the most important distinction between the reviews by
Barber and Tart is that the former was written without substantial
reference to the emerging wave of electrophysiological studies, whereas
Tart's evaluation takes full cognizance of this development. This point
of contrast between the two papers bears eloquent testimony to the

impact that these newer methods of investigation have made in recent years. Tart's main thesis in his critique is cogent and persuasive: Experimental studies of the hypnotic dream should be carefully monitored, not only with the electroencephalograph but with a full battery of other psychophysiological measuring devices as well.

Thus the most noteworthy contribution in Tart's reprinted paper is his evaluation of the physiological evidence of the comparability of hypnotic and spontaneous dreams. He appears considerably more confident than some others that the EEG pattern accompanying hypnotic dreams can invariably be differentiated from stage 1 sleep. At the same time he does not entirely discount the possibility that some hypnotic dreams may occur in sleep onset. The contention that the hypnotic and nocturnal dreams occur in distinctive neurophysiological states according to the galvanic skin measure, is not as clear cut either (refer to Hawkins et al., 1962; Green, 1965; and Montagu and Coles, 1966.)

Tart has pioneered in the application of the newer electrophysiological techniques to the study of the hypnotic dream, and a perusal of his earlier 1964a study is informative, because it provided the data from which he concluded that fundamental differences exist between hypnotic and natural dreams. It reveals the rather extraordinary fact that Tart did not actually compare hypnotic and natural dreams, but instead contrasted two types of hypnotic dreams—those experienced immediately in the hypnotic state and those occurring later, in sleep, as a consequence of posthypnotic suggestion! Clear conceptual distinction must be observed between the several varieties of hypnotic dreams and natural dreams if confusion is to be avoided. Evidence now available indicates that the posthypnotic suggestion may effect both quantitative and qualitative changes in the dream. Tart, himself, acknowledges that "the extent to which the suggested narratives exercised almost total control over the content of some of the stage 1 dreams was striking . . . and indicate great promise for the use of posthypnotic suggestions as a technique for controlling the content of stage 1 dreaming." It is difficult to reconcile Tart's equation of posthypnotic and ordinary nocturnal dreams, other than on the basis of his earlier definition of spontaneous dreams as occurring in stage 1 sleep, whereas hypnotic dreams are accompanied by a waking EEG pattern.

Tart's experimental study gives rise to other interesting and methodological issues. Only one will be dealt with here, and it is selected because of the space Tart devotes to the discussion of the Freudian concept of the disguise function of dreams. His tentative conclusion is that a hypnotic dream will not be disguised unless it is explicitly or implicitly demanded. This is a difficult proposition to test because the demand might well be inferred by a sophisticated subject from the simple instruction "to dream." Assuming that Tart's position is founded to a considerable extent on personal experience, it is again instructive to look at his earlier experiment.

Tart found no indication of the presence of any Freudian dream work mechanisms in dreams produced in either the hypnotic state or stage 1 sleep. This judgment was derived exclusively from an examination of the manifest content of the dreams. The finding that nocturnal dreams were much less influenced than were hypnotic dreams by a suggested narrative was similarly based. Tart also equated disguise with any form of distortion or indirect representation in the dream, although it will be recalled that Freud maintained that disguise is accomplished almost entirely via the mechanism of symbolization.

In any event, the asserted absence of dream work mechanisms becomes understandable when the nature of the task assigned to the subjects is considered. They were provided with an exceedingly detailed narrative (consisting of no less than 23 different action units) as the stimulus for a "dream." It was assumed that, because the theme contained-elements of danger, subjects would experience fear and anxiety, hence a need to disguise the content. This whole procedure is loaded with questionable assumptions.

First, the complexity of the stimulus would seem to provide an essentially cognitive problem—the challenge to recall as many of the two dozen action units as possible. Second, that a personal sense of danger was stimulated by the narrative would appear extremely doubtful. Subjects typically possess a basic trust in the investigator and a high level of confidence in the experimental situation as one that is safe. Third, it is well established that hypnotized subject is not a symbolizing automation. The more ambiguous the instructions, the greater the latitude for response; however, the narative employed in Tart's experimental study is so highly defined as to practically preclude its becoming incorporated into the dream life of his subjects in any meaningful manner. Tart's observation that his subjects' personal dynamics were manifested only in dream episodes divorced from the assigned task of dreaming about the suggested narratives, would appear to verify this construction.

These issues have been raised not in criticism of the work of Barber and Tart, both of whom have displayed an exemplary hardheaded attitude toward the phenomenon in question, but as an indication of the unsettled state of affairs in the field and the hazards involved in attempting prematurely to force closure in the face of the incon-

*sistent, inconclusive, and downright contradictory evidence that exists
at the present time.*

SOME FUNDAMENTAL EXPERIMENTAL ISSUES

The articles by Barber and Tart are highly instructive regarding
the safeguards that must characterize any responsible hypnosis experiment and if their efforts are susceptible to criticism, then most other
investigations are doubly vulnerable. In addition to the fact that the
vast majority of studies involving hypnosis have neglected the essential
detail of an adequate waking control group, Barber's added stipulation
that experimental and control groups must be either possessed of equal
amounts of susceptibility or randomly chosen from a group unrated
in terms of hypnotizablity is well taken, because there is reason to
suspect that hypnotizable people may differ in certain essential respects
from those who are not. There is also a consensus among researchers
in the field that control subjects should be as well motivated as experimental subjects and that the experimental situation must be structured
so as to sanction the act of "dreaming" for experimental and control
subjects alike.

Orne (1959) has labeled the totality of cues, implicit and explicit,
which communicate the hypotheses or expectations of the investigator,
the *demand characteristics* of the experimental situation, and he has
emphasized the need for a control group composed of highly motivated
subjects who undertake to simulate the requisite behavior in order
to identify the exact and unique contribution of hypnosis. Judges of
such a performance are, of course, not informed as to who are the
experimental and who are the control subjects. A practical problem
involved in experimental studies of dreaming is that there can be no
really naïve subjects. Everyone has a lifetime of practice with this
phenomenon and is highly familiar with his own dreams and those
of a great many others. What does it mean, then, if a control group
composed of such well-rehearsed simulators can produce dreamlike
content? What is really astonishing is that not everyone can contrive
a reasonable facsimile at will and on demand.

In fact, a rather sizeable control group that exactly meets Barber's
requirements already exists, namely, those many "good" hypnotic subjects who have been unable to produce the requested dreams despite
being highly susceptible, seemingly well motivated, and exposed to
a situation which not only approves but actively encourages this behavior. It would appear that, although hypnotizability may or may

not be a necessary condition for this type of performance, it is hardly a sufficient one.

A complication considered peculiar to all hypnosis research is the hypersuggestibility of the subject. It is assumed that subjects are highly motivated to comply to the best of their abilities with the explicit and implicit, real and inferred, demand features of the experimental situation. Orne has repeatedly demonstrated in his search for the essence of hypnosis that it is most difficult to separate the intrinsic and extrinsic properties of hypnosis. The very real possibility exists that most behaviors thought to be characteristic of hypnosis may be purely artifactual; for example, the resemblance between sleep and hypnosis may be largely attributable to the popular "sleep" method of hypnotic induction. It is somewhat less apparent that the frequent failure to control significant research variables may be attributable to the "credulous" attitude of experimenters who, in their uncritical acceptance of the validity of hypnotic phenomena, trade upon their subjects' suggestibility in order to effect confirmation of their own expectations (Sutcliffe, 1960). Information provoked by Barber's careful interrogation of his subjects' introspective experience in complying with the demand "to dream" points up another deficiency of many studies.

Although some of the methodological problems involved may be unique to hypnosis research, it is apparent that the majority of issues are similar to those encountered in the objective evaluation of any psychological manifestation, namely, adequate sampling, the need for proper control groups, valid and reliable measuring instruments, complete and detailed reporting, and so forth. The potent influence of experimenter expectations as a source of contamination is simply more obvious in hypnosis research. It is a common failing of researchers to forget that the specific variables under study are embedded in a larger psychosocial context, and, as a consequence, they fail to assess, control, or systematically vary those factors associated with set and setting which distort their results. Elaboration on this issue by a few specific examples will serve to establish the essential identity between the hypnotic and more conventional areas of research.

The criticism has been frequently advanced that, irrespective of other issues, the hypnotic relationship must invariably intrude into and distort the content of the hypnotic dream. Newman et al. (1960), in an article reprinted on pages 168–184, used artificial complexes as stimuli for hypnotic dreams. The experimenters were not concerned initially with the unconscious meanings that the complexes had for the subjects, but with the more formal aspects of representability and in the contrast of immediate hypnotic with posthypnotic dreams. However, many of the more obscure aspects of the reported dreams became intelligible only when the experimenters developed an awareness of the importance of the hypnotic situation itself as a dream stimulus. Dreams often depicted intense ambivalent feelings about the hypnotist and the hypnotic situation, and the investigators concluded that "the meaning of the experimental situation for the subject has been overlooked in much hypnotic work." That this complication is not unique to the hypnotic study of the dreaming process will be made clear.

The rapid proliferation of electrophysiological studies has promoted a widespread recognition that the very act of harvesting dreams even under laboratory-controlled conditions may distort the phenomenon being investigated. Whitman et al. (1962) concluded that two thirds of the dreams dreamed by 10 subjects over 40 nights in the laboratory dealt with the experiment in either an obvious or indirect manner. The elaborate electrical instrumentation was particularly distressing to the subjects, and neither reassurance nor continuing exposure to the situation was sufficient to decrease anxiety.

In contrast, Dement (1965) reported that only 30 per cent of the dreams of his subjects dealt with the experimental situation even on the first night in the laboratory, dropping to about 10 or 15 per cent thereafter. The content of a large sample of dreams was examined by Dement, Kahn, and Roffwarg (1965). A marked degree of habituation was again found: dreams on the first night in the laboratory tended to be concerned with the experimental situation, but on subsequent nights this influence was sharply reduced, although never completely eliminated. There was also a greater tendency for the early dreams of the night to be related to the experiment.

Other studies have found the influence of the experimental situation to be substantial and sustained. In a triad of articles, Domhoff and Kamiya (1964a, 1964b, 1964c) used the classification schedules developed by Hall in a comparison of dream narratives collected in a laboratory setting and at home. Results show the marked impact of the laboratory experience to be one of the most important methodolgical problems that must be resolved before objective indicators of dreaming can be fully exploited as a method of studying dream content. The experiment was generally perceived as threatening and embarrassing by female subjects and annoying and exhibitionistic by the males. The experimental situation is so distressing an experience, the authors suggest, that it should at least be conducted in a more natural, homelike environment. An obvious minimal control in this procedure would involve an extended period of adaptation to the strange experimental situation. Studies by Tart (1964b) and Sampson (1965) also depict the contaminating influence of subtle, inadvertent, implicit demands of the experimental situation on the conduct of dream research.

The hypnotic dream is evidently only a member of that larger class of dreams produced by subjects with an awareness that they will be scrutinized by persons possessed of expertise in dream analysis. This consideration highlights again the problem of selective recall in dream studies. Most of what we thought we knew in the immediate past was derived from dreams obtained in clinical settings. Thus a paper by an analyst who uses patients whom he knows well and has treated for a long time, is quite different from that of an experimental psychologist who uses subjects with whom he has had little or no previous contact and who do not have the same kind of transference involvement. It is a common experience in psychotherapy that some patients can be readily taught to notice and to value their dreams and thus to increase the frequency of recall. What determines which of 10 or 20 dreams per night will be recalled and reported? Is it simply the last dream experienced each night, or the most singular and dramatic, or are they those which are least revealing or most compatible with the theoretical predilections of the therapist? The propensity of patients for producing dreams consonant with the theoretical proclivities of their therapists is well known, so that, as Zubin (1964) put it, Freudians get Freudian dreams, Jungians get Jungian dreams, and Rogerians get no dreams at all.

The sea voyage dream, depicted on page 186 (Moss, 1961) neatly captures the influence of the therapeutic situation on even the natural night dream. It may well be asked whether the role of the therapist in such circumstances parallels that of the hypnotist in the suggested dream. And is the hypnotic dream really more susceptible to environmental influence than those produced in psychotherapy or, for that matter, even in the laboratory situation? Horowitz and Rashid (1965) have commented on the virtue of dreams captured via EEG cues in providing insights into their patients' problem areas, as contrasted with the usual reliance on volunteered dreams. Dynamic patterns were often revealed with remarkable clarity in a rich concatenation of dreams. There is obviously need for the systematic recruitment of dreams from large numbers of subjects in a variety of settings and in all phases of REM sleep throughout the night, if we are to establish with any degree of confidence the characteristics of spontaneous dreams.

DELIBERATE MANIPULATION OF DREAMING

In contrast to the foregoing unplanned or accidental effects, the deliberate manipulation of dreaming behavior has interested many investigators. If the impact of the experimetal situation is so profound, it is rather curious that Tart (1966b) reports that psychologically trained judges were unable to discriminate hypnotic dreams about "anything" from those about "the meaning of being hypnotized." Some dreams about the hypnotic situation did occur in reaction to both sets of instructions, but the majority in either instance bore no apparent relation to the hypnotic situation. Either the subjects failed to dream about the "meaning of hypnosis" even when so instructed, or they did so in such a thoroughly disguised fashion as to be undetectable.

Dement and Wolpert (1958) were also relatively unsuccessful in efforts to influence dream content using physical stimuli such as a tone, a flashing light, and sprays of cold water, although it is again possible that these external stimuli were incorporated in transmuted or symbolic form. In contrast, Berger (1963) did find that outside events were frequently interwoven with dreams, and Bolcert (1965) documented the influence of thirst on dream content.

As in the case of hypnotic investigations, studies generally can be divided into those which have attempted to influence ongoing dreams directly and those involving presleep stimulation. As examples of the latter approach, Witkin and Lewis (1965) found evidence that elements of a presleep film were incorporated into the dreams of that night, elements from the film being interwoven with significant events in the dreamer's personal life. In an investigation of the effect of viewing two films, one violent and the other neutral, prior to sleep, Foulkes and Rechteschaffen (1964) found little direct incorporation of the film content into the dream, although the traumatic film seemed to have a generally stimulating influence, resulting in longer, more vivid, and imaginative dreams.

It might be well to recall at this juncture that Freudian theory did not assume a monotonic relation between the intensity of the day residue and the intensity of the dream. Rather it is the incidental day residue that is assumed to have highly excitatory dream effects precisely because it is incidental and has become associated with certain drives or impulses activated during the day. To put it another way, these studies should serve to remind that in order to achieve significant impact on a dream, the input stimulus must either be left intentionally ambiguous (incidental) or be carefully tailored to coincide with the psychodynamics of the subject. In the latter instance, a hypnotic suggestion cannot be equated with latent dream content unless it is the equivalent of an actual latent wish of the particular subject. An effective dream stimulus is one that serves to provoke associational chains radiating in many directions, so that the stimulus becomes more or less immediately embroidered with idiosyncratic meanings by the dreaming subject.

In an imaginative effort to capitalize on the undoubted "intraserial effect" occasioned in most electrophysiological studies of dreaming by the expedient of requesting a report from the subject after each dream, Davison, Breger, and Fahrion (1966) tape-recorded the dreams collected on one night and presented them as the predream input stimulus to the same subject the next evening. It was assumed that dreams have a close proximity to unconscious, conflictual material and that confrontation with one's own recent dreams would be highly threatening, activating defensive processes which would be apparent in the manifest content of subsequent dreams. Preliminary results indicate striking differences in certain content variables between baseline control dreams and those reported after exposure to dreams of the preceding night. The effect was particularly evident in an increase in the fragmentation of dream episodes and accompanying contradictions and inconsistencies. GSR ratings showed no relationship to alterations in the dream content, but physiological reactivity increased progressively during periods of free association, supposedly due to an increasing sensitivity to the dynamic content of the dream material.

Research has already clearly established that under certain conditions the sleeping person can be mentally alert, capable of appropriate interaction with his environment, and successful in the performance of a variety of refined behaviors. Kamiya, using money as a reinforcement, motivated sleeping subjects to respond to signals and to press switches; Williams et al. (1963, 1964) have encouraged performance of the same type of tasks using aversive stimuli; Mandell et al. (1965) reported success in training sleeping subjects to learn some information; and Oswald (1960, 1961, 1962) demonstrated that subjects are capable of relatively fine discriminations during sleep. A consistent and highly provocative finding throughout these and other studies is that although subjects may or may not be trained to respond during all phases of sleep, the most consistent, high-level quality of performance is invariably elicited in the REM period.

Another significant observation is that it takes a relatively intense peripheral stimulus to arouse a person in the REM phase of sleep, *except when the stimulus has personal significance*, in which case even a slight stimulus may quickly alert him. REM sleep is obviously not deep unconsciousness, but a state in which attention is concentrated internally, so that although the person is ordinarily oblivious to external stimulation, he remains reaction-sensitive to meaningful stimuli and may be capable of prompt and proper response with minimal arousal. The success of a number of sleep-conditioning experiments would appear to increase the credibility of the assertion that posthypnotic suggestion can influence dream content.

There are undoubted wide individual differences in responsiveness to the manipulation of sleeping behavior. People seem to vary considerably in the depth or soundness of sleep. It is commonly accepted that some people have an unusual ability for inducing sleep or waking themselves up. Some people seem to retain greater contact with their external surroundings and, although behaviorally asleep, will assert that they were awake and thinking. Some individuals also claim that they are capable of controlling even their dreamlike thoughts and experiences. Even though little is known yet about the reasons why one person can be influenced in his sleep and another cannot, a recent observation which should pique the scientific curiosity is that the capability for superior performance during sleep may be correlated with hypnotic susceptibility.

Many investigators have emphasized the individual differences they have observed and the by no means uniform success in sleep-conditioning. Some people awaken. Others do not respond. When asked to recall dreams or words heard during sleep, people have displayed a readiness to forget rather than remember. In general these results dampened the hope of accomplishing very much by sleep training and surely the unsophisticated attempts and commercial programs of the past had not been encouraging. There is, however, a singular group of people who seem to react differently to sleep instruction and display facilities of memory for sleep learning. Nobody has determined what properties of mind distinguish these people, only that they are capable of being hypnotized (*U.S. Public Health Serv. Publ.*, 1389, 1965).

This statement has reference to a study by Cobb et al. (1965) which indicates the possibility of eliciting complex behavioral responses to meaningful suggestions administered during various stages of physiological sleep as defined by EEG monitoring. Four subjects who had previously demonstrated high hypnotizability gave accurate responses while remaining asleep, but four low-hypnotizability subjects did not. Consistent with the results of related studies, responses could be elicited clearly only during emergent stage 1 periods.

In a second study (Evans et al., 1965) 20 additional subjects with no previous experience in hypnosis were similarly tested. Typically, subjects responded to some but not all of the suggestions and subsequent cue words, specific responses being limited to stage 1; they did not recall any of the suggestions the following morning, although they did respond to some of the cue words administered in the context of a free association test; and they responded with increased frequency to cue words the next night. As so frequently happens in hypnosis experiments, the perfect relationship between susceptibility and performance obtained in the first study was not observed in the second one. There was a low positive correlation with hypnotizability on night 1 but not on night 2. A possible interpretation of the earlier results is that previous (success-failure) experience in the hypnotic situation may have produced ongoing sets in subjects toward subsequent suggestion-type experiments.

Nevertheless, a rekindled interest in the possible relationship between sleep and hypnosis is being sparked by these and other recent experiments. Brady and Rosner have found that the hypnotic suggestion to dream produces a waking brain-wave pattern accompanied by the rapid eye movements characteristic of nocturnal dreaming. Simulating subjects were able to manufacture dreams but had no conjugate eye movements (*U.S. Public Health Serv. Publ.*, 1389, 1965, pp. 64–65). Jenness (1965) reports that sleep walkers average better on visual and kinesthetic imagery tests than nonsomnambulists and also score significantly higher on tests of hypnotic susceptibility. Arkin, Hastey, and Reisner (1966) are in the process of carefully documenting their success in conducting dialogues with sleeping subjects. Sleep-talking can apparently be initiated during all times of the night and in all sleep phases, and subjects are amnesic of these exchanges on later awakening. Based on an evaluation of Soviet hypnopedia experiments, Hoskovec (1966*b*) concluded that learning during sleep is possible when a "presuggested set" is employed, concerning the capacity of the subject to perceive and remember the material to be learned during sleep. Selection of subjects according to their hypnotizability or primary suggestibility seemed to be an important prerequisite.

THE NATURE OF DREAMING

The technical breakthrough pioneered by Aserinsky, Kleitman, and Dement represents a brilliant new tool for behavioral science that may be as catalytic to the field of dream research as were Freud's effulgent contributions at the turn of the century. As Foulkes (1964) has stated it, "there is reason for optimism that present investigations may lead not only to the testing and modification of psychoanalytic and other theories, but to the generation of altogether new theories solidly based on experimentally derived data."

Results at this time are of a very preliminary nature, of course, lending themselves to a wide variety of constructions and interpretations. Fundamental questions permeating all of the preceding electrophysiological studies are the nature of the sleep mechanism, how the dreaming cycle develops, and what purpose it serves. The presence of the sleep cycle at all age levels in human beings and in the whole gamut of mammalian species indicates that dreaming sleep must serve some vital biological function. In fact, REMP sleep has such distinctive neurophysiological properties as to suggest two kinds of sleep or a third state of consciousness, along with waking and NREM sleep. (Refer to articles by Snyder, 1963, 1965, and Hartmann, 1965, for comprehensive reviews of studies on the physiologic state concomitant with dreaming.)

Dement (1964) now suspects that there is a biochemical basis for the sleep cycle and that stage 1 sleep quite possibly serves the purpose of eliminating some hypothetical toxic substance. Dreaming sleep may well be a homeostatic mechanism of sorts in a biologically determined cycle involving alternating periods of energy discharge and conservations. One captivating conjecture is that NREM mentation contains the stream of preconscious day residues and that dreaming may be the means of collating, interpreting, and storing the millions of impressions which bombard the perceptual apparatus daily. Other investigators are convinced that dreams are little more than an epiphenomenon of stage 1 sleep.

Findings are far from definitive regarding assessment of basic Freudian postulates, such as the statement that dreams serve to discharge instinctual drive energies while at the same time functioning to protect sleep. Fisher (1965) has recently undertaken to reinterpret and to integrate the major findings of these studies into psychoanalytic theory. He correctly asserts that Freud saw no incompatability between these different levels of discourse and that he never relinquished a belief that some day a link would be established between psychoanalytic conceptions and the underlying physico-chemico-biological processes.

The weight of evidence argues strongly against a strictly or even predominately psychological interpretation of dreaming. The most plausible position is that it is a *psychobiological* process and that sleep (NREMPs) and dreaming (REMPs) each has psychological and physiological components, the interaction of which must be painstakingly teased apart. The most tenable assumption for those concerned with the "meaning" of dream content is that, as a natural consequence of growth and development, the physiological mechanisms involved are taken over and utilized by an essentially psychological process of dreaming.

As Snyder (1963) commented in his commendable article "The New Biology of Dreaming"; "Thus far, there have been few and tenuous bridges between the psychodynamic and physiological levels of discourse. The aim of this presentation is to suggest that the beginning made this past decade, and the promise of future developments in the experimental study of dreaming, may be such a bridge   perhaps a *via regia* between the two domains."

Enthusiasm for these fruitful new electrophysiological techniques must be tempered by a note of caution. It should not be forgotten that the relation of the various physiological measures to dreaming is complex and the associated behavior and experience are diverse. It needs to be recalled, for example, that the newborn infant spends a higher proportion of sleep time in REMP's than do adults, the mature congenitally blind adhere to the same sleep cycle as do non-afflicted people, dream reports do not accompany 20 to 30 per cent of REMPs, and dreamlike episodes do occur in a fair proportion of NREMP's. Among a host of other anomalies is the fact that although it ordinarily takes an hour for subjects at night to reach the first dream stage, people who nap during the day frequently report involved dreams following a brief interval of sleep. Also, some laboratory subjects give every evidence of being asleep, including snoring, yet when awakened will insist that they were only relaxed and their thoughts were ordered and controlled, whereas under certain circumstances others will show sleeping brain waves while seemingly wide awake. Furthermore, there is the puzzling fact that sleep walking incidents, long assumed to be the acting out of a dream, occur in sleep stages 3 and 4 and are thus divorced from "dreaming" stage 1. Shapiro writes:

The association of dreaming with REM periods is soundly based on experimental data. But the concept that dreaming occurs only during REM periods or that time spent in REM period sleep is always associated with dreaming in every individual of every mammalian species under every natural or experimental condition is far from being so firmly based. Furthermore, the Dement and Kleitman classification of the stages of sleep which was so convenient and useful in the early investigations of sleep and dreaming in healthy young adult human volunteers leads to many contradictions, exceptions, and ambiguities (when applied to different subjects under varying conditions) . . . . In addition to this, there is substantial evidence of quantitative and qualitative differences in dreaming and dream recall at different times of the night and under different experimental conditions. Data on other physiological parameters also do not fit simply into the original concept which led to the use of REM time and percent REM in total sleep time as measures of dream time and amount of dreaming (Shapiro, 1966).

In brief, then, electrophysiological measures are imperfect indicators of dreaming, although they offer advantages far superior to earlier methods. At the same time it should be borne in mind that dependence on these physiological indicators of sleep and dreaming in no way relieves investigators of a responsibility to continue development of increasingly specific and objective behavioral and experiential indices of the types of thinking and cognition associated with each differentiable EEG pattern (Kamiya, 1961). Persons specifically interested in the interpretive significance of dream content must continue to rely for the foreseeable future on a skillful, well-considered, and imaginative interpolation of older methods and techniques with those now in process of development.

Chapter 6
Hypnotic Dreaming and the
Nature of Hypnosis

COMPETING THEORIES OF HYPNOSIS

The discussion of any hypnotic phenomenon must inevitably concern itself with the nature of hypnosis per se, and the extreme differences of opinion within the professions of psychology and psychiatry are too well known to require detailed elaboration. Several of the more widely held theories have already been touched upon: the motivational explanation advanced by psychoanalysis in terms of susceptibility as an outgrowth of regressive infantile dependency and libidinal needs; the Pavlovian concept of hypnosis as a physiologically determined state of inhibition akin to sleep; trait theory which presupposes possession of certain requisite aptitudes or skills, such as the selective attention required in hypnotic amnesia; social role theory with its emphasis on subject responsiveness to the direct or implicit demand characteristics of the hypnotic situation; and the nihilistic stance of those who maintain that hypnosis possesses no unique identity at all and should not even be dignified as a special psychological state.

Sharp divisions of opinion thus exist as to whether hypnosis is a "state," or a relationship, or merely a myth. Each authority pits his expertise against that of the others, and although a plethora of clever, imaginative, and well-articulated theories are available, there are few incontrovertible facts on the basis of which to discriminate and choose among competing systems. Except as an academic exercise, it would be profitless to review again the many extant theories of hypnosis. Suffice it to say that each theory illumes certain aspects, but none adequately explains hypnotic susceptibility, the peculiarities of behavior attendant to hypnosis, and the relationship of hypnosis to other, often remarkably similar life events.

HYPNOSIS ABROAD

Despite the popularity of social-psychological explanations of hypnosis in the United States today, we cannot lightly dismiss the fact that in the Soviet Union psychologists and psychiatrists are convinced that hypnosis is a form of selective cortical inhibition closely related to normal sleep. Dominance of the Pavlovian theory of hypnosis in the Soviet Union is perceived by American psychologists as a stultifying influence; however, an undoubted virtue is that this physiological conception of hypnosis has acted to dilute the usual association with mysticism, to reduce public and professional resistances, and to promote a much greater acceptance on the part of general medicine than in any other country. In contrast to the United States, there is a close compatibility of psychiatry with the mainstream of medicine, and as a result psychotherapy, including the use of hypnosis, is widely applied in medical practice.

Soviet psychiatrists see themselves as directly and indirectly intervening in the elimination of centers of excessive inhibition or excitation in the central nervous systems of their patients through medications, environmental manipulation, and such psychotherapeutic techniques as advice, guidance, reassurance, persuasion, and suggestion. Treatment may best be characterized as superficial, directive, and rational. There is broad acceptance of the hypnotic state itself as being conducive to physiological repair, and prolonged hypnotic sleep is regarded as possessing undoubted curative value. The basic merit of the hypnotic state, however, is thought to be the patients' heightened responsiveness to therapeutic suggestion.

Hypnoanalysis in the western usage of the term is never used as a technique, and psychoanalytic theory is an anathema, especially the Freudian concept of a dynamic unconscious, which probably accounts for the paradoxical interest in sleep therapy and an absence of interest in the hypnotic manipulation of dreaming. According to Ziferstein (1965), Soviet psychotherapists may recognize some of the latent meanings of their patients' dreams, but they do not ordinarily interpret them, responding instead with remarks intended to counteract possible antitherapeutic influences of the dream.

Although it is acknowledged that the degree of hypnotic suggestibility varies in accordance with the subject matter, setting, and the state of rapport between doctor and patient, hypnosis is perceived as clearly physiological in essence. The impact of hypnosis on biological reactions and somatic processes has been studied extensively, and research into the relation between hypnotic, natural, and even drug-induced sleep has flourished. It is the consensus that a close similarity exists between these states. An important qualification is that the authoritarian method of induction ordinarily employed by the Soviet hypnotist with an emphasis on the patient's absolute passivity and submissiveness doubtlessly encourages the finding of marked similarities. It may also be suspected that a careful differentiation between hypnosis and natural sleep is not always observed. Russian research in the field of hypnotic physiology has employed chiefly the conditioned reflex and EEG studies, which, because of their objective nature, invite replication, but the absence of critical studies by competent investigators in the United States renders impossible an evaluation of these many seemingly significant studies at this time (Gorton, 1962).[1]

The third country in addition to the Soviet Union and the United States, in which hypnosis has met with relative acceptance in recent years, is Japan. The public attitude is reportedly mixed, both negative and highly positive, and, although the majority of physicians are skeptical or cautious and do not publicize the use of hypnosis in their practice, hypnosis has been fairly well accepted in the universities and psychologists have been active in research. A receptive disposition in the general population has been nurtured by long familiarity with the practices of Zen Buddhism, Indian Yogi, and more primitive religious ceremonies. Many Eastern religions provide training in mental discipline and the tranquil contemplation of inner experiences, and priests on occasion even engage in frank hetero- and autohypnotic practices.[2]

This background may account for the unusual prevalence of psychotherapy patients who request training in self-hypnosis as an aid to inner perception. Another consequence has been a considerable interest in J. H. Schultz's Autogenic Training Technique (1964), a procedure based primarily on relaxation exercises, which provide a step-by-step introduction to meditation. Unfortunately, the "higher stages" are described only in cursory form, but at the advanced levels highly elaborated symbolic fantasies can reputedly be induced by the meditator.

Japanese investigators have displayed a considerable interest in hypnotically induced hallucinations or imagery. Naruse and Obonai (1952,

---

[1] Readers interested in hypnotherapy in the Soviet Union are advised to consult the following: Platonov, 1959; Andreer, 1960; Winn, 1961; Svorad and Hoskovec, 1961; Field, 1961; Brozek, 1962; Rokhlin, 1963; Sabot, 1965; Lewis, 1965; Hoskovec, 1966a, Hoskovec and Svorad, 1966. See also: E. A. Volpert, *Dreams in Natural Sleep and Hypnosis* (Med. Publ. Hse., Leningrad, 1966).

[2] Readers should also consult G. Naruse's chapter in F. L. Marcuse's book, *Hypnosis Throughout the World,* as well as his chapter on hypnosis as a state of meditative concentration in *The Nature of Hypnosis* (ed. M. V. Kline).

1953, 1954, 1956; Naruse, 1960, 1965), for example, have engaged in a program of study of imagery modification and alteration, using a relatively simple sensory conditioning procedure. An early, elementary approach involved the presentation of paired stimuli, one auditory and the other visual, to subjects in deep hypnosis. In a subsequent posthypnotic hallucinatory state, presentation of the auditory stimulus alone resulted in a vivid visual hallucinatory experience. Hypnosis appeared to facilitate the process; the deeper the preceding trance, the clearer the imagery. Many variations of this procedure are possible, and studies have been conducted of single images, overlapping images, perception-imagery interaction, the influence of attributing meaning to the images, and so forth. In this manner it has been possible to scrutinize the process involved in the decomposition, fusion, distortion, and reformulation of images.

Naruse (1962a) has turned his attention to the nature of the altered state of consciousness which facilitates such imagery production. A unique feature of his presentation is the emphasis placed on autohypnosis. He charges that the process of induction in heterohypnosis has a great influence on the induced state and colors decisively the phenomena that are evoked. In comparison, autohypnosis is a much more neutral, tranquil, and deeply introspective experience—a state of meditative concentration—in which there is typically a relaxation of reality testing, a readiness to shift from a perceptual to a hallucinatory level of functioning, and a passive preoccupation with imagination. Naruse believes that this self-induced state of passive contemplation is nearer the "essence" of hypnosis than is the typical product of more familiar heterohypnotic techniques.

A technique for eliciting and observing a form of visual free association which results in a series of unique, personalized images similar to the experimentally induced dream is also described by Naruse (1962). The training procedure and stages are related to the meditative exercise of Autogene Training, and the imagery elicited has been profitably employed in the conduct of psychotherapy. EEG studies have shown a close similarity between the patterns found in the autogenic process, Zen meditation, and self-hypnosis. According to Naruse, all three might well be considered as a "presleep state," characterized by a sustained alpha rhythm even when the eyes are open.

STUDIES OF PERCEPTUAL CONCENTRATION AND ISOLATION

Investigators in the United States have evidenced an increased interest in the meditative stage. Using the electroencephalograph as a teaching device, Kamiya (1961, 1962) has demonstrated the feasibility of training subjects to readily identify, induce, or suppress the subtle alpha state in a manner reminiscent of the outcome of extended Zen training. His results suggest that people might be more easily trained to induce this pleasant, tranquil state than had previously been thought possible and, in this way, to sharpen self-observational faculties or even to control sympathetic-autonomic bodily functions.

Also in this country, Deikman (1963) is studying the meditation phenomenon via an experimental procedure that involves quite simply the contemplation of a neutral stimulus object (for example, a small blue vase) in a setting devoid of distractions other than taped auditory stimuli introduced to test the disruptive effect of calibrated background stimuli. A remarkable finding is the ease with which phenomena of depersonalization, visual distortion, and quasi-hallucinations can be stimulated.

Over short periods of time, ranging up to half an hour, subjects perceive marked alterations in the objective stimulus and in their general surroundings, a sharp diminution in the distracting effect of the extraneous stimuli, development of a sense of highly personal involvement with the object of concentrated attention, and so forth. These results indicate that many people have a capacity for distinctive alterations in their customary perception of the world and themselves under conditions of minimal manipulation. The experimenter actually found it necessary to assume an active role in allaying anxiety arising from these strange perceptions, although the overall quality of the experience was quite pleasurable and not unlike experiences recounted in autohypnosis.

A host of studies this past decade in the areas of sensory, social, and cultural deprivation have documented persuasively that the human organism requires a continually varied sensory input for normal intellectual development and the maintenance of ongoing adaptive behavior. Experiments designed to reduce and monotonize stimulation reportedly result in cognitive and perceptual disorganization, typified by painful feelings of loneliness, anxiety, and unreality and eventuating in hypnagogic experiences, dreamlike states, and possibly hallucinations. Stimulus impoverishment will not itself produce these major disruptive psychological effects; the amount of stimulation is apparently less important than the need for varied experience. A complex interaction of subject personality, experimenter expectations, situational variables, in combination with a condition of minimal, diffuse, and monotonous stimulation, is a primary requisite for the disorganization of cognitive and perceptual functioning. The importance of set and setting is attested to by Peña (1963), who found a significant enhancement of hypnotizability associated with perceptual isolation; the greater the duration of isolation, the greater the susceptibility. Heightened vividness in thought and imagery was a common report of subjects.

One of the more remarkable and seemingly contradictory findings developed in the course of research in sensory deprivation, according to Brownfield (1965), is that under certain, as yet not well-delineated conditions, the isolation procedures may have beneficial effects. Some subjects not only show no evidence of cognitive or perceptual disorganization but even exhibit a facilitation of performance. Experiments are now underway to verify reported positive therapeutic effects for certain classes of psychiatric patients. A suggestive finding is that characteristic modes of interacting with the external environment may contribute to a determination of how a subject reacts in the isolation experience: subjects who are "field-dependent" in terms of an excessive reliance on external cues for a frame of reference tend to react with discomfort and disorganization when environmental cues are minimized or lacking (Cohen et al., 1958). The possible virtues of social and perceptual isolation are testified to by the many adherents of mystical Eastern religions, who engage in a carefully cultivated form of sensory deprivation, far more extreme than that employed in the research laboratory, in an effort to shut off the world and free the mind to experience a transcendence to a state of higher spiritual enlightenment.

HAWTHORNE HOUSE STUDIES

A firm advocate of the position that hypnotizability is a relatively stable component of personality structure, Ernest Hilgard in recent years has advanced a theory of hypnosis which attributes susceptibility to a developmental process, probably closely related to occurrences in early childhood, particularly in interpersonal relationships among family members. In a concentrated program of research this past decade, centered at Hawthorne House on the Stanford University campus, Hilgard and a host of collaborators have labored over a long-range investigation of hypnotic phenomena. One phase of this program of research has had as its objective the development of scales for the quantitative assessment of hypnotic susceptibility, scales which are needed to provide criteria for the study of hypnotizability and the parameters and correlates of hypnosis. Among the representative hypnotic phenomena studied has been the hypnotic dream, an aspect of study in which Hilgard and Charles Tart collaborated closely.

A recent book by Hilgard (1965) summarizes this program of research, providing pertinent quantitative information on individual differences in hypnotizability, the interrelation between representative hypnotic phenomena, and the nature of hypnosis. The investigators found that dreamlike hallucinations could be produced in somewhat over two-fifths of their student sample $(N = 203)$ when first tried and that repeated trials did not increase the proportion of dreaming. Differences between hypnotic and night dreams were observed; for example, many of the dreams reported lacked a convincing experiential quality. However, the more hypnotizable subjects provide both a higher incidence of dreams and the most dreamlike productions.

Normative data on a wide variety of individual items of hypnotic behavior demonstrate anew that hypnotic susceptibility is not a unidimensional ability or trait. Item clusters based on face validity and confirmed by the statistical method of factor analysis identified the following significant dimensions: a general factor accounting for one third to one half the variance in any set of item correlations, an ideomotor factor, a closely related factor of cognitive and sensory inhibition, positive hallucinations, the production of fantasies from memory and imagination, and the persistence of effects through time.

The *Stanford Hypnotic Susceptibility Scale*, Form C, includes a test item calling for the production of a hypnotic dream. It is of interest that this task occupies an intermediate position in order of difficulty of compliance, correlates 0.57 with total score, and has a reliability of 0.63[3] The ability to produce dreams has a substantial relationship to direct-suggestion motor items (such as arm rigidity) on the one hand, and to age regression on the other. On the *Stanford Profile Scales*—a later instrument designed to provide a configuration of scores that would indicate relative susceptibility in special areas of hypnosis—the prominence of fantasy, memorial revival, and visual imagery in dreams, hyperamnesia, and age regression resulted in the assignment of these items to a dream-regression (DR) subscale. Each of six such subscales correlates positively, as might be expected from the common factor that pervades them, and the DR subscale also correlates 0.70 with the total scale.

Experiments at the Hawthorne House laboratory have not yet dealt

---

[3] In a study of the reliability of scoring the *Stanford Hypnotic Susceptibility Scale*, Form C (Evans and Schmeidler, 1964), the correlation between the total scores of two observers was 0.95. Nevertheless, there was disagreement on 25 per cent of the total sample $(p < 0.001)$ as to whether subjects passed or failed the dream item. Quite obviously the judges applied differing criteria, which points up again the need for well-developed, objective standards on what constitutes a dream.

with posthypnotically induced dreams, although studies are underway involving the influence on dreams of artificial conflicts induced by hypnosis. For example, in a study of the concept of repression, Imm (1965) used hypnotic suggestion both to implant sexual or hostile conflicts and to control awareness. It was hypothesized that word association disturbances and disguised and distorted references to the experiences in hypnotic dreams would appear under conditions of induced amnesia for the conflict but not under conditions when the experience was remembered or the experience was resolved. More word association disturbances were noted under the Repression Condition than under other conditions. Hypnotic dreams from each subject revealed a tendency for elements of the conflict to appear in these dreams following a sexual rather than a hostile suggested experience, particularly if the subject was amnesic. Subjects possessed of greater tested hypnotic susceptibility provided clear evidence of the conflict situation both in their dreams and on word associations. Results tentatively support the psychoanalytic notion that conflicts not in awareness produce disguised references which appear in primary process dominated thought.

Hilgard's conclusion regarding the hypnotic dream is noteworthy:

Although hypnotic dreams are not night dreams, the two dream categories overlap and they undoubtably have much in common. Barber's (1962a) interpretation that hypnotic dreams are merely fabricated to please the hypnotist is an extreme one, unjustified particularly by the dreams dreamt in sleep as a result of posthypnotic suggestion. Even though some amount of fabrication goes on, it may be as revealing, as indeed the deliberate fabrication of a TAT story is. In any case the dreamer is the author of his own dreams; how deeply "unconscious" any dream production is can only be a matter of speculation at the present time. All evidence points to the fruitfulness of hypnotic dreaming as an area of investigation" (Hilgard, p. 163).

THE PHENOMENOLOGY OF DREAMING

In the absence of agreement regarding the nature of hypnosis, it might have been hoped that hypnosis could be identified by the manner in which it is brought about; however, it should be clear by now that nothing approximating a standardized method of induction exists. If there is a common denominator, it is the technique of perceptual concentration: by capturing and controlling the focus of a subject's attention, he can be enticed to relinquish his customary critical and evaluative mode of thinking and perceiving in favor of a receptive attentiveness to suggestions from the hypnotist.

If hypnosis cannot be defined by either *what it is* or *how it is induced*, neither can it be precisely indentified by *what it does*. It is a well-documented fact that strikingly similar performances can be elicited in quite disparate circumstances and settings. As has been seen, vivid imagery, hallucinations, and other dreamlike phenomena can be generated in relation to such altered states as acute psychoses, hallucinogenic drugs, and Zen meditation, not to mention sensory deprivation experiments, fugue states, the capacity for creative synthesis, and just plain drowsiness and sleep.

Because the hypnotic state is obviously achievable by other than the single route called formal trance induction, some authorities have found it tempting to interpret these many other related states as implicitly hypnotic in nature. It might be less parochial to admit that hypnosis is by no means as singular or unique as it first appears and is often chauvinistically represented. It may well be that an interrelationship exists between waking imagery, daydreams, hypnagogic and hypnopompic experiences, night dreams, psychotic hallucinations, and hypnotically induced visualizations. On the other hand, these other parallel forms of behavior may at best be only analogues, similar in certain respects to hypnotic phenomena, but not really identical. The underlying mechanism remains to be elucidated. In any event, quite apparently the hypnotic induction procedure is only one method of guided awareness to a potentially perceivable inner panoply of hallucinatory fantasy.

At this juncture it would seem fruitful to give further consideration to the relationship between hypnosis and sleep and the fantasy derivatives of each, from a phenomenological perspective. Liberal reference will be made in this regard to recent statements by Dement (1965), a respected representative of those engaged in the psychophysiological study of sleep and dreams. Dement points out that the common conception of sleep in the past was one of a period of minimal functioning that fulfilled a need for rest and restoration, and that most of our established notions about the distinction between sleep and wakefulness were based on a comparison of the physiology of the NREM phase as contrasted with its extreme opposite, the active waking state. Dement goes on to remark:

> The fact that levels of activity in the waking state are usually higher than in NREM sleep is because the former state is ordinarily a time of interacting with the environment. When this interaction with the environment is being voluntarily suspended, we may achieve a low level of activity but we are still awake. When the suspension is *involuntary*, we are asleep (Dement, p. 164).

In other words, people deliberately restrict the amount of afferent stimulation to the nervous system, and at a certain critical level sleep ensues. Is this procedure too different from the popular "sleep method" of hypnotic induction? Kubie and Margolin (1944), for example, speak of hypnosis as resulting from the creation of a focus of central excitation with surrounding areas of inhibition. "According to this description, the onset of the hypnotic state can be defined as a condition of partial sleep, in which one or more open channels of sensorimotor communication are maintained between the subject and the outside world" (p. 611). A distinction is made between the induction and established phases of the hypnotic state. In the induction phase the hypnotist momentarily becomes the sole representative of the external world, but, once hypnosis is achieved, the subject's normal boundaries in both time and place can be reestablished, although the hypnotist supposedly remains incorporated within his conscience as an "experimentally induced superego figure." How does this differ from reported instances in which "rapport" is established with a subject normally asleep who is then induced to engage in hypnotic-like behaviors?

Phenomenologically speaking, up to a point hypnosis is a purely voluntary venture in which the subject (passively) cooperates, but then a remarkable thing happens, judged by either behavioral or subjective standards—the subject appears to forfeit a substantial degree of responsibility for direction of his subsequent behavior to the hypnotist. The act of dreaming in either sleep or hypnosis, according to many investigators, possesses such an involuntary or nonvolitional quality.

Dement identifies another distinctive feature of the dream experience as "the conspicuous lack of critical judgment on the part of the dreamer." He states that the most incongruous, illogical, and impossible happenings are accepted as "real," although he goes on to agree with Freud that at a certain level we probably retain awareness that we are actually dreaming. The hypnotized subject, too, is characterized by credulity or hypersuggestibility so that he seems quite literally to accept and to act in accordance with the perceptual structuring instigated by the hypnotist. The experienced hypnotist knows, however, that a subject's needs and wishes must be consistently respected, because the subject has the ability to abrogate the contractural relationship in whole or in part any time the demands become excessively burdensome (Moss, 1965).

In analogous fashion it might be said that an individual volunteers for sleep, relinquishes conscious control, and, once the sleep state is established, he is subjected to experiences that are very real and often quite discontinuous from his normal routine, but there he retains a capacity to arouse himself or shift the scenario if the dream content becomes too distressing. As Dement has repeatedly emphasized, *dreaming is experientially the same as being awake*, except that endogenous neurological activity is substituted for sensory input and the motor outflow is ordinarily blocked.

This description of events would appear highly compatible with the reports of those who would define hypnosis in terms of subjective or psychological criteria. Orne comments:

> No reliable objective criteria have yet been developed which will un-equivocally identify the hypnotic state. This is particularly true in regard to physiological criteria. In the absence of reliable objective criteria, it becomes necessary to describe hypnosis in terms of the subjective events which the hypnotized individual experiences. The cardinal characteristic of the state is that a potentiality exists for the subject's perception of reality to be distorted in accordance with the hypnotist's cues. This distortion may affect any and all modalities of perception in regard to both internal and external events (Orne, 1961, p. 170).

Other attributes of the hypnotic state, according to Orne, are that the subject experiences it as discontinuous from his normal waking life and there is a quality of compulsion associated with the hypnotist's demands.

In recent years evidence has accrued that the "good" hypnotic subject may be characterized by a propensity for unusual, imaginative, hypnotic-like subjective experiences in everyday life (Shor et al., 1962; Barber and Glass, 1962; Ås, 1963). The most comprehensive study to date on the relation of imagery and fantasy to hypnosis is currently being conducted by Sutcliffe and his associates (1966). In accordance with the fantastic and delusory character of hypnotic experience, it was hypothesized that vividness of imagination and proneness to fantasy are two specific aptitudes involved in trance behavior. Results of this study are only now being analyzed.

In summing up his position on the relation between the waking and sleep states, Dement provides small comfort to those who advocate a sharp demarcation:

> We can only say at the present state of our knowledge, the similarities between REM sleep and wakefulness seem far more striking than the differences. In other words, whatever degree of uniqueness it may eventually be found to possess, at the present moment the salient feature of the dream state is its neurophysiological similarity to active wakefulness (Dement, 1965, p. 210).

Whether hypnosis is eventually established as essentially a waking or sleep state or as something in-between, the differentiation between stage 1-REM and that in which hypnotic dreaming occurs can never again be regarded as distinctly separate, as was once maintained.[4]

REPRISE AND CONCLUDING COMMENTS

If the preceding paragraphs do not constitute a wholly convincing argument for the physiological equivalence or even the phenomenological identity of the REM and hypnotic dream states, it is because major portions of evidence are lacking. No one now knows the answers to the many issues raised, and that is exactly the point. The intent has been only to accurately mirror the tangled skein of available evidence. The need for an open-minded approach to the facts is attested to by a poll of those psychologists best qualified to express an opinion on the subject in the fields of both clinical and experimental hypnosis.

A summary of the survey made of the diplomates in clinical and experimental hypnosis created by the American Board of Examiners in Psychological Hypnosis (listed in the 1965 Directory of the American Psychological Association) is provided in Table 1. Forty-six responses were received from a total of 52 diplomates canvassed in reply to two questions:

TABLE 1

Tabulation of answers of forty-six diplomates in clinical and experimental hypnosis to questions concerning hypnosis and dreams

	Hypnotic and night dreams are essentially similar	Hypnosis can increase a subject's understanding of dreams
Yes	25	22
No	10	14
Uncertain (no opinion)	10	9
Unclassifiable	1	1

1. What is your opinion as to whether hypnotically induced dreams are similar in essential respects to nocturnal dreams?

[4] Readers are referred to Milton Erickson's 1965 article on an inquiry conducted into the experiential nature and character of different levels of the hypnotic state, with and through the finely tuned introspective faculties of Aldous Huxley.

2. Do you believe that hypnosis can facilitate the ability of some subjects to intuit the meaning of primary process thinking (for example, symbolism)?

It is noteworthy that a number of respondents had no opinion regarding either question, and even many of those who did qualified their answers with statements of limited or frankly clinical personal experience.

Some respondents took issue with the general nature of the questions, stating that they would have to differentiate between the validity of dreams provided in the immediate hypnotic situation vis-à-vis those stimulated by posthypnotic suggestion in regular sleep, and also between the interpretation of one's own dreams as contrasted to those derived from external sources. Nine of those who agreed that hypnosis can increase interpretive ability volunteered that this was because hypnosis facilitates a freer flow of associations. The firm conclusion is that a wide variance in opinion exists even among those possessed of unusual experience and expertise in the clinical and experimental applications of hypnosis.

What then is known with even a modest degree of probability regarding the hypnotic dream?

1. The hypnotically induced dream is likely to range from a deliberately contrived hoax, through spontaneously experienced static images or a simple daydream, to a product replete with symbolism and closely resembling a natural dream.

2. An uncontrolled variable in most studies has been the precise form of the instruction "to dream," which can vary in significant ways. The subject may be asked to respond to the suggestion immediately or it may be given as a posthypnotic suggestion to be activated at night when the subject is asleep. In the first instance, the resulting product is usually quite brief in duration and often does not even sound very much like a night dream. An individual during hypnosis may also be instructed first to go to sleep and then to dream, and under these conditions he may appear to have a true dream. In the case of the posthypnotic dream during the night, the product may possess many features in common with the normal night dream, but the contribution of the implanted stimulus to the dream is obscured. It is entirely possible that the hypnotically suggested content may function only as a day residue or may at least have no greater impact than any other "transference" suggestion.

3. There is some circumstantial evidence that the hypnotic subject may produce dreams in the immediate hypnotic state by a transitory

immersion into descending stage 1 sleep; however, this contention remains to be critically examined.

4. It is unresolved at the moment as to whether the subject carries out the posthypnotic suggestion while actually in stage 1 sleep or momentarily reenters the hypnotic state. Repeated determination of the fact that among the various sleep stages REM sleep is uniquely responsive to exogenous stimuli, lends credence to the possibility of manipulation of dreaming by either hypnotic or waking suggestion.

5. The dream stimulus itself may be specific and detailed or deliberately ambiguous. It is generally agreed that subjects typically embellish the dream stimulus with a substantial personal contribution, and the more unstructured the suggestion, the greater the degree of elaboration. A nonspecific posthypnotic suggestion "to dream" is thought to result in a product indistinguishable from the spontaneous night dream, but, again, it is almost impossible to determine the exact contribution of the stimulus suggestion under such circumstances.

6. It has been argued by clinicians that hypnosis facilitates trance logic or primary process thinking and that the hypnotized individual has an enhanced facility for interpreting symbolic material. Of course, the difficulty of objectively establishing the "real" meaning of dream symbols is a complicating issue, but the hypothesis that a hypnotized individual is more capable of interpreting imaginal productions correctly than the nonhypnotized individual is open to empirical test, and much more easily by other means than by the use of hypnotic dreams. The important point is that there is very little literature which has demonstrated the hypothesis to be valid.

7. It does seem possible to conclude that the hypnotic stimulation of dreams and their hypnotically induced interpretation result in clinically valuable projective material. Irrespective of the nature of the hypnotic dream or the veridicality of the interpretations of symbolic productions generally, these methods may have real therapeutic utility. These techniques free the psychotherapeutic procedure from a passive dependence on spontaneous nocturnal dreams, because a state of expanded consciousness leading to the activation of symbolisms is actively cultivated. Obviously, much more work needs to be done in objectifying the therapeutic value of these techniques.

8. When it comes to hypnotic dreams and their relationship to night dreams on the basis of the electrophysiological findings, particularly those dealing with EOGs and EEG, the amount of empirical research that has been reported is in no way adequate to establish the neurophysiological similarity of these two types of dreams. A start has been made and even very preliminary findings are provocative of specula-

tion; however, much work remains to be done in exploiting the potential inherent in these newer techniques. Generally, electrophysiological data do not support the assertion that the nature of hypnosis and sleep is quantitatively the same. There is no identifiable difference from the alert, waking EEG pattern when the subject is in communication with the hypnotist or acting in compliance with most suggestions. It is the nature of the hypnotic state during dream production (or the nature of the sleep state at the moment of carrying out a posthypnotic suggestion "to dream") vis-à-vis the natural REM period that demands careful scrutiny. Other physiological correlates of dreaming, such as EOG, GSR, respiratory changes, and plethysmographology on the male organ, remain to be investigated in relation to the hypnotic dream.

9. A primary obstacle to a meaningful comparison and contrast of normal and hypnotic dreams is the lack of any agreement as to the nature of hypnosis. It may well be that dreams should be defined by the character of their manifest content rather than by the circumstances of their occurrence, but until more is understood about the essence of the hypnotic state and its relationship to stage 1-REM sleep, extreme caution should be exercised in generalizing from one product to the other. Hypnosis is obviously not a necessary condition for the stimulation of dreaming and, furthermore, it is certainly not a sufficient one. Dreamlike productions are elicitable under a wide range of conditions, and it is quite possible that some persons have this special capacity with or without hypnosis. The majority of even "good" hypnotic subjects apparently do not possess an ability to comply with the suggestion "to dream," although a positive correlation to measures of susceptibility or hypnotic "depth" has been reported. The requisite traits of those subjects who do succeed remain to be determined. Certainly, variations in the hypnotic state must be taken into account. It is as gross a form of simplistic thinking to regard hypnosis as a totality as it was heretofore to consider sleep a unitary entity. Superficial degrees or depths of hypnosis are almost indistinguishable from wakefulness, whereas others border on and gradually shade into normal sleep. Left to his own devices, a hypnotized subject will drift into natural sleep, and hypnotists beginning with Hippolyte Bernheim have reported the existence of unsuggested or spontaneous dreams. In any event, the term hypnosis quite possibly covers a spectrum of altered states of psychobiological functioning, and it is probable that the nature of associated mentation may vary accordingly.

In addition to the many difficult technical problems that plague the hypnotic study of dreams, there is yet another complication of a more subtle, attitudinal nature. The fascination regarding the dual phenomenon of hypnosis and dreams has an undeniably ambivalent quality, a mingled reaction of wonderment, perplexity, and apprehension, from which even the behavioral scientist is not exempt. Deep-seated patent reservations on the part of many professional persons with respect to the serious investigation of hypnosis does not merit further elaboration. Less palpable is the tendency to employ the critical and skeptical faculties to minimize the reality of the inner life and, when these processes do break through, as with hypnosis, to attempt to discount them as artificial products that are intentionally contrived.

Contemporary Western man prides himself on a consciously organized and rational *Weltansicht,* which encourages a sharp distinction between the worlds of waking and dream experience. In contrast to other societies, past and present, in which hallucinatory experiences are accepted as completely normal events and even institutionalized and rewarded, in our culture a compartimentalization of experience is demanded. The American society has always been irrevocably extratensive in temperament. Dreams are sanctioned by their occurrence in the sleep state, but if visions or imagery intrude too vividly into our waking world, we tend to regard them as pathognomic. This may contribute to the long-standing, erroneous attitude that hypnotic susceptibility is related to psychopathology and that even the employment of hypnosis presages some form of neuroticism on the part of the professional person.

Perhaps this strict demarcation in required by the always difficult distinction that we feel forced to maintain between internal and external reality. Modern-day psychology is only too keenly aware of the degree to which perception is an interpretation determined by past experience and fraught with possibilities for projection, rather than any direct revelation of external reality in the objective sense. Man might easily mistake his dreams for reality, were they not so clearly embedded in the familiar context of sleep, and it is an undoubted convenience on awakening to be able to dismiss these often discrepant and potentially distressful experiences as purely illusionary. Witness the confusion and consternation of the poor narcoleptic who suffers vivid and realistic dreams in the midst of his workaday world.

Although dreams are regarded as the characteristic mental activity during sleep, the concurrences of multiple independent observations compel the conclusion that sleep is not a necessary condition for the activation of the dream-producing mechanism. As Dement puts it, "The identical mechanisms might also be responsible for such waking state phenomena as hallucinations, images, visions, daydreams, and so forth" (Dement, 1965, p. 140). It is common knowledge that the distinction between the conscious and unconscious is relative at best; all thought that is conscious from one angle is unconscious from another, and there is a continuous and fluid transition between the extremes.

The question of the equivalence of hypnotically induced and spontaneous dreams is, in the final analysis, correctly viewed as only one aspect of a still broader issue that pervades the whole field of hypnosis studies. Hypnosis research can be broadly categorized as either intrinsic or instrumental in nature (Reyher, 1962). The instrumental research employs hypnosis as a tool or independent variable in the study of personality, psychopathology, and psychophysiological alterations as, for example, in the hypnotic investigation of dreaming. However, a great many psychologists have felt constrained to ignore the results produced by this kind of research, because they remain unconvinced that hypnotically instigated behaviors are sufficiently comparable to their natural counterparts to allow valid comparisons. Because so few unequivocal facts have been established about hypnosis per se, they adhere firmly to an intrinsic position, namely, that at this stage in our knowledge it is both more judicious and productive if research is done *about* hypnosis rather than *with* it. If interested in the hypnotic dream at all, they would insist that it be studied for its own sake, as a distinctive fantasy form peculiar to the subjective or altered state of consciousness, called hypnosis.

The author would agree that this is a sound, prudent, and defensible position. It is hoped that this book has demonstrated the desirability and plausibility of a serious examination of the proposition that hypnosis can attenuate the ties with external reality and promote access to an inner world of fantasy, creative imagination, and dreams, and that an evident enthusiasm for such exploration has served to clarify rather than obfuscate the basic experimental issues involved.

Part Two
Selected Readings

The Translation of the Cryptic Automatic Writing of One Hypnotic Subject by Another in a Trance-Like Dissociated State

BY MILTON H. ERICKSON AND
LAWRENCE S. KUBIE

During the training of a subject for a particular experiment in hypnosis, a unique observation was made upon the ability of one person in a spontaneous trance accurately to decipher and to translate the mysterious and cryptic automatic writing of another. In their conscious states neither individual could understand the script. In trance-like states each one quite independently reached identical interpretations of it. Cryptic automatic writing is found to suffer from processes of distortion identical with those seen in dreams; and the translation of such writing, to involve the same principles as those involved in dream analysis.

In chronological sequence in the protocols detailed below there is portrayed both the general situation and the series of events leading to these observations: (1) the subject as an incident in his training and while in a deep trance was told by an assistant in the absence of the investigator, to forget all the vowels but not the fact of their existence. (2) In another trance a week later he was given additional suggestions to the effect that he would replace the seventh (g), eighth (h), and ninth (i) letters of the alphabet with their respective numerals and that henceforth his name would be "Jack Young." (3) He was then asked to write his name. In doing this he omitted the vowels and substituted the numeral "10" for the letter "J," declaring emphatically as he completed this task that something was wrong.

Assuming in the interpretation of hypnotic productions as in the interpretation of dreams, that every trivial detail has meaning, the assistant sought to secure from the subject an explanation both of his use of the numeral *ten*, and of his comment that something was wrong. The subject wrote the letters "N" and "F" and the numerals "7," "7," "8," and "9" automatically in his effort to explain these phenomena, apparently offering them as an adequate explanation of everything. Dissatisfied, the assistant demanded a more understandable writ-

SOURCE. Reprinted by permission from *The Psychoanalytic Quarterly*, 9 (1) 51–63 January, 1940.

101

ten explanation. This resulted in still more abbreviated and cryptic automatic writing; and further requests produced merely a repetition of that writing, despite the assistant's efforts to compel some alteration of the written characters by active physical interference.

External circumstances then terminated the interview at this point but not before the subject had demonstrated his complete lack of any conscious understanding of what his written "explanation" meant, or of what the "mistake" had been, and whether it was the substitution of a "10" for the "J" in his written name.

After the subject left, the investigator came into the laboratory and while he and his assistant were puzzling over the cryptic writing, a second subject, Alice, entered the laboratory and showed an immediate interest in the problem. This subject has the rare capacity to develop spontaneous hypnotic trances during which she functions adequately in whatever situation she finds herself. Upon awakening from them she has no awareness of her trance activities. Because of her interest in the problem, she was given an outline of the essential facts and the writing was shown to her by the assistant who then departed leaving this second subject, Alice, to puzzle over the writing with the investigator.

Thereupon Alice developed a series of spontaneous trance states interspersed with ordinary waking states. In the trance states she interpreted the writing item by item and explained it step by step to the investigator who maintained essentially a passive, receptive role. This passive role was forced upon the investigator by the brevity of the spontaneous trances, the difficulty of trying to carry on a conversation with her at all, and the necessity constantly to meet her at two different levels of awareness in a single situation. Alice's spontaneous trances tended to be so brief that she would have time to offer only an explanatory remark or two and would then awaken with no awareness of what she had just said. In the waking state she would continue her puzzled wonderment over the writing which had just been interrupted by the spontaneous trance, or she would become interested in some totally unrelated topic and discuss that until some remark of the investigator disclosed to her his own unclear state of mind regarding the last bit of explanation she had given. There would follow another spontaneous trance in which, briefly and concisely, Alice would make another remark to clarify the investigator's mind. As a consequence, it was necessary for Alice to develop a large number of spontaneous trances and to repeat her explanations many times before she could feel satisfied with the investigator's comprehension of what had been said. In addition, Alice's explanations were often as cryptic to the investigator as the writing itself, as for example her use of the word "sign" to explain the correctness of the letter "H" (cf. the protocol below).

In the intervals between the spontaneous trances, investigation showed that Alice had a complete and persistent amnesia for all of her trance disclosures, even after the entire interpretation of the writing had been secured; furthermore, when her own interpretation of the writing was presented to her, she regarded it purely as a product of the investigator's own reasoning. However, when questioned about it in an induced trance state, she not only recognized the explanation as her own but meticulously corrected the slightest change in wording introduced by the investigator.

Why Alice resorted to this devious and uncertain method of communication instead of permitting herself to develop flashes of conscious insight, is a matter for speculation not wholly explained by her statement that the writing represented her own unconscious way of thinking and writing.

The following day the first subject, T. L., came to the office unexpectedly to report what he termed "an amusing hypnagogic experience." Unaware that the assistant had told the investigator of the original situation, and unaware also of the investigator's subsequent experience with Alice, he described fully his own experiences with the assistant on the previous day, corroborating the details given by the assistant and including others which were later verified. He emphasized in particular his own argumentativeness, his insistence that there was a mistake in the written name, his feeling of absolute certainty about his conscious understanding, and his feeling of irritation with the assistant whose manner seemed unwarrantedly to imply that there were unrecognized meanings in the writing. He related that after his departure he had forgotten about the incident until, falling asleep late that evening, he had a "hypnagogic experience" in which he "saw" the episode exactly as it had occurred with a new interpretation of it all. He expressed much amusement over his earlier belligerency and defensiveness, and also about his new realization of "how intensely you can believe something that is totally wrong, when right in your subconscious you know the truth." He went on to explain that along with his original "conscious explanation" he now "saw" the "true subconscious explanation" which was not at all similar to his "conscious explanation." Asked to restate his original "conscious explanation," he claimed that because it was "so wrong" he could no longer remember more than a vague outline of it, but that now he was ready to give the "correct explanation of the whole thing."

In response to the investigator's manifest interest, he proceeded to give his explanation, but not with the confidence his manner had led the investigator to expect. It became apparent at once that the subject's conscious grasp of the problem was limited and that he only thought he understood it. Actually his method was to offer sudden, brief, dogmatic statements as if each were the complete explanation, only to discover spontaneously that his explanation was inadequate. Then there would follow another sudden flash of conscious insight and another dogmatic statement.

After a number of such steps the subject took the attitude of one solving a puzzle and began to search for the explanation of his various dogmatic statements and for the significance of the writing. As he studied the writing and tried to fit his various statements to it, additional flashes of insight developed, sometimes relevant to the immediate question he was trying to solve, and sometimes pertinent to another item not yet touched upon. Thus bit by bit in an unsystematic fashion, a complete explanation was developed which was in full accord with the one given by Alice. In this episode the investigator's role was again a passive, receptive one.

Of marked interest is the fact that neither subject volunteered any interpretation of the first 'explanation' written as four digits. Both subjects ignored that particular writing completely until it was called to their attention. Alice remarked simply that everything was included in the writing she had explained, while T. L. commented briefly, "That's [the digits] not so good; the writing's better."

PROTOCOL I

FIRST WEEK

1 Subject T. L. was told while in a hypnotic trance to forget the vowels of the alphabet but not the fact of their existence.

SECOND WEEK

2 Subject T. L. was again hypnotized and told this time to replace the seventh, eighth and ninth letters of the alphabet (g, h, and i) with their respective numerals.

3 T. L. was then told that his name was "Jack Young" and he was asked to write it.

4 T. L. wrote his name "10 ck Yng" (cf. Figure 1).

Figure 1

5 Upon inspection of his writing, T. L. declared it to be incorrect,
   that the "J" was a mistake, and he became disputatious when
   the assistant suggested that it might be correct.
6 The assistant asked, "Is what you wrote correct?"
7 T. L. wrote automatically the character "N," which was interpreted by the assistant as a "No," but this T. L. did not confirm
   (cf. Figure 2).

N

Figure 2

8 The assistant asked if the writing was apparently incorrect.
9 T. L. wrote automatically the character "F" which the assistant
   interpreted as a "Yes," but this again was neither confirmed nor
   corrected (cf. Figure 3).

7

Figure 3

10 The assistant then asked why the writing was only apparently
   incorrect.
11 T. L. wrote automatically the construction, "7 7 8 9," very faintly
   and somewhat illegibly (cf. Figure 4).

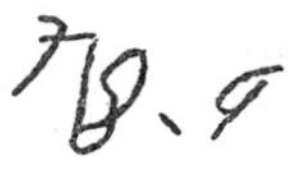

Figure 4

12   The assistant asked that the explanation be rewritten plainly and clearly and in a fashion understandable to both of them.

13   T. L. then added to the "N" and the "F" already written a peculiar group of letters (cf. Figure 5).

Figure 5

14   The assistant, after scrutiny of this writing, asked T. L. to rewrite on another sheet of paper his explanation in a more clearly understandable and readable fashion.

15   T. L. complied with this request by producing a second graphic construction, essentially a repetition of the previous one, ignoring and resisting as he did so the assistant's attempts to compel an alteration of the writing by forcibly moving the paper while T. L. was engaged in his task (cf. Figure 6).

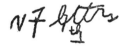

Figure 6

16   No further verbal explanation of the writing was obtained at this time except an argumentative repetition of his previous declaration that the written name contained a mistake namely, the use of 10 for J. External circumstances then brought the interview to an end.

PROTOCOL II

ENTRANCE OF ALICE

1   The written name was exhibited to Alice by the assistant, and a rapid explanation was given of the posthypnotic suggestions regarding vowels and the replacement by numerals of the seventh, eighth and ninth letters, and of T. L.'s insistence that there was a mistake in the writing of the name. Following this the assistant left.

2   Alice studied the name as it was written and then counted the letters of the alphabet rapidly.

3   Alice's explanation: "J" has the ordinal position of "10" but the omission of the vowels gives it the ordinal position of "7." "7" however is actually identical with "G" and, hence, it cannot be used to designate "J". Therefore, "J," the seventh letter, must be written as "10." In brief, J is both the seventh and the tenth letter, but it can be written numerically only as "10."

4   Alice was then shown T. L.'s written production, Figure 6. This she promptly read as "Numbers for letters," illustrating this significance by immediate reference to the use of a "10" for a "J" in the written name.

5   The investigator then gave Alice the additional information about the assistant's interpretation of the letter "N" as signifying "No" (cf. Figure 2).

6   The writing was read then by Alice as, "Not letters; numbers for letters."

7   Alice's explanation: The second character in the written explanation actually is a "T" as well as an "F" and may equally well be read as a "4." T. L.'s passive acceptance of the interpretation of a "No" serves to transform the first two characters of the writing into the word "Not" with the vowel omitted; furthermore, since the second character is obviously an "F," and also a "4," emphasis is thereby placed upon the second character and this is indicated doubly by the fact that the letter "F" actually is the fourth letter in the alphabet with the vowels omitted. Hence, "F," by virtue of all this, can be used to signify "*for*" as a simple pun as well as an abbreviation.

8   Therefore, on first reading the written explanation, one reads "Not letters," but since this is only part of an explanation, one must reread the written characters for their additional meanings; hence on second reading, one reads "No 4 lttrs," or "Numbers for letters."

9   The investigator accepted this reading unquestioningly, but asked what the "*th*" meant, since it appeared in both of T. L.'s written explanations.

10   Alice first explained with the single word "sign," but finally declared that it was connected "by the sign," which she identified by gesture as the line underneath the "*th*," with the second character of the written explanation and that it "explained" the "mistake."

11   Alice's explanation: The second character reads "T," "F," "4,"

and "for," but in relation to the "*th*" it also reads "7." "G" is the seventh letter of the alphabet. "G" should be written as "7." "G" is written "G" in the name, hence, "G" is a mistake.

12　The investigator then asked Alice to read aloud the written explanation, which she did as follows: "Not letters; numbers for letters; not 7; seventh letter; 7 in place of letter," and as this explanation was read, Alice declared that there was a concealed "7" in the word "lttrs," an item which had been consistently overlooked by the investigator.

13　As an additional explanation, Alice added: "7" should be in the place of the letter "G" in the name, but a mistake was made and "G" was written. So to explain what he meant by "a mistake," "7" is written here [pointing to the concealed "7" in the character "lttrs"] so that you can see that there is really a "7" in the place of "letters" where you should read it, but where you really read just "lttrs."

14　The investigator asked if there were any further explanation of the "*th*" since "H" is the eighth letter.

15　Alice explained: It is a sign. You read "7-th" not 7-t-h. To this was added, "Not mistake like "G." It [*th*] is a sign.

16　The investigator then raised the question of "G" becoming the fifth letter of the alphabet with the vowels omitted. Alice explained that "G" could not be the fifth letter because the difficuly about the "J" had definitely established "G" as the seventh letter.

17　Alice was then asked about the letter "K." Again she explained that the establishment of the letter "J" as number "10" provided a point of orientation for all of the letters in the alphabet, regardless of the omission of the vowels, and she restated the fact that the vowels had only been forgotten, but not the fact of their existence. Therefore, the letter "J" established as number "10" would automatically cause "K" to be letter number "11" and "G" to be letter number "7."

18　Alice then was asked about the identification of the letter "F" as the number "4" by virtue of the omission of the vowels. Alice pointed out immediately that this was purely for purposes of punning and that anything was permissible in a pun.

19　Alice was then asked to explain how it was that she could interpret such cryptic writing.

20　Alice's explanation: Oh, that's easy. That's just the way I always think and write. Just a little means a lot.

21　Alice was asked, "How could you know that the writing could be interpreted?"

22 Alice's explanation: When you knew about the vowels and the numbers, then you could see lots of meanings all at once right there and you could just read them.

23 When asked about the written digits in Figure 4, Alice explained that they meant the same as the writing, but not so clearly.

PROTOCOL III

THE NEXT DAY

1 Subject T. L. reported to the investigator an "amusing hypnagogic experience" in which "I remembered the whole situation. I had a complete conscious explanation at the time. I was so sure of it, too; I wanted to argue. I said there was a mistake. I remembered every little detail of that whole situation, and, at the same time, in that hypnagogic state I could see the whole thing in an entirely different way. Half asleep there, I could see my conscious understanding of that whole situation and at the same time I could see my subconscious understanding. The two were so different and I had been so sure of my conscious understanding, but it really was all wrong. I didn't have anything right in my conscious understanding at all, and yet I wanted to argue; I was looking for an argument."

2 The investigator asked T. L. for an account of his conscious understanding.

3 T. L. declared that he could not remember anything about it except that it was all wrong, nothing right. "I wasn't even thinking about the things I thought I was thinking about." The investigator asked him to explain this more fully. T. L. replied, "Consciously I said there was a mistake but the mistake I thought I was talking about wasn't a mistake at all. I thought I was talking about J but in that hypnagogic experience I knew that J was right but that G was a mistake. J was just a mistake to my consciousness even though it was not a mistake to my subconsciousness."

4 The investigator asked T. L. to give an account of his subconscious understandings.

5 There followed then an explanation of the writing in which item by item was accorded the same interpretation as had been given by Alice. The method by which his explanation was achieved was one based upon sudden flashes of insight, such as obtained in the solving of a puzzle. Thus in relation to the second character (cf. Figure 3) he declared he could explain it best by writing it from memory, whereupon he proceeded to write the French form of

the numeral "7" (the subject has studied French). In the usual position, elevated above the line, he added to this numeral a "*th*." When the accuracy of his recollection was questioned, he became decidedly disputatious and insisted that it was right because of the line underneath the "*th*." From these disconnected flashes of insight partial understandings of several different aspects of the problem were obtained. Alice, on the other hand, recognized the numerical quality of that character along with its other attributes without resort to intermediary steps.

6   The order in which T. L. built up his interpretations of the written explanation shown in Figure 6 was as follows:

(*a*) Declaration that the use of a "10" for a "J" in the written name was not an error but that the "G" was an error.

(*b*) Statement that the writing (Figure 6) read both "Not letters" and "Numbers for letters."

(*c*) Elucidation of the use of a "10" for a "J." "Without the vowels J was the seventh letter and I had to put a number for that letter, but I couldn't put a 7 because even if there were no vowels you had to count their places and that would make G the seventh letter just as J was, so I just wrote the correct number for the letter J."

(*d*) Identification of the "F" (Figure 2) as a "T," and "F," a "4" and as "for" followed by its identification as a "7" as described in Item 5, and by relating this explanation to the clarification of the 'mistake' contained in the letter "G."

(*e*) Declaration that there should be a "7" in addition to the one contained in the second character of the written explanation, to be read with the "*th*" as "seventh letter."

(*f*) Discovery of the concealed "7" and the reading of the message as "Not letters, numbers for letters, not 7, seventh letter, 7 in place of letter."

(*g*) Clarification of the question of the "K" and the "H" in the same fashion as Alice had done.

(*h*) Discovery of the pun on "4" and "F" contained in the second character of the written explanation, since previously he had regarded the "F" as a simple abbreviation for "for."

7   Declaration that the four digits, illustrated in Figure 4, constituted a similar but less satisfactory explanation than the writing in Figure 6.

8   Explanation that Figure 6 differed from Figure 5 only because of the assistant's interference. Alice had declared them to be identical in meaning.

DISCUSSION

I. The main event of this unplanned and unexpected experience is in itself worthy of record for it is an arresting fact that one human being while in a dissociated trance-like condition can accurately decipher the automatic writing of another—writing which neither of the two subjects was able to decipher while in states of normal consciousness. The observation stresses from a new angle a fact that has often been exphasized by those who have studied unconscious processes but which remains none the less mysterious—namely, that underneath the diversified nature of the consciously organized aspects of the personality, the unconscious talks in a language which has a remarkable uniformity; furthermore, that that language has laws so constant that the unconscious of one individual is better equipped to understand the unconscious of another than the conscious aspect of the personality of either.

If this is true, and it seems to be a fact attested from many sources, it must give the psychoanalyst reason to wonder as to the wisdom of confining himself exclusively to the technique of free association in his efforts consciously to penetrate into the unconscious of his patient.

II. When one turns to the details of this experience, one finds several points which need more specific emphasis, and certain basic questions which remain wholly unanswered:

(1) In the first place it is striking that in the translation of automatic writing, as in the interpretation of dreams, each element may be made to do double and triple duty: to wit, the several purposes subserved by the letters N and F.

(2) Again we see that here, as in dreams, puns, elisions, plays on words and similar tricks that we ordinarily think of as frivolous, all play a surprising and somewhat disconcerting role in the communication of important and serious feelings. We accept this type of thought and language in simple jokes as for instance in the old conundrum of childhood: "How do you spell 'blind pig'? to which the answer is 'b l n d p g—leave out the 'eyes'." But it is ever a source of fresh amazement when the unconscious processes express weighty and troublesome problems in a shorthand which has in it an element of irreverent levity.

(3) In the whole episode there are two untouched problems—why in the first instance the "mistake" occurred at all (the slip is seemingly trivial, a tempest in a teapot) and second why when the mistake had

occurred, the first subject, T. L., could not have recognized it and corrected it simply and directly. Perhaps it is of importance that the mistake concerned the patient's own identity, i.e., the automatic spelling of his own name. It will be recalled that in the course of the experiment his name had been changed by suggestion to "Jack Young."

It is possible that a highly charged rebellion against the implantation under hypnosis of this alternative personality, struggling with a co-existent attitude of passive submission to the authority of the hypnotist may account for several things: the exaggerated tempest, the curiously evasive quality of some of the replies, the ambiguities (as if he did not know whether to correct the error or not) the elements of malicious humor, the literal-mindedness, the hiding. All of this seems to indicate that, both in the automatic writing and in the subsequent efforts to translate it, the subject is struggling simultaneously to explain and to hide his meaning. In support of this hypothesis there is one possible explanation of the writing, which neither subject offered although it is a rather obvious alternative: if N equals "not," and if F is also a "T," and if we consider that the first letter of the following group of letters is L, then the first three letters would read "not T. L."—in other words, not the subject's own initials.

It may well be that if we knew enough about the subject, T. L., and the identifications which must make up the basis of the structure of his whole personality, this otherwise mysterious little episode would then become quite understandable.

Commentary

My interest in the ability of the unconscious mind of one person to understand the unconscious behavior and communications of another person began in 1929 at the State Hospital for Mental Diseases, Howard, Rhode Island. It was there that I conducted my first planned experiment. This happened as follows. I was admitting a new patient who was in his early twenties and was entering a mental hospital for the first time. He was mute, stuporous, unresponsive, showed *flexibilitas cerea*, and stared unblinkingly straight ahead. He did not show a blink reflex nor seem to be aware of stimuli except to be passively responsive in simple matters. As I studied him, I realized that in appearance and behavior he was an excellent counterpart of another patient I already had on the ward who was also in his early twenties and was also blond. Both patients had a strikingly similar history of latent homosexuality and both had developed their mental disturbances under comparable situations. For each of them this had been an overt homosexual seduction. For each the aggressor was a man over 40 years of age. In the instance of the newly admitted patient, the aggressor had a bushy black beard.

My ward patient invariably spent the day sitting in a certain chair in a certain place on the ward. I instructed the ward attendants to set up a screen in front of that ward patient to conceal him. After the ward bath and the routine admission physical examination, the new patient was led to a chair in front of the screen and was so positioned that when the screen was removed, the two patients would be directly facing each other at a distance of five feet. Both patients were sitting with their arms hanging straight down.

Half an hour later, one of the attendants, upon instruction, called to another attendant, "Bring that screen over here. I need it." I was seated, engaged in talking to a patient some 30 feet distant but with a good view of the two patients made to confront each other suddenly by the screen removal. Twenty minutes later the new patient was perspiring freely. Slowly he raised his right hand and pointed at the other patient. At a signal from me, the attendant called out, "Hey, Bill, I'm through with the screen. You can put it back." This was done.

The newly arrived patient was then slowly led by me to another ward. There he was asked, "Why did you point?" Slowly, laboriously, the reply was given, "He troubles me. He makes me afraid. Afraid something will happen to me. Something bad . . . bad . . . bad." Questioned insistently, the patient seemed unable to voice anything more.

Two hours later I sat down beside the ward patient, something I had been doing regularly in an effort to induce him to talk. The opening gambit had always been a comment on some patient on the ward, but not necessarily in sight. (This opening gambit with mute patients had often proved fruitful). He was asked, "What do you think of that new patient?" He answered with the first words that he had spoken since his entrance into the hospital months previously, "He is evil . . . most evil. I want to kill him . . . I couldn't move. He is evil . . . very evil." Nothing more was elicited.

The two patients were kept on separate wards. Months later, when both were occasionally slightly communicative, they were carefully confronted with each other. Immediately the "new" patient declared, "You are like me. You are better. You want to kill. Not me." As if after deep thought the "old" patient stated, "Yes, kill, not you . . . that man who did that to me . . . to you."

I asked both what they meant. One answered, "We understand." The other answered, "He is my brother in unhappiness." Neither would elaborate. Nothing more could be elicited from either.

With this sort of an introduction to the ability of one person to comprehend another at a nonverbal level, I then became intensely interested in the remarkable capacity of the unconscious mind of one person to understand that of another. Dr. Kubie, I knew, shared my interest and this led to our collaboration on the paper reprinted here which seemed to present an utterly clear demonstration of the capacity of the unconscious mind of one person to understand even highly symbolic unconscious behavior or expression of another person.

Since publishing that paper with Dr. Kubie, I have done much experimental and clinical study of this phenomena. I have created situations in which dual personalities would meet at a bona fide social gathering so that I could watch them recognize each other, although only I knew them to be dual personalities. I have handed a dual personality a letter written by another dual personality and watched the startled reaction of recognition when the meaningful change in the handwriting done by the secondary personality was inserted into the body of the primary personality's letter without that primary personality being aware of it.

I have asked psychotic patients to interpret pictures, verbalizations, and posturings of other patients, often with confirmable and remarkable accuracy. I have done the same with neurotic patients innumerable times with confirmable results. Most particularly, I have done a great deal of experimental work with hypnotic subjects comparable to the Kubie-Erickson study. Some of this work I hope to publish some day for its instructive and revealing significance.

This entire field of unconscious communication is an area for investigation that should be extensively explored both for underlying principles and for the advancement of psychotherapy. Research should prove most rewarding, and new understandings both academic and clinical would be the result.

MILTON H. ERICKSON

Phoenix, Arizona
1966

An Experimental Approach to Dream Psychology
Through the Use of Hypnosis

BY LESLIE H. FARBER AND
CHARLES FISHER

INTRODUCTION

Because of the difficulty of investigating emotional processes experimentally, the investigation of dream psychology has progressed little since the publication of Freud's *The Interpretation of Dreams*, a fact which Freud noted in 1933 when he complained that analysts "behave as though they had nothing more to say about the dream—as though the whole subject of dream theory were finished and done with" (1931*b*, p. 16). He called attention, as an exception, to the pioneer work of several Viennese investigators who, using hypnosis (Schroetter) and other methods, had made a start in the experimental confirmation of the theory of dream symbolism. Unfortunately, this research was not pursued. The last two decades have seen considerable development of hypnotic techniques in the study of various unconscious processes. Erickson (1939*a*, *b*), Kubie (1934), Erickson and Kubie (1938, 1939, 1940), Luria (1932), Eisenbud (1937, 1939), and others have contributed to this literature.

To develop a method of dream study which might be more objective than the interpretive technique used in analytic therapy, a group of average college students were used as hypnotic subjects. With them as subjects the following problems were investigated:

1. *The capacity of normal individuals under hypnosis to understand dream language and the factors which might influence this understanding.* In hypnotic and other dissociated mental states, individuals show capacity for understanding and interpreting the uncon-

SOURCE. Reprinted by permission from *The Psychoanalytic Quarterly*, **12**, (2), 202–216 (April, 1943).

This paper was presented at a special round table at the convention of the American Psychiatric Association in Boston, 1942.

This investigation was made possible by the generosity of Marshall Field III. The authors would like also to express their gratitude to Dr. Gregory Zilboorg, and to Dr. Winfred Overholser, Superintendent of St. Elizabeths Hospital, who have encouraged this work from the beginning.

scious psychic productions of others. It is well known that schizophrenic patients are able to interpret dreams. Some artistic individuals manifest a special faculty for understanding the unconscious import of artistic creations. Erickson found that a hypnotized subject in one instance was able to read and understand the automatic writing of another person.

2. *The production of experimental dreams under hypnosis.* Earlier workers have found that they could partially control the form and content of the dream by suggesting under hypnosis what was to be dreamed about. Their suggestions were restricted to a limited number of grossly sexual situations. We hoped to confirm this work and extend its scope to include a variety of dream stimuli.

3. *The nature of the relationship between hypnotist and subject.* Hypnosis fell into comparative disuse as a therapy largely because of the lack of understanding of the hypnotic relationship.

The students who participated in the project as hypnotic subjects were recruited from a Washington university by the professors, who announced to their classes that two psychiatrists were doing research with hypnosis. The volunteers were from 18 to 21 years of age. Those who seemed unstable were immediately excluded, and only those who proved to be naïve about psychology, ignorant of any knowledge of the theory of dreams, were chosen. They were asked not to read about the subject for the duration of the project. Those selected were average students, with no conspicuous personal problems and no special talents, either artistic or intellectual.

DREAM TRANSLATION

Under hypnosis the subjects were directly presented with dreams, of which some were fantasies of the experimenters, some produced by other subjects during hypnosis, some were the dreams of friends and patients, and a few were myths and psychotic productions. For example, an eighteen-year-old girl was told under hypnosis: "Dreams have meaning. Now that you are asleep you will be better able to understand them. A girl dreamt that she was packing her trunk when a big snake crawled into it. She was terrified and ran out of the room. What do you think the dream means?" Almost before the question was finished, the subject blushed, hesitated a second, then said, "Well, I guess she was afraid of being seduced. The snake would be the man's sex organ and the trunk hers."

As a control, subjects were always questioned about the dream before and after hypnosis, and in no instance did the subjects in the waking state make any comment comparable to that obtained under hypnosis. Care was taken not to ask leading questions nor to reveal the experimenters' interpretations of the dreams.

Several female subjects were given this dream: "A boy was sitting at his desk studying when the waste basket caught on fire. He ran and got a pitcher of water and put the fire out." Their immediate response was, "Oh, he wet his bed," or, "He should have gone to the bathroom." However, a dream about a girl putting out a fire made no sense to them.

It was suggested to one subject that as a child she had wet the bed and been severely scolded by her mother. In response to this stimulus she dreamed of falling into a pond in winter and being scolded by her mother. This dream was then related to a second girl, under hypnosis, who was entirely ignorant of the genesis of the dream. Without any hesitation the second subject said, "Oh, that girl must have wet the bed!" thus recovering the stimulus that had produced the dream.

A second example illustrating the sexual differentiation of symbols is the following dream given for translation: "A man is sitting in a dentist's chair while the dentist tries to pull his tooth. He pulls and pulls. The dreamer is in great pain when the dream ends." Several subjects said the dream meant that a man was having his "vital organ" cut off. When the dental patient was a woman, the dream was translated as "giving birth to a baby."

An exclusive appetite for mushrooms, developed by a psychotic patient, was described to a subject under hypnosis, and she was asked what it would mean if it were a dream. She answered, "He was very sexual. He might even be homosexual." Since one of the authors later treated this patient, he can attest to the validity of this student's hypnotic interpretation.

During the first World War, one of the authors had the following vivid nightmare: "I had been captured by the Kaiser and he made ready to execute me. He placed my head on a chopping block and was about to swing the axe which would end my life, when the dream ended." Under hypnosis a student said the Kaiser was really the dreamer's father who was going to chop off his penis, not his head. She believed it was a punishment for something—probably some sexual act.

The story of Moses and the bulrushes presented as a dream to a girl subject evoked the response, "I think somebody was going to have a baby," adding that the bulrushes stood for pubic hair.

Because of the startling unanimity of response offered by hypnotic subjects, one might at first conclude that dreams are like puzzles which have only one answer—a sexual one. We have come to believe that these uniform sexual responses were influenced by the nature of the hypnotic relationship. Hypnosis is not only a state of consciousness, like sleep, in which dreams occur, but it is also a very striking interpersonal relationship. The most obvious characteristic of this relationship is the extreme dependence of the subjects and their feeling that the hypnotist is omnipotent. Their critical capacities, while not eliminated as Freud once thought, are certainly restricted. The hypnotist too is reacting, not only to the subject, but to the hypnotist's role of omnipotence. His reaction will in turn influence the subject. The relationship contains all the complexities of any relationship between two people, although the belief has developed, because of certain extraordinary aspects of the process, that in hypnosis one deals with something outside the bounds of normal human experience. The unique interaction at any given moment between the personality of the hypnotist and the personality of the subject will necessarily determine the experimental results. Even under what seem to be the same experimental conditions, different hypnotists evoke totally different responses.

Many observers have compared hypnosis to sexual seduction or assault, (cf. de Saussure, 1943) and it is a commonplace that a male hypnotist can hypnotize women much more easily than men. It is noteworthy that practically all the erotic dream translations cited were obtained from comparatively uninhibited women, and from one male subject who was a rather passive individual with a marked attachment for the hypnotist. Jung is said to have abandoned hypnosis when an awakening subject coyly thanked him for being so decent. "That demonstrated to me," he said, "the true nature of hypnosis." We have not found that hypnosis is very different in this respect from other transference relationships. Recognition of this factor does not detract from the method, as Jung feared, but increases its scientific validity.

The following example will illustrate how the form of the dream translation will depend on the interpersonal factors described. A shy female subject in hypnosis was told, "Some time ago you were packing your trunk when a snake crawled into it. You became terrified and ran out of the room." She then dreamed, "It was night and I was lost in the jungle. It was muddy and the mud came up to my waist so that I could not move in any direction. There were little snakes on the branches of the trees above me, which kept falling on my arms and shoulders. They kept getting nearer; some of them touched me. Only the mud kept the snakes from going below my waist; they could not touch me where the mud was; they could not get in. I felt safe in the mud." Questioned about this dream when awake, she said that the snakes were something harmful and the mud signified safety—a mere paraphrase of the dream. Hypnotized again, she was questioned by a person other than the hypnotist. Now the snakes represented something desirable, the mud a barrier to the satisfaction of her desire. First she spoke of the snakes as ideas which attracted her but which other people thought too radical; then as people whose political and social beliefs made them attractive, but who were disapproved of by others; finally, she referred to the snakes as experiences she wished to have but which convention, as represented by the mud, denied here. At this point the interlocutor left the room and the subject's hypnotist questioned her alone. There was then a general relaxation of her facial expression and quite spontaneously she said that the snakes represented a pollution which came from the phallic branches of the trees, and this was the experience she desired. Questioned by a person other than the hypnotist, her translation was on a conventional social level. The dream was perceived in sexual terms in relation to the hypnotist. Both translations are of course parts of the total dream significance.

A similar variation in translation was obtained while attempting to discover how pregnancy would be portrayed in an experimental dream. A hypnotized girl was told, "Not long ago you discovered that a friend of yours had become pregnant; she came to you and told you how terrified she was to be caught in this way. You were shocked and did not know what to do." She then dreamed, "I was on an island and all around me waves were swelling; there were mountains up and down and around. There was a sudden downpour of rain. I felt that everything around me was so powerful that I was just insignificant. I did not know what to do." Several days later the dream was recalled to her under hypnosis by a person other than the hypnotist. Although she felt the dream was about pregnancy, the small island was the social ostracism and isolation enforced by her predicament, while the rain was the gossip and insinuation which fell on her. When her own hypnotist questioned her, she said that the rain was the downpour of semen.

This difference in response raises some interesting questions. Are the sexual translations due to some direct or implied suggestive influence by the hypnotist? Although it is difficult to eliminate this factor, our impression is that neither the hypnotist nor the substitute exerted any suggestion. Or can the dominant-submissive relationship of hypnosis be a sexual experience to the subject and does this serve to determine the form of his translations? It is undoubtedly true that a number of subjects seem to regard hypnosis as a sexual experience. We believe that this specific characteristic of the relationship with the hypnotist makes for a sexual interpretation, but this cannot be stated with certainty.

Only five, or about 20 per cent of the subjects carefully studied, proved to be able translators of dreams. The explanation for the failure of the remainder of the group is not clear. It can be said, however, that these individuals were quite inhibited and rigid compared to the translators. The reasons for both the ability and inability to translate dreams will be elicited only through careful personality studies of the individual subjects.

Even among the selected group it often happened that a hypnotized subject was unable to make any statement about a dream. This type of resistance could usually be overcome by one of two opposite methods. Sometimes a subject was able to translate his own dream only when it was presented as that of another person. At other times it was necessary to transform another person's dream into his own, by suggesting that this was an actual experience which had happened to him, and then asking him to dream about it.

A pregnant woman of our acquaintance dreamt that she lay in bed one morning she was horrified to find a number of small white worms crawling over her arm. This dream was offered to a hypnotic subject with no result. The subject was then told that she herself had recently suffered the same horrible experience. She dreamt, "There was a white candle resting in a small dish beside my bed. The candle burned lower and lower and little wax particles kept dropping into the base of the dish." When asked about the new dream, she said, "The man came and that's what the dripping of the wax was." The first dream about the worms was recalled to her and she said, "That was the same thing." With another subject, who was likewise unable to find any meaning in the worm dream, this same maneuver of re-dreaming elicited a dream that the subject was driving alone in a car with her arm resting on the sill of the open window. It was snowing and snowflakes kept dropping on her exposed forearm. After this dream she commented, "Now I know what the dream about the worms meant. Some girl had had relations with a man and she was afraid of getting pregnant. They hadn't taken any precautions. The worms refer to sperm." For some reason these two subjects translated the worm dream only after they had in effect restated the dream in their own dream language.

THE PRODUCTION OF EXPERIMENTAL DREAMS

The production of experimental dreams under hypnosis was first successfully accomplished many years ago by Karl Schroetter (1912). In 1912 this investigator reported a series of dreams containing the symbols with which psychoanalytic dream interpretation has made us familiar, and the work was offered as experimental proof for the Freudian theory of symbols. This theory received additional confirmation in the investigations of Roffenstein (1923) and Nachmansohn (1925). As in sleep, the hypnotized subject will dream spontaneously, and he will also dream about situations that are suggested to him.

The production of such experimental dreams under hypnosis depends, however, upon the capacity of the individual subject to accept in fantasy and live through an emotionally toned situation suggested to him by the hypnotist. While the situation is being outlined, his facial expressions and bodily movements show that he is experiencing genuine emotion—often painful and sometimes very intense.

The experimental procedure we finally evolved, after considerable trial and error, is as follows: Under deep hypnosis the subject is told, "I am going to recall an experience that happened to you some time ago. You have probably forgotten it, but as I describe it, you will remember it in all its details." The experience is then described and the subject is told: "A dream will come to you. Raise your right hand when the dream begins and lower it when the dream is finished." After one or two minutes of dreaming, the subject will relate his dream. It should be noted that the subject is not instructed to dream about the suggested situation, but merely told that a dream will come to him. We have been more successful in eliciting dreams with this method, probably because it permits greater freedom of fantasy on the part of the subject.

The dream stimuli we have used fall into two categories: first, those which were sexual, comprising experiences of pregnancy, intercourse, bedwetting, masturbation and homosexuality; second, nonsexual stimuli, including experiences of hostility, false accusation, competition, being taken advantage of, and others. Dreams obtained by hypnosis or by posthypnotic suggestion have all the characteristics of spontaneous dreams, and the subjects do not make a distinction between them. Following the dream stimulus, the subject usually first gives us a dream which is a paraphrase of the suggested stimulus, slightly modified by the inclusion of incidents from his own life experience. As he continues dreaming his subsequent productions have more and more the bizarre and pictorial character of dreams.

Why all subjects are not able to dream under hypnosis is not clear. The reaction to a dream stimulus seems to depend upon a combination of factors which include the nature of the dream stimulus, the personality structure of the subject, and his relationship to the hypnotist. Roffenstein had great difficulty in finding a hypnotic subject who would dream, probably because he utilized dream stimuli involving highly traumatic experiences as, for instance, suggesting to a woman that she dream about a homosexual relation. We have used a more indirect method calculated to spare the moral sensibilities of the subject. To elicit a dream about pregnancy, we suggested an experience in which a friend had become pregnant. Since the dream is always personalized, we achieved the desired result in the end. Another method of bringing about the acceptance of reprehensible experiences was to place them in childhood. From one subject we were able to elicit excellent dreams by the instruction: "I am going to recall a certain experience. This did not actually happen to you, but as I tell you about it, you will live through it as if it had." As a final precaution, we always attempted to remove the stimulus at the end of the experiment by telling the subject that the suggested experiences had not really happened to him.

The following experimental dream involves the play on words that is so frequently encountered in dreams. A young woman was told, "When you were a little girl you wet your bed and when you awoke in the morning your mother scolded you." The subject then dreamed that she told a lie which made her parents so angry that they spanked her. In her first account, she omitted the bedwetting, the substance of the lie. Only after considerable questioning by us, and evasion on her part, did she state that what she had lied about was risking being "run over in order to go to the A and P."

We have sometimes asked subjects to draw certain objects or figures that appear in their dreams, which frequently helps to clarify their meaning. Marcinowski (1911–12) first demonstrated that landscapes in the dreams of his patients represented parts of the body, unrecognizable from the verbal descriptions. Kubie (1934) likewise reported a very instructive case, in which the meaning of a dream was revealed in a drawing representing an airplane as the male genitals.

To investigate symbolization of the female breast, a male subject was given the dream stimulus: "One day you were walking down a street in one of the poorer sections of town and you happened to see a young woman sitting on the steps nursing an infant. Her breast was exposed and you could see the baby take the nipple in its mouth and suck at it." His dream was: "I came to the corner where there

Figure 1. Mt. Pleasant.

was an old, rundown store. I went in to look for a magazine called Famous Fantastic Mysteries. I saw some fruit—apples and oranges— and tobacco and candy. They did not have the magazine so I bought some pipe tobacco and went out. I took the Mount Pleasant street car and rode to the top of a tall hill; it was flat on top; the other side was steep. It was the end of the car line. I got off and stood on the edge and looked down." Under hypnosis he drew a picture of the hill (Figure 1).

The same subject was told that he had once wet his bed and had felt very much ashamed because that was the sort of thing a child did. He dreamt that he called his mother and told her about wetting the bed. The doctor came and advised an operation. He went to the hospital in a cab with his mother, was prepared for the operation, and was greatly frightened as he was taken to the operating room. Next he was walking out of the hospital and down 13th street to a hardware store in order to buy a woodworking tool. Asked under hypnosis to draw the tool, he drew the head of a hammer.

Past experiences are sometimes incorporated into the dream. A girl, given the dream stimulus of an experience in which she had been caught masturbating by her mother dreamed: "My sister and I, dressed in our best clothes, were making mud pies with mud which we kept in a rusty tomato can. We splattered the front of our dresses and mother scolded us, saying that it was my fault that my sister was doing it too." She later remembered this to be an incident from her childhood, possibly a screen memory.

Another subject, told that while walking through the woods she had been frightened by seeing a snake, dreamed that she and her father climbed a steep, winding path to the top of a hill on which there was a reservoir. As they walked back she leaned on her father's arm. When awake she recalled having made such an excursion to a reservoir with her father. Shortly afterward she went home on vacation and in describing to her father her work with us, she mentioned this dream. He was startled and visibly upset but unwilling to give any explanation. The father's reaction permits the speculation that the girl's casual recollection is a screen memory for an early trauma. As an association to snake, it suggests seeing the father's penis. That experimental dreams might be used to recover forgotten experiences was proposed by Nachmansohn who made similar observations.

We gave a male subject the dream stimulus of having eaten some green apples and developing a severe diarrhea. We suggested to him in detail the nature of his symptoms and described the number, kind, changing color and consistency of his stools. All through his subsequent narration he coughed and spluttered. This symptom had not been present before, and it disappeared after the experiment. He dreamed that he was ill in bed. The light was turned on and off several times. It got "lighter and then darker." He started and stopped reading several times. He turned on the radio but it kept running on and on, interrupting his thoughts. There was no music—only talk—until finally he turned it off. We believe that the cough and the manner of speaking were symptomatic equivalents of diarrhea by displacement, similar to the verbal diarrhea of the radio which ran on and on.

Many subjects will, when asked, produce a dream without any dream stimulus. These spontaneous dreams often have a manifest content corresponding to the chief conscious interests of the individual. A geology major, with a marked interest in architecture, dreamed repeatedly of architectural groupings and landscapes.

On several occasions we asked a woman physician to be present during hypnotic sessions. During these sessions the subject's spontaneous dreams changed in character. With a woman present, he dreamed of climbing a staircase; of a sewer pipe running through a tunnel; of driving a car around the left side of a mountain into a tunnel.

The hypnotic subject is thus found to be not simply a passive object whose dreams can be manipulated at will by an omnipotent hypnotist. Hypnotic behavior is a meaningful, goal-directed striving, its nature determined by the dynamic unconscious. The subject's spontaneous dreams are influenced by his own unconscious needs and the interaction of these with the hypnotist and any other persons included in the hypnotic situation. Similarly, the dreams elicited in response to dream stimuli are not simple reflections of the stimulus but reveal the needs and wishes of the subject

Manifestly nonsexual dream stimuli usually evoke dreams expressing the social situation in terms of "body language." A young girl was given as a stimulus a situation in which, falsely accused by a friend of cheating in an examination, she became very angry but because of circumstances was unable to deny the accusation. The subject then dreamed that a dentist was trying to pull her tooth despite her frightened protests that the nurse had taken the anaesthetic out of the wrong bottle. In her dream the humiliating accusation is portrayed as bodily assault and deprivation.

A boy was told that he had a rival in his geology class with whom he had trouble competing because he refused to defer to the teacher as the other boy did. The subject then dreamed: "The geology class went on a field trip. We came to an outcropping of rock and I started chipping at it with my hammer. A flying fragment of rock hit the other boy in the face, cutting him. That made me feel fine." Here academic competition becomes a bodily assault on his rival. The examples indicate how a familiar dream symbol may portray a variety of human experiences. Thus, tooth-pulling may represent not only castration and childbirth but also socially insulting predicaments; the attack with the hammer may represent not only homosexual assault but also scholastic rivalry.

SUMMARY

A method is presented for the study of dreams and other unconscious processes by hypnosis. In hypnosis certain subjects have more awareness of the meaning of dream language than in the waking state. This awareness is influenced by the relationship between hypnotist and subject. The similarity of this relationship with other interpersonal relationships was pointed out, as well as the possibility of using this method for the study of transference. A number of experimental dreams, evoked by both sexual and nonsexual dream stimuli, are presented and their special characteristics discussed. The results obtained illustrate the great plasticity of the dream language and argue against too narrow interpretation of symbols.

Commentary

I have not done any work in hypnosis for many years and have kept up with the literature in only a casual sort of way. In regard to the paper by L. H. Farber and myself, it seems that the several attempts over the years which have been made to replicate the aspect of this study that has to do with the ability to hypnotize subjects to interpret dreams have not been successful. I am unable to understand why this has been the case. Perhaps our result was due to a combination of youthful enthusiasm and the particular subject group that we worked with. Some twelve or fifteen years ago I did do an extensive study on the nature of suggestion demonstrating that suggestions will be incorporated into dreams when given in the waking state, especially if the subject is in the relatively regressed position of the psychoanalytic situation.

There is a good deal of recent work utilizing the REM-EEG method, which confirms the finding that suggestions can be incorporated into nocturnal dreams when the suggestion is given in the hypnotic state. Many investigators, because of their absence of knowledge about the psychoanalytic formulation of the primary process or their lack of skill in detecting primary process transformations of day residues, are, as a consequence, unable to detect the incorporation of a suggestion into a dream because this may occur in a distorted manner involving condensations, displacements, and so forth. It is, of course, methodologically difficult to work out objective ways of demonstrating the connections between such transformations and the original day residue and to rule out the possibility of subjective *ad hoc* interpretations. But it is possible to do so.

CHARLES FISHER

New York, N. Y.
1966

Dreams and Hypnosis

BY MARGARET BRENMAN

Since Schroetter's fragmentary, unfinished investigation (1911) of so-called "hypnotic dreams," there has been a good deal of glib talk regarding the power of hypnosis to create dreams which, according to most researchers on this problem, are in all ways like spontaneous night dreams. The classic example, often quoted by Freud and by many others since, is that of Schroetter's female subject, presumably an unsophisticated person, who was told while in a deep hypnotic state to dream of having homosexual relations with a lady friend; she promptly reported a "dream" in which the friend appeared, carrying a shabby traveling bag, on which there was a label with the printed words: "For ladies only." This was certainly a provocative outcome but scarcely proof that the response to a hypnotic suggestion to "dream" is a psychological product comparable in all significant qualities to the condensed, delicately wrought content which issues from the dream work during sleep.

It is curious that investigators appear to have taken it for granted that the hypnotic suggestion to "dream" actually issues in a dream (Farber and Fisher, 1943; Wolberg, 1945, 1948). It is as if the belief in the magic power of hypnosis overwhelms the investigator as well as the subject and thus, when the subject responds with a production which often resembles a night dream, it is assumed without further question that there is no difference between the two. The hypnotist might as well assume that were he to command his subject to fly, the resulting activity, whatever its nature, could be called "flight." Assumptions of this sort preclude any fruitful investigation of the true nature of "hypnotic dreams."

We believe, from our observations, that varying depths of hypnosis

SOURCE. Reprinted by permission from *The Psychoanalytic Quarterly*, 18, 455–466, (1949).

From a joint research project with Merton M. Gill, M.D., on the nature and applications of hypnosis. *This study*, previously supported by the Menninger, Macy (New York), and Hofheimer Foundations, *is now being supported by a grant from the United States Public Health Service*. Robert P. Knight, M.D., has served as consultant for this work.

Read at the meeting of the American Psychoanalytic Association, New York, December 1948.

involve significant and varying changes in ego functioning (Brenman et al., 1947); moreover, it is likely that the suggestion to dream produces further alterations. We are not in a position to study the precise nature of these changes, however, so long as we assume that our instruction has an inevitable result.

Before proceeding to a presentation of our preliminary hypothesis regarding the characteristics of the various forms of hypnotic "dreams," we must comment parenthetically on the fact that it is still an open problem as to whether even all night dreams have precisely the same structure, formal qualities, and kinds of distortion. In his chapter, The Dream Work, Freud says: "Thus, for example, I remember a dream which on waking seemed so particularly well constructed, flawless and clear that I made up my mind, while I was still in a somnolent state, to admit a new category of dreams—those which had not been subject to the mechanism of condensation and distortion, and which might thus be described as fantasies during sleep. A closer examination, however, proved that this unusual dream suffered from the same structural flaws and breaches as exist in all other dreams; so I abandoned the idea of a category of dream-fantasies (Freud, 1938, p. 355). In a footnote added later he comments, "I do not know today whether I was justified in doing so."

Freud's persistent doubt about the uniformity of psychic productions during sleep is further indicated: "A dream without condensation, distortion, dramatization, above all, without wish fulfilment, surely hardly deserves the name. You will remind me that, if so, there are other mental products in sleep to which the right to be called dreams would have to be refused. Actual experiences of the day are known to be simply repeated in sleep; reproductions of traumatic scenes in dreams have led us only lately to reverse the theory of dreams. There are dreams which by certain special qualities are to be distinguished from the usual type, which are, properly speaking, nothing but night fantasies, not having undergone additions or alterations of any kind and in all other ways similar to the well-known daydreams. It would be awkward, certainly, to exclude these imaginings from the realm of dreams (Freud, 1959, p. 421).

In still another connection he says, "Indeed the natural dreams of healthy persons contain a much simpler, more transparent and more characteristic symbolism than those of neurotics, which, owing to the greater strictness of the censorship and the more extensive dream distortion resulting therefrom, are frequently troubled and obscured, and are therefore more difficult to translate" (Freud, 1938, pp. 381–82).

We include these comments to suggest that it is probably a meaningless formulation to ask whether hypnotic dreams are the same as spontaneous night dreams, as if *all* hypnotic dreams have certain formal qualities in common which distinguish them as a group from *all* night dreams. We have observed in our hypnotic work that there is a great range of psychic production at the instruction: to dream. Perhaps such a range exists for the spontaneous night dream as well. Rapaport is at present engaged in a study of the problem of night dreams, the preliminary findings of which promise to elucidate this question.

From our preliminary study of the verbatim recordings of the productions of both normal subjects and patients we have the following impressions: (*a*) the response to the suggestion, "You will now have a dream," ranges from a slightly embellished reminiscence of an actual event to a production which at least on the surface resembles a classical night dream; (*b*) by and large, these productions employ "primary processes" more than does normal, conscious, waking thought but less than does the "typical" night dream described by Freud. It might be said that often the hypnotic dream is a kind of second-rate poetry in comparison to the tight, complex outcome of the dream work. Thus, although a wide range of phenomena appears, it may be said, from the point of view of the formal qualities, that the average hypnotic dream takes a position which is intermediate between the conscious waking daydream and the night dream, with considerable overlapping at both ends of the range. In spite of the many similarities to night dreams in the formal structure of some of the hypnotic dreams, it must not be forgotten that while the primary function of the night dream is to guard sleep, the motive power for the hypnotic dream derives from the need to comply, in so far as possible, with the expressed wishes of the hypnotist; thus to guard an interpersonal relationship. We do not yet know what all the implications of this difference are, but we can suppose that it will prove to be an important factor in establishing the differing dynamic roles of the two productions. Although we have not conducted experiments designed to test this problem, we can report that no one of our subjects reported anything remotely resembling a night dream if left to himself. The hypnotic dream, so far as we now know, does not occur spontaneously but only at the explicit or implicit behest of the hypnotist. Another significant difference lies in the fact that whereas one of the prerequisite conditions for night dreaming is the withdrawal of motor cathexes, the maintenance or withdrawal of motor cathexes for the hypnotized "dreamer" is determined by the hypnotist.

With these important differences, there seem to be significant similarities between the hypnotic state and the state of consciousness which gives rise to spontaneous night dreams. In both there are significant alterations in the defensive and in the synthetic functions of the ego. It has been our observation, however, that these alterations in hypnosis are highly variable in different subjects and fluctuate a great deal from moment to moment (perhaps they do in sleep as well); they by no means imply an obliteration of ego functioning (Brenman et al., 1947). Freud has compared the hypnotic state to a state preceding sleep. In his discussion of the necessary conditions for free association, he says: "As will be seen, the point is to induce a psychic state which is in some degree analogous, as regards the distribution of psychic energy (mobile attention), to the state of mind before falling asleep—and also, of course, to the hypnotic state" (Freud, 1938, p 192).

Although we are as yet unable to establish a strict continuum in the range of hypnotic dreams, we offer a rough classification of these productions which will provide illustrations of their great variety. Before proceeding to these, a technical point of procedure should be clarified. Suggestions to "dream" are given in many different ways. The most frequent techniques described in the literature are: (1) the subject may be told simply, "Now you will have a dream"; (2) he may be posed a specific problem or topic about which to dream; (3) a posthypnotic suggestion may be given to have a night dream on a specific theme; (4) he may be asked to recall a repressed night dream; (5) he may be instructed to continue 'dreaming' where a night dream has broken off. We believe that all of these techniques are, in a sense, what Ferenczi called "forced fantasies" brought about in an altered state of consciousness or, better, of ego functioning. We shall indicate in each of our examples which of these techniques was used.

First, an instance of the *embellished reminiscence* was produced by a woman of hysterical character who was being treated for symptoms of anxiety, depression, and multiple somatic complaints. She complained, while in hypnosis, of a pervasive sense of failure and deficiency in the ability to make people like her. She was given the suggestion to dream about this problem and reported: "I saw two of my girl friends on the porch of my home. I was there too. I seemed to be about fifteen years old. They told me they were not going to come back that evening as they had planned, but would come another time." This dull and rather banal response was not typical for this patient, who frequently reported highly condensed hypnotic dreams of a sort to be described later.

Another variety of response is the *static pictorial image*. The following examples are from the records of a middle-aged man with a well-compensated, compulsive character, who was being treated for torticol-lis. He was not deeply hypnotizable, but at the suggestion to dream in hypnosis he sometimes produced static pictorial images which he found startling. A surprising number of them dealt with his being gazed at intently. In one of the most striking he saw a vivid picture of a figure of indeterminate sex nailed to a cross, with head turned to the right and down, the same position into which the torticollis had twisted his own head. As he watched the figure, the head slowly lifted and the eyes fused into one which gazed at him intently and with great sorrow. The patient had not had, since early childhood, any interest in religion. This image, while it has a dreamlike quality, is relatively static and brief. In another such image he saw an owl watching him intently with great, wide eyes—"as though telling me not to be a fool."

Still another level of production which appears to us distinct both from the reminiscence and the static pictorial image is the *quasi allegory*, a hybrid form, resembling the conscious daydream, but includ-ing, in a rather obvious and primitive fashion, some elements of uncon-scious symbolism. An example of this variety of hypnotic dream is taken from a case, recently reported by McDowell (1948), of a veteran with the presenting symptoms of severe anxiety and ejaculatio praecox. This man was an unsophisticated person who, as far as is known, had no knowledge of the unconscious meaning of symbols. The pro-duction we will now describe occurred shortly after the disappearance of his ejaculatio praecox. He was told by the therapist that he would have a dream in hypnosis which would explain the meaning of his previous symptom of "being like a jack rabbit" as he called it. The therapist left the room and when he returned the patient reported the following.

"There were long white stairs going up into the sky, as far as I could see. There were women lined up on both sides of the stairs. They were all reaching out for me as I was running up the stairs as fast as I could run, always running. At the top of the stairs is a beautiful girl with no clothes on, lying on a big, white, soft bed. I reached her, got into bed with her, "came" in a hurry and started running up the stairs again just like before. I looked back and she was still lying there with her arms raised toward me, looking disappointed, but I kept running." This sequence is repeated several times, and he concludes: "I got off the bed the last time and started walking." Now all the other girls were gone, the beautiful woman was waiting and after he had "calmly climbed the stairs, began intercourse calmly—no hurry. We were still doing it when the dream ended."

There is a shallowness and transparency in this response which gives it a rather contrived flavor. At the same time, the presence of the classic symbol of ascending the staircase in this naïve man links this production to the regressive, archaic night dream.

Still closer to the night dream is a variety of response which we will call the *quasi dream*. Our example is taken from the record of the analysis of a young hysteric. This young woman was possessed of an intense ambition to become a famous writer, having written many elaborate novels while working as a saleswoman. She came for treatment of "spells" during which she became rigid and talked wildly. During the initial interviews she had been told by a young and inexperienced resident physician that if she wanted to be cured of her "spells" she might have to give up her writing. Though dismayed by this prospect, she agreed to come for therapy. She was hypnotized occasionally during the course of the analysis, in periods of great resistance. In one such period, when it seemed that her unconscious competitiveness with the analyst as a defense against her strong passive wishes was fairly close to consciousness, she was hypnotized and told simply, "You're going to have a dream." Her response (in part) follows.

"I'm in a hospital bed . . . I like the room . . . it's not an ordinary hospital . . . it's way up high with a beautiful view . . . the walls are tinted pale green . . . I see the nurse's face or something . . . and it ought to startle me because her finger tips are gone . . . on the first two fingers, down to the second joint . . . and I was going to interrupt and tell the nurse . . . if it is a nurse . . . that part of her fingers are gone . . . but I hate to interrupt when they're talking ['they,' unidentified at this point] . . . so I don't say anything . . . they're talking pleasantly and I'm comfortable."

She was asked directly, still in hypnosis, what she thought the dream meant; she could make nothing of it. Accordingly, she associated in the usual way, and it then appeared to the analyst that she was expressing both her wish for and her fear of the analyst's power over her, the specific threat to her own power being expressed in the symbol of the missing fingers, which on one level meant she could no longer type her novels, and would thus be deprived of her most important weapon. The dream was not interpreted, and she was given the posthypnotic suggestion to have a night dream which would embody the same meaning as this hypnotic dream. The next day she reported a night dream which seemed to state more clearly her intense defensive strivings for power. This was also not interpreted and again, on successive days, she was told to "dream" in hypnosis, with the instruction that these "dreams" would state even more clearly the same conflict (still not interpreted to her). Finally, she produced the following in hypnosis.

"I am sitting at a desk . . . a big desk . . . outdoors, looking down . . . I'm high up . . . looking down over beautiful scenery . . . there's a lake, a lot of trees . . . but no other person . . . just me . . . my desk is smooth and polished and large . . . I don't know how it got there."

This seemed a simpler dream than the one about the missing fingers. Her associations in hypnosis made it clear that she was attempting to usurp the analyst's position. Her wish to be lofty and godlike, the *defense* against her passive needs and against her fears of helplessness now obliterated the wishes to be taken care of.

We have presented this series to illustrate two points: (1) this is a variety of hypnotic dream which seems fairly close in quality to night dreams; (2) that in such series there appears to be a progression either in the direction of accenting the defensive aspect of a conflict or, as we shall see in the next series, in the direction of exposing more sharply the underlying need or impulse which is being defended against.

A successful young surgeon, a morphine addict, who was gradually losing his practice because of his addiction, "dreams" the following in response to the unstructured suggestion, "You will now have a dream." He is in the operating room, performing an extremely difficult appendectomy and executing it with the utmost delicacy and skill. He describes, largely in the present tense and with relatively little affect, all of the complications and his successful techniques of handling them, lapsing occasionally into the past tense and finally, in response to direct questioning, confirming our impression that he was embroidering an actual experience. This kind of production, while obviously meaningful and perhaps even potentially helpful in therapy, is a far cry from the rebuslike character of the night dream.

In a subsequent session, in response to the same unstructured suggestion to "have a dream," he again produced an actual experience, this time, however, wholly in the present tense and with intense feeling. He re-enacted the birth of his son who had not begun to breathe spontaneously. Over and over he shouted, "You've got to make it, Tommy! Breathe, boy! I'm gonna help you! You've just got to!" He went through all of the motions of holding the newborn infant up to his mouth and helping him to start respiration. Tears rolled down his face, and finally he announced (still in the present tense) that the baby had begun to breathe and that he knew he had saved him.

On the next occasion, given the same instruction, he reported a production of a different order. The following is an excerpt.

"I am falling asleep now and all of a sudden there is a monster, a terrible monster [voice choking with genuine panic] . . . I can't breathe, it's choking me, it wants to mash me to pieces [breathing with great difficulty] . . . on my chest . . . weighting me down . . . it's horrible, horrible . . . I must fight it . . . it's smothering me, what shall I do? . . . a terrible thing . . . great big body and lots of legs . . ." As he continued this *quasi nightmare,* he began to clench his fists and became frantic. Suddenly, he shouted, I want to fight it, I have to fight it, can I fight it?" [Therapist: "Yes, you can."] At this point he began to flail his arms in the air, still breathing with great difficulty, and finally gave a great lurch which landed him on the floor. As he hit the floor he looked around him in amazement, and somewhat sheepishly, no longer in hypnosis.

It is evident that these three productions, all in response to the suggestion to "dream," are significantly different from each other not only in their manifest content, and in the degree of uncontrolled affect, but also in the degree to which primary and secondary processes are employed. It would appear also that there is a progression from the defensive position taken in the first hypnotic dream (where he denies his terror of helplessness by performing a delicate operation with utmost skill) to the second where the defense seems still in evidence, though somewhat shaky, in saving his child who cannot, at first breathe; and finally to the third where there seems no longer to be any defense against the overwhelming anxiety associated with his feeling of helplessness and inability to breathe, an anxiety so intense that he breaks out of the hypnotic state altogether.

In the first of these two series (the hysterical girl), we see a progressively clearer statement of a defensive position, and in the second (the surgeon), an increasing disclosure of an underlying terror. Perhaps these progressions are analogous though not identical with the progression described by Freud in his discussion of dreams of the same night. He says: "All dreams of the same night belong, in respect of their content, to the same whole; their division into several parts, their grouping and number, are all full of meaning and may be regarded as pieces of information about the latent dream thoughts. In the interpretation of dreams consisting of several main sections, or of dreams belonging to the same night, we must not overlook the possibility that these different and successive dreams mean the same thing, express-

ing the same impulses in different materials. That one of these homolo-
gous dreams which comes first in time is usually the most distorted
and most bashful, while the next dream is bolder and more distinct"
(Freud, 1938, p. 537). Freud does not discuss whether the increasing
'boldness' of the night dream refers only to the underlying impulse,
or whether the defense may sometimes be clarified in this way also.

We cannot say from the preliminary survey of our material that
this progressive clarification (whether of the underlying need or of
the defense) is characteristic for hypnotic dreams in a series.

SUMMARY

We question the assumption that the hypnotic dream is a psychic
production which duplicates, either in function or structure, the spontaneous night dream. We suggest instead that there is a wide range
of response to the hypnotic suggestion to "dream," the average production having a structure which seems intermediate between the daydream and the spontaneous night dream, in that primary processes
are used more than is common in waking thought, but less than in
the typical night dream. We add further the tentative suggestion that
hypnotic dreams in a series may progressively clarify either the defensive aspect of a conflict or the impulse (or need) which is being
defended against.

Commentary

My interest in the hypnotic dream has been sustained for over
twenty years now, and I have expressed my most recent thoughts
on the matter in the book by Merton Gill and myself (1959, pp.
236–244). We have argued that there is no necessary connection between hypnosis and sleep as physiological states, although there may
be a common psychological equivalence.

We believe that the regressed subsystem of the hypnotic state is
akin to the ego system which is active during sleep. The mechanism
of the production of hypnotic dreams may include three distinguishable elements: First, use of a suggestion as a content day residue,
whether or not it activates a "natural day residue"; second, a transference day residue, which refers more to unconscious and infantile impulses characteristic of the subject's personality; third, some comments
on the hypnotic situation itself.

It is our conclusion that whatever the comparability of hypnotic and spontaneous dreams, and the reprinted article shows that the suggestion to dream results in a whole range of phenomena, of all the specialized hypnotic techniques, the use of dreams in hypnosis is probably the most clinically fruitful. A person is usually able to state his unconscious conflicts more sharply through the hypnotic exploration of dreams than by an investigation in the normal state.

MARGARET BRENMAN

Stockbridge, Massachusetts
1966

An Experimental Study of the Hypnotic Dream*

BY MILTON MAZER†

Investigations of the symbolism occurring in spontaneous dreams are limited by the fact that the interpretation of the dream symbols can only be made by inference, supported more or less by the patient's associations and an understanding of his personality. Such interpretations suffer from the additional limitation that they may include not only that which is supplied by the patient but may also reflect an attitude or bias on the part of the observer. An early attempt to overcome this difficulty in the study of dream symbolism was that of Schroetter (1911), who published a study of hypnotically induced dreams. Schroetter suggested the latent content of the dream to a hypnotized subject and recorded the manifest dream and its duration. He determined the duration of the dream by having the subject signal by hand the beginning and end of each dream. Dreams secured in this manner were often highly symbolic, and they provided a clear advantage over spontaneous dreams in that the symbols could be interpreted with some assurance since the dream stimuli were known. In 1923 the work was extended by Roffenstein, who was able to secure a more consistent symbolization by instructing his subjects to dream in symbolic language. He did this by telling them to distort the dream so that others would not be able to understand its meaning. A further paper on the subject by Nachmansohn appeared in 1925.

Farber and Fisher (1943) reinvestigated the use of hypnosis in the

SOURCE. Reprinted by permission from *Psychiatry: Journal for the Study of Interpersonal Processes*, 14, (3), 265–277 (August, 1951).
* This paper has been reviewed by the Veterans Administration and is published with the approval of the Chief Medical Director. The statements and conclusions published by the author are the result of his own study and do not necessarily reflect the opinion or policy of the Veterans Administration.
† B.A. 32, M.D. 35, Univ. of Pa.; Interne, Mt. Sinai Hosp., Philadelphia 35–36; Asst. Res. in Internal Medicine, Montefiore Hosp., New York 36–37; Clinical Asst. in Internal Medicine, Mt. Sinai Hosp. 37–39; Ward Surgeon in Internal Medicine Assoc., Chief, Cardiovascular Research Unit, VA, Washington, D.C. 39–43; Physiologist 8th Air Force, Editor Air Surgeon's Bulletin, U.S. Army Air Force 43–46; Res. in Psychiatry, Bronx Veterans Hosp., New York 46–49; Candidate, William Alanson White Institute of Psychiatry 47-; Attending Consultant in Psychiatry, Bronx Veterans Hosp. 49-; Lecturer in Psychology, New York Univ. 51-. For bibliography, see Reference Lists section of this issue.

study of dream psychology. They studied the production of experimental dreams under hypnosis, the nature of the relationship between hypnotist and subject, and the capacity of hypnotized subjects to understand dream language. They reported a number of dreams evoked by both sexual and nonsexual stimuli in which the dream stimuli were highly symbolized, and they stated that the hypnotically induced dreams had all of the characteristics of spontaneous dreams. The conclusion that hypnotic dreams have all of the significant characteristics of spontaneous night dreams has recently been questioned by Brenman, who believes that they stand structurally between the conscious day dream and the night dream.

The purpose of the study here reported is to extend and elaborate on the previously published work, with particular attention to the symbolization of emotions, the self, and interpersonal relations, particularly the relationship of subject to hypnotist. A secondary part of the study comprises an attempt to determine the depth of hypnosis required for the production of hypnotic dreams, and to investigate the process of symbolization.

PROCEDURE

The subjects of the study were 26 of the 30 employees of a general hospital who had volunteered for the purpose. In most subjects eye fixation and verbal suggestion was the method of induction; hand levitation was used with a few subjects. In order to determine the depth of hypnosis required for hypnotic dream induction, suggestions for dreaming were given to the 26 subjects at various levels of hypnosis. Dreams in which the dream stimuli were symbolized were secured from 10 subjects. Of these, 3 were nurses, 3 were physical rehabilitation aides, and the others were a ward attendant, a clerk, a minister, and a social worker.

When the subject was in a hypnotic state, he was told that hypnotized persons are able to dream on suggestion and that he would now dream about things suggested by the hypnotist. He was further told that he would raise his right hand when each dream began and lower it when the dream ended. After each dream ended, the subject was asked to relate the dream while still in the hypnotic state. A number of dreams were secured in this manner in one hypnotic session. After the subject was awakened from the trance, with complete amnesia except in one case, his dreams were read to him and his immediate associations recorded. These were occasionally useful in determining the nature of the dream symbols, though as a rule the symbolism was obvious since the latent content of the dream (the stimulus) was known.

A time record was kept from the moment the stimulus word or phrase was spoken to the beginning and end of the dream. The interval between the stimulus and the onset of the dream is designated the latent period. The duration of the dream itself is called the dream time.

The first dreams of any particular subject were usually not symbolized but were generally paraphrases of the dream stimuli, utilizing material from his life experience. The method generally used for producing symbolic dreams was that of Roffenstein. Depending upon the subject's sophistication, he was told that his mind would symbolize the dream stimulus, disguise it, or hide its meaning so that others would not be able to tell what he had dreamt about. Once a subject had produced a few symbolic dreams, he generally dreamt symbolically thereafter without further instruction. In a few hypnotic sessions, two of the methods described by Farber and Fisher (*Ibid.*, pp. 209, 210) were used.

DEPTH OF HYPNOSIS AND DREAM INDUCTION

There were three types of response to the suggestion to dream: no dreams, nonsymbolic dreams, symbolic dreams. The relationship between the depth of hypnosis and the type of response is shown in Table 1. The depth of hypnosis is shown in order of increasing depth according to the Davis-Husband scale (Friedlander and Sarbin, 1938), which was found to be a valid rating scale, with the one exception that simple posthypnotic suggestions were occasionally elicited at less deep levels than the scale indicated.

It is seen from analysis of the data in the table that neither symbolic nor nonsymbolic dreams were produced in subjects who were not in at least a light hypnotic state as represented by a depth of 6 (eye catalepsy). Only one of 10 subjects whose trances were at a depth of 10 or less was able to dream, and in that case nonsymbolically. It was only in subjects whose trances were as deep as that represented by complete posthypnotic amnesia, or deeper, that dreams could be produced with any consistency. Of 13 subjects who were hypnotized to depth 20 (complete posthypnotic amnesia) or more, 9 dreamt symbolically, 3 nonsymbolically, and 1 did not dream at all.

These data demonstrate that the ability to produce hypnotic dreams is largely determined by the depth of trance, and that a fairly deep trance is required before any significant proportion of subjects can

TABLE 1

Hypnotic dream production versus depth of hypnosis

Depth of hypnosis	Number of subjects	Types of dreams elicited*		
		None	Non-symbolic	Symbolic
Fluttering of eyelids (3)† Closing of eyes (4) Physical relaxation (5)	5	5	0	0
Eye catalepsy (6) Limb catalepsy (7) Rigid catalepsy (10)	5	4	1	0
Partial amnesia (13) Simple posthypnotic suggestions (18)	3	1	1	1
Complete posthypnotic amnesia (20) Somnambulism (25) Posthypnotic hallucinations, visual and auditory (26, 27)	13	1	3	9

* In each instance, the highest form of production for that particular depth is given for the subject, with symbolic considered the highest form.

† Numbers in parentheses refer to Davis-Husband scale. Reference footnote 8.

be induced to dream symbolically. The fact that subjects in the hypnoidal state or in light trance did not, save in one case, produce dreams is evidence against the possibility that the dreams secured were simply fabrications designed to please the hypnotist. Moreover, subjects who were asked to invent dreams in the waking state were either unable to do so or produced themes which did not significantly resemble dreams produced under hypnosis. Additional evidence on this point will be given in the discussion.

SYMBOLIZATION IN THE HYPNOTIC DREAM

Individuality of Symbolization. Three hundred and thirty-three dreams were recorded from the 10 subjects who could dream symbolically; 274 were symbolized and 59 were paraphrases of the stimulus. Almost every hypnotic dream contained two readily recognizable elements: the symbol, and the attitude of the dreamer toward that which he symbolized. The symbol used for a particular dream stimulus varied greatly for different subjects, and the use of the same symbol was rare. The only significant exception was in the symbolization of the female breast: out of the 10 subjects, 4 dreamt about hills or mountains when asked to dream about the breast. The symbols used were often highly specific for the particular dreamer, coming out of his own segment of the culture and based upon his own experiences. City-bred subjects used city scenes for the dream framework, as contrasted with those who had lived much of their lives in the country. How a specific segment of the culture influenced dream content is illustrated by the dream of a male subject who was asked to have a dream about the penis. In his dream he made a particular point of rejecting a frankfurter that was offered to him and instead demanded a "special," the latter being a colloquialism in certain parts of New York City for an unusually large and well-seasoned frankfurter. The influence of education upon the dream content is shown in a dream by the same subject about a vagina. In this dream he utilized his knowledge of organic chemistry and dreamt of taking an examination in which he was having difficulty in finding a place in a benzene ring (a hexagon) for a methyl radical. Another example of cultural determination is that of a male subject who was asked to dream about the female breast. He dreamt of a young boy in overalls and straw hat, walking barefoot over a very soft feather quilt. On interrogation he related the dream to a fantasy which was common amongst his childhood friends and which was also known to the experimenter. The fantasy ran, "Gee, I'd like to walk barefoot on a floorful of tits." In the dream the soft feather quilt apparently represented the breast.

Precision of Symbolization. The detailed precision of symbolization found in many hypnotic dreams is shown in the following example of a dream about masturbation.

(1) This fellow's taking an exam. It's a very hard exam. He gets tense. As he looks at the paper he gets more tense. His face gets flushed and his hand begins to shake. He knocks the paper and pencil off the desk and drops his head on the desk from exhaustion.

The subject's immediate association to the dream was, "I remember myself becoming tense during an exam. I'd place my hands between my thighs and tighten up to relieve my tension." Since it is his looking at the paper which increases his tension, one may suppose that the paper in the dream represents the fantasy which induced the masturbation. The shaking of the hand may symbolize the manual manipulation of masturbation. As the pencil is knocked from the desk (the orgasm), the paper (the fantasy) goes with it and the act is completed.

Another example of the detailed precision of the hypnotic dream is shown in the following dream about intercourse. The subject was an unmarried woman in her early thirties.

(2) I'm down in the country walking along the side of a railroad track at a whistle-stop sort of place. There's a man in the tower. His job is to pull the switch. I hear the toot of a whistle. A train's coming and there's another one coming the opposite way from around the bend, head-on on the same rails. There's no brakeman to pull the switch. It surely looks as though there will be a head-on collision.

The subject woke from the hypnotic trance before the dream was completed. She showed signs of anxiety. She related the dream in the waking state but it remained vivid enough to require the present tense. In this dream she symbolized intercourse as a collision and by this indicated that she conceived of it as a dangerous experience. She also showed this by waking from the trance before the dream was completed. Before she hears the two trains approaching, she sees the switchman in the tower; but once the trains are approaching head-on, the switchman is no longer there. This would seem to be a symbolized statement that once coitus is begun, control of the situation is lost.

Attitude of the Dreamer. One of the notable things observed in the large series of dreams studied is the consistency with which the dreamer reveals his or her particular attitude toward the thing, emotion, person, or relationship symbolized. When a series of dreams to the same stimulus was collected from one subject during a number of hypnotic sessions, there was a remarkable consistency in the attitude expressed even though the actual symbols chosen showed considerable variation. This is illustrated by the dreams of a 32-year-old male subject, who on a number of occasions was asked to dream about the penis.

(3) This fellow starts to write with a pencil. The point is sharp but he writes until it gets dull. He tries to sharpen it in a sharpener but each time something happens to it. He tries and tries until he finds he has no pencil left.

(4) This fellow walks into a Jewish delicatessen and orders franks and sauerkraut. But the frank they give him doesn't suit him. It's too small and thin. He orders a big "special."

(5) A softball game. This fellow's up at bat. Every ball thrown he swings and misses. Everyone laughs at him. Someone yells, "Pick up a bigger bat. That's what you need to hit it with."

(6) This fellow was having trouble with his fountain pen. He tried to fix it and couldn't. He took it to a repair shop, and they said it would

be as good as ever. He took it home and it wouldn't write. He became angry and threw it away.

(7) This man walks into a lunch counter with some of his friends. They all order coconut pie but the cuts are all different in size. They argue about the cuts and the man says, "I should have the biggest piece. You know why." They all laugh when he says, "You know why."

(8) It's a crowded subway, rush hour. I have a big package in my hand. It's getting squeezed. I don't know what to do with the package. It had flowers in it. I offer it to an old lady but she doesn't want to take it. I offer it to everyone but no one wanted to take it. Finally, I dropped it on the floor and stood on it, and I was comfortable.

Even in dreams secured when the subject was regressed hypnotically to earlier periods in his life, he showed the same attitude toward his penis. The following dreams were secured during hypnotic regression to ages 20, 15, and 5 years, respectively. The subject was regressed in the usual manner to the birthday of the age given (Spiegel et al., 1945), and after the authenticity of the regression had been checked by questioning him about the date, events of his life, current events, and the like, he was given the dream stimulus.

(9) [Age 20] A fellow fills up his fountain pen with ink and tries to write and can't. He opens the cover and exposes the tube. When he tries to examine the tube, the contents roll all out over the table.

(10) [Age 15] The whole gang goes to the cruller bakery. They have the round doughnuts. We wait for the long ones. Then the tray comes out. Everybody tries to pick the biggest. Then we watch for the guy so we can shoot the jelly in them.

The following dream was secured at regressed age five. The subject did not know the word penis, so he was asked to dream about "the thing you pee through." Though he did not symbolize the stimulus in this instance, he nonetheless expressed the same attitude that he had in the dreams already cited.

(11) [Age 5] All the kids are coming home from school. We all live in the same block. We take out the things we pee with to see who can pee the longest. Everybody holds back to squeeze it far. I don't win. The big boy wins.

In each of the 9 dreams described above, the subject makes the same statement about his penis; namely, that he feels that it is inadequate or unacceptable. In none of the total of 11 dreams secured from him about the penis does he make a contrary statement. In dreaming about the vagina, he expresses an attitude which complements the one he expresses toward his penis.

(12) My locker was worked with a combination lock. I opened it with the combination lock a thousand times. This time I did the combination but it wouldn't open. I tried and tried but it wouldn't open. I got mad and got a crowbar and banged and banged until I opened it. But I couldn't use it any more. It wouldn't work after that.

(13) This fellow walks into a restaurant and orders a steak. It is brought to him and it looks very appetizing. He starts to cut it but the harder he tries the tougher it gets. He finally cuts a piece but the whole thing spatters over the table.

(14) Taking an exam. Organic chemistry. Have to convert ethyl alcohol to methyl alcohol. There's one little thing missing. Think it's a CH_3 radical. Don't know where to put it. I look at a benzene ring and they're all filled up. I attempt to put it alongside another radical and let it go at that.

The following dreams about the vagina were secured from the same subject at hypnotically regressed age levels of 25, 20, and 10, respectively. The dream elicited at the regressed age of 15 was similar to that given for age 25 years.

(15) [Age 25] This fellow decides to go swimming in the choppy water. He swims to the bell buoy. About three quarters there he gets tired. But he must make it or he isn't worth a cent. Finally, when he's almost out he tries again and makes it. He's so tired he lays there for hours and hours.

(16) [Age 20] This fellow received a strong, small fibre carton. He looks for a knife to break the seal but there's no knife. So he tries to open it with his fist but it's too strong. Finally, he uses every effort and smashes it wide open.

The subject, not knowing the word vagina at regressed age 10, was given the colloquialism "cunt" as the dream stimulus.

(17) [Age 10] This girl is walking along Avenue B. She walks funny with her legs close to one another. She can hardly walk. Everybody looks at her and some sons of bitches go over and try to spread her legs apart but they can't. She still walks with her legs close together.

In each of the six dreams about the vagina, the subject makes the same statement; namely, that the vagina, with reference to the whole complex of meanings it has for him, is difficult to attain. In four of the dreams he attempts to attain it by force, and in three of them the force is so excessive as to defeat his purpose.

Symbolization of Parts of the Body. Despite the individuality of symbolization by different subjects, there were certain similarities in the mode of symbolization. Thus, parts of the body were usually symbolized by objects similar in form to them. The penis was symbolized by a cruller, a baseball bat, a frankfurter, a bandaged finger covered by a rubber sheath, a piece of Danish pastry, a sword, a banana, a flaming torch, a cannon, and a man's foot going into a shoe. The germinating function of the penis was suggested in its being symbolized as a package of flowers. Among the symbols used for the vagina were a valley, a locker, a circus poster of an open mouth, a funnel, a slipper, a bay, a steak, cherries, a fibre carton, and a benzene ring. The female breast evoked the following symbols: an ice-cream sundae topped by a cherry, a many-tiered cake, a soft feather quilt, an ice-cream cup, a flowing water pump, a hill, a mountain, a pillow, and a bell being pulled. It will be noted that the penis, vagina, and breast were frequently symbolized as food.

Symbolization of Biological Functions. Activities such as intercourse, masturbation, childbirth, menstruation, and urination were generally described symbolically by other activities. Thus a female subject described intercourse as a head-on collision of two trains (Dream 2), and the male subject who described his penis as inadequate and the vagina as difficult of attainment (Dreams 3–17) described intercourse as a competitive activity.

(18) This fellow and girl go horseback riding. They're taking it easy, just riding along. Then, the girl decides to race her horse. He races his. They race for a mile. Both horses are foaming. The fellow and the girl are laughing.

(19) This fellow and girl go to an ice-cream parlor. He only has enough for one ice-cream cone. But they get straws. They are selfish so they start to race. At the end they are both suffering from exhaustion, sipping all that stuff.

A more literal and impersonal symbolization of intercourse came from a male subject whose dreams about himself were, in general, impersonal also.

(20) I saw a young man in his teens. At a lake there was a barrel of water. He took an oar and kept stirring the water in the barrel with it. He kept going faster and faster until he got tired. The he stopped and sat down and had a cigarette.

Masturbation was symbolized by a boy being surprised by a girl while urinating, a piston going in and out of a cylinder, a spiked wheel revolving against velvet, and the process of writing an examination paper (Dream 10). When a subject was instructed to dream about someone being punished for masturbating, he dreamt about a boy with a bandaged finger standing in the corner of a room.

The act of giving birth to a baby was symbolized in a number of ways. A male subject described a cement mixer which was mixing gravel and cement in the proper proportions and depositing the mixture into a wheelbarrow. At another time the same subject dreamt of a coffee machine filling coffee bags. Another male subject dreamt of a male friend who was severely constipated and was in the act of defecation. He described the pain experienced by his friend and repeatedly urged him to strain. Finally, with the completion of defecation, he described the relief felt by his friend.

Urinating in bed was often symbolized by an accident, as a glass of water spilling, a faucet turning on by itself; another symbol was a man perspiring excessively due to fever. Occasionally, as in the following dream, the idea of punishment for urinating in bed was introduced.

(21) I dreamt about a young boy who comes home from school with a note saying he talks too much. His father says he'll put a zipper on his mouth if he ever does it again.

Symbolization of People. The subjects symbolized specific persons by other individuals, or by making allusion to an absent person about whom emotion is felt. The following are the dreams of a male subject to the stimulus "you will have a dream about a father."

(22) This boy is playing for a baseball team. It's the last inning and it's two out. The coach walks over and says he must get a hit. He strikes out. The coach berates him for not having done the right thing.

(23) This boy decides—he sees a horse and wagon. He decides to take a ride even though it doesn't belong to him. He's riding and he hears someone say, "Stop." It's the policeman. The policeman starts slapping him across the face.

(24) You just found some money. You're going toward the movie. You're about to pay. There's a door there. We pocket the money and run home. You're not allowed to go to the movies. You should be at school.

In the dreams recorded above the subject sees his father as an obstacle to his desires and as a punishing figure. During these experiments, the subject's father died. In the session a few weeks after his father's death, four dreams about the father were elicited. In none of these did he describe the punishing, obstructing figure portrayed in Dreams 22 to 24. The dreams secured after the father's death showed other and nonthreatening aspects of him. He was symbolized as a self-sacrificing, hard-working man, as a man suffering from ill fate, as an exceptionally powerful man, and as an old man involved in political discussion.

One subject's dreams about the mother included dreams about an absent person, an empty bed in a hospital room, being examined in school and receiving punishment because his head was full of lice, a cleanliness inspection at school in which his hands were dirty. In the last two dreams the mother is alluded to by the dirty hands and the infested head, since she was the person who should have protected the subject from the events described in the dreams. The subject's mother had been an invalid and had died when he was still a child. A female subject dreamt of the mother as a whirlpool that drew everything into it. Her waking associations to the dream were: "Something that was being destroyed or disintegrated. My association is my own mother who is ill, and her illness I see as self-destruction and sometimes I think it is destructive of me."

A female subject, asked to dream of the father, symbolized him as an empty chair before the fireplace. Her father had deserted the family when she was two years old. Another female subject dreamt of a field in which there were long stalks over which a man with a long knife was standing. Her immediate association was: "My feeling of something impending, some kind of doom."

Symbolization of Emotions. The emotions were symbolized by activities, by natural phenomena, and by objects in certain relationships with each other. A female subject asked to dream about punishment had the following dream:

(25) I was a little girl and had a nice ice-cream cone I was licking. It was winter. My mother found out about it, so she licked me because I wasn't supposed to have an ice-cream cone in the winter.

Her associations were: "My mother never punished me physically but my father did once. The ice-cream cone probably symbolizes something I was forbidden besides that. I don't know what. Probably something to do with sex. Maybe a woman's breast. I don't think I was nursed much when I was born." In the dream she makes the statement that punishment results from indulging in perverse activity, symbolized by eating ice cream in the winter, and her associations suggest that the activity referred to is sexual. The idea of impotence was elicited in a dream by using one of the stimuli of Farber and Fisher, namely, "falsely accused of cheating in an exam, you became angry, but because of the circumstances could not deny the accusation."

(26) I was playing first base. Someone hit the ball and I started to run. I covered first base and he knocked me over. I got up and started

to hit him but I couldn't hit him. I kept swinging but couldn't hit him. I felt clumsy and awkward.

Another subject was given the same stimulus and dreamt about the false accusation aspect, ignoring the impotence theme.

(27) It appears to be raining and a man is carrying an open umbrella. He closes it and the ground is dry. It's not raining and it's not wet. [*Association:* Something, it must be a false situation. It isn't true. If it is open, why isn't it wet?]

The two dreams cited above point up the desirability of using simple stimuli in studying symbolization by this method.

In general the symbols used for the emotions were conventional. Thus, fear was symbolized by a black cat, by a destructive fire, by a speeding, shaking subway train, and by thunder and lightning.

Symbolization of the Self. In order to investigate the subject's concept of himself each subject was instructed to "have a dream about yourself." Dreams elicited by this stimulus appeared to reveal the subject's image of himself. The following dreams to this stimulus were secured from a 32-year-old male subject. The first listed is at his current age, and the others at hypnotically regressed ages of 25, 20, 15, 10, and 5 years, respectively. They show two related concepts: the omnipotent individual and the constant benefactor.

(28) I'm playing ball with the New York Giants. No one knows it but me, but I have a way of hitting home runs in every game. I get up there and by a turn of the wrist hit a home run. No one knows it but me.

(29) [Age 25] Things are bad economically. All this fellow's family are not doing too well. He gets a job in a doll factory and makes good in a big way. Soon he gets all the men in his family jobs in the doll factory. They all make a living. He feels good and they do too. No troubles.

(30) [Age 20] This kid is very sick and all the doctors have seen him and they all shake their heads. There's one doctor left and they call him. He looks at the child and gives him some medicine. The child immediately gets better and everybody thanks the doctor.

(31) [Age 15] All the fellows in the block to get some money are carrying clothing up to the fifth floor of the clothing factory on our block. A big fellow comes along. He tells them all to rest and he carries the clothes up and down, up and down. He gets the money and divides it among all the kids. He doesn't take any for himself, not even for a soda.

(32) [Age 10] The kids have got a baseball team. Pretty good ball players. They don't have gloves or uniforms. One day while they're play-

ing, a boy comes along and takes them to a store and gets them bats and balls and uniforms and two gloves apiece, and everybody thanks him.

(33) [Age 5] Very hot summer day. Everybody's sitting outside, the kids and mothers and fathers. Everybody's thirsty. Suddenly a man comes on a big brown horse with packages of ice cream. He's a good man.

A male subject who from the experimenter's knowledge of him appeared to be a rather detached person did not portray himself as a human being in any of the seven dreams he had about himself. In each he sees himself as solid, strong, or self-possessed, but nonhuman.

(34) I see a giant log sawed through so you see the entire circumference. It's white and spotless and in the center is a line dividing it into two halves. The line denotes the age of the tree. Then you see it as an old and mighty tree. It must have been a long time spreading its shade over the countryside. Branches resemble southern moss. Underneath the tree, I see a small deer, a fawn. One, two, three. They're grazing at the foot of the tree. The mother deer has her head up looking for danger. The tree is big and the protector, so they are not afraid. They feel safe in the shadow of the tree.

(35) I saw a gray squirrel with a busy tail like a feather. It was looking around. [*Association:* Alone, self-dependent, feeding itself.]

(36) I saw a silver cup that was floating in the air, rising higher and higher It took the image of an eagle with silver wings. It alighted on the Capitol and then the eagle was transposed on the Capitol. Then the Capitol was immense as seen through a telescope.

(37) I see an arched bridge like the Golden Gate. Under it is a body of water covered by ships sailing up and down. In the distance I see a tall, well-constructed building that's solidly constructed, that's built to remain a long time. It's limestone and has large windows. It extends up to the sky, has autos around it, people entering it, air traffic flowing past. The spire on top resembles the Statue of Freedom in Washington. Light comes from the statue. The sun is shining on the back of it.

(38) Saw a monoplane with silver wings and red body and one wheel, soaring in space, no one at the controls, maintaining an even keel. It wasn't out of control. When it came in for a landing, two wheels appeared instead of one. It came in evenly for a two-point landing. It was in control. No excitement. [*Association:* Single wing, wheel, and body denotes oneness. Steady flight, steadiness, everything under control. I keep a lot to myself, I don't get excited.]

(39) See a picture of a statue resembling winged victory. It's on top of a golden ball. The ball is perched on top of a flagpole.

(40) I see a road on one side of a mountain that goes into space. Then it stops by a tunnel and goes no further. Then the dream repeats itself. This time it goes into the tunnel, deeply through hills and valleys. The

sides of the road are illuminated but there are no pedestrians and no traffic.

The following are four dreams by a female subject to the stimulus "have a dream about yourself."

(41) I see a large ball. It seems to be growing larger and larger. After a while I have the feeling that someone is pushing it.

(42) I saw a road close to or part of the side of a mountain which kept getting steeper and steeper. Someone was walking up the road and finding it harder and harder to go up, and protecting itself from slipping down.

(43) It's jumbled. I could see a volcano. The figure of a person beyond and walking alone. [*Association:* Someone is very lonely. Overwhelmed or overpowered by something.]

(44) Hard to describe. Saw something of stone or marble. A large stone that would be used for a piece of sculpture. It was high and wide as though in the process of being formed.

Symbolization of the Hypnotic Relationship. It has long been recognized that hypnosis occurs within the framework of an interpersonal relationship, but the complete implications of this statement have probably not been realized and have by and large been limited to a consideration of the sex of the hypnotist. Thus, Farber and Fisher noted that spontaneous hypnotic dreams occurring in the presence of a male hypnotist were altered when a female physician was introduced into the situation.

A simple, yet effective, method of studying the nature of the hypnotic relationship was devised for this investigation. Subjects were instructed to have dreams to the following stimuli: "You will have a dream about me" (the experimenter), "about you and me," "about being hypnotized," and "about how you feel now" (in the hypnotic state). By such stimuli it was hoped that the subjects might be induced to symbolize in dreams the meaning to them of the interpersonal situation involved in hypnosis.

A female subject whose first induction occurred during a demonstration of mass hypnosis by the experimenter had the following dream in response to the stimulus "have a dream about me."

(45) I see a man. He's whistling and all the mouses are following him. He's leading them out of town. They keep following him and finally he drowns them.

This dream will be recognized as the story of the Pied Piper of Hamelin. In a dream to the stimulus "have a dream about being hypnotized," she also expressed the feeling that hypnotic control is dangerous.

(46) I see a black horse with a man on it. The horse wants to go but the man won't let him. The horse runs off anyway.

Her immediate associations were: "I don't like horses. I'm afraid of them. I was riding on one and he tried to bite me."

That some subjects conceive of the hypnotic relationship as a controlling one is shown in the dreams of three different subjects.

(47) A large amphitheatre. There's an orchestra playing. Before it starts playing everybody was milling about. It was bedlam. As soon as the conductor raised his baton there was silence among the audience. There are thousands of people. If the numbers they play are close together, they remain silent. In the intermission they mill about, but when the conductor comes out again and raises his baton they get quiet again.

(48) I could see a fly going into a web and struggling. He couldn't free himself. A spider appeared. He kept staring at the fly.

(49) I'm walking through a garden. All the flowers are bending down as if somebody just struck them down. If you touch them, they'll wake up again.

Two subjects indicated that the hypnotic relationship was conceived of by them as a protecting one. Dreams 51 and 52 are from the same subject.

(50) I could see a person who had fallen into the ocean. Approaching him was a shark. Suddenly, out of nowhere a fish came who held off the shark. Then a boat came from over the horizon and took the person out of the water. Then, the victim waved to the fish who protected him from the shark.

(51) A busy city street. There's a crowd of people on one corner. A car hits a little dog. It's not seriously hurt but it's in pain and whining. A vet, a man in a white suit, comes along and gives him an injection and the dog stops whining. The crowd goes away and he picks up the dog and takes him away in a car.

(52) Seems to be a very extensive fire. A little village is being laid to ruin. Every home is partially burnt. It's rural. The homes are far apart. It's hilly country that the people have fled. Families go together. They've taken their livestock with them. The fields are entirely ruined and most of the livestock are thirsty. They drink milk from the goat and two cows. But it's not enough for the number of people. The children are crying. There's a truck coming down the road, like a milk truck. The type that looks like a big thermos jug. A man jumps out and starts running water out of it and the people run down and drink the water.

Two of the subjects in their dreams described hypnosis used in this experimental study as a cooperative experience.

(53) I see a manager of a baseball team. He has a coach, an assistant. Both work with the team to win games and get the pennant. They have a successful season, and then they have a victory dinner, and at the dinner the manager gave the coach credit for helping him with the team.

(54) I see two snakes entwined between themselves and they resemble the medical caduceus. They're wrapped around the pole. There's a vivid light, and it's full of life and light. [*Association:* A friendship and companionship and the caduceus is your being a doctor and I'm working with patients.]

Three of the subjects also expressed in four dreams the feeling that hypnosis as here used was a means to knowledge. Among the dreams was one of a book with its pages successively turning over until it was finished.

CHARACTER STRUCTURE AND THE HYPNOTIC DREAM

While formal personality studies were not part of this investigation, there was some opportunity both before and during the investigation to make observations on some of the subjects. It has already been shown that there is a remarkable consistency in the attitudes expressed in the hypnotic dreams of any one subject, and that through them the subject reveals his emotions toward the stimuli offered, whether they be parts of the body, natural functions, people, himself, or the hypnotic relationship. It was clear that many of the attitudes revealed in this manner were outside the subject's awareness. It should be possible from a review of a sufficient number of hypnotic dreams on varied themes to construct an outline of personality for an individual. There was, however, no opportunity to attempt to validate such an estimate of personality for any of the subjects used in this study.

By casual observation the experimenter noted early in the study that one subject appeared to be rather detached with great strivings for self-sufficiency. Strikingly his dreams assumed this consistent pattern: The human figure was rarely used as a symbol, though it was common in the dreams of other subjects. Analysis of the data shows that his difference from the other subjects in this respect is statistically significant. Of 38 dreams secured from him, only 4 (11 per cent) contained human figures. Of the 236 dreams from the nine other subjects, 177 (75 per cent) contained human figures. The difference is highly significant by the Chi Square test. To the stimulus "have a dream about yourself" he had seven dreams (Dreams 34–40), and in none of these did he portray himself by a human figure. These data suggest the possibility that dehumanization of the latent content of the dream in its translation to the manifest dream may be a significant finding in detached personalities. A study of the dreams of a series of analytic patients with respect to the nature of the manifest content might provide evidence on this point.

THE DREAM WORK

After the dream stimulus was given, there was always a latent period before the beginning of the dream, which was signalled by raising of the hand. The latent period was rarely longer than 90 seconds, and 71 per cent of the latent periods were within a 15-second to 60-second range. It was, presumably, during this period that the dream work, the translation of the latent to the manifest dream, occurred. It seemed desirable, therefore, to investigate whether the subject was consciously aware of the formulation of the dream during the latent period. Subjects who were questioned about the experience said that, though they tried to think about the dream stimulus as soon as it was given, the content of their thoughts had little or no relation to the dream when it appeared; and, further, that the dream seemed to appear without any effort on their part. Moreover, the experimenter's occupying the subject's awareness with neutral material during the latent period did not inhibit the formation of the dream. In order to further investigate this point a number of experiments were done. One subject was on two occasions instructed to recite a poem from memory as soon as the dream stimulus was given and to cease reciting as the dream began to appear. This did not prevent the formation of the dream. Two other subjects in deep trance were able to read aloud from a book without preventing the production of dreams. A fourth subject was able to read aloud from a book and simultaneously to perform automatic writing, unintelligible to him at the time, without inhibiting dream production. These experiments appear to indicate that the formation of the hypnotic dream occurs outside of hypnotic awareness and is not prevented by concentration of the subject on activities in awareness.

Farber and Fisher have noted, and this was confirmed, that the early dreams of a subject in response to a stimulus may be simply a paraphrasing of the stimulus by material from the subject's life experience, but that if he is induced to continue to dream, the dream elements become more and more disguised until the final production is a symbolized, distorted dream. This suggests that the dream work may occur in a similar manner. If this is true, one might expect that the latent period would be longer for disguised dreams than for undisguised dreams since the work of translation is greater. This was found to be the case in this study.

DISCUSSION

In any investigation involving hypnosis it is necessary to make certain that the data are secured in a hypnotic state and are not simply fabrications designed to please the investigator. Since most hypnotic phenomena can be reproduced volitionally, the only positive assurance that a subject is hypnotized is his ability to perform in a manner not possible in the nonhypnotized state. Hypnotic age-regression represents such a performance. Two of the subjects of the present study were regressed on a number of occasions and were then able to recall material not available to them in the nonhypnotized state—for example, the day of the week of the birthday to which they had been regressed. Moreover, they were able to dream in the regressed state. Dreams secured at regressed age levels, some of which have been cited, did not differ in any significant respect from those secured from the same and other subjects in the hypnotized but nonregressed state. Further evidence that the dreams reported were not simply fabrications designed to please the experimenter is threefold: first, nonhypnotized subjects who were asked to invent dreams were either not able to do so or were unable to produce themes that had the character of those produced by hypnotized subjects; second, the dreams of any one subject to the same stimulus showed a remarkable consistency, indicating that the significant determinants lay in the reaction of the subject's personality to the stimulus rather than to his need to please the experimenter; and third, the fact that the capacity to produce the dreams reported has been shown to be a function of the depth of hypnosis.

The next question that arises is whether the productions described in this paper have any relationship to dreams occurring during sleep, and whether they should be called dreams at all. If one insists that the term dream be limited to phenomena occurring only during sleep, he defines the term in respect to the circumstances in which it occurs rather than in respect to the nature of the productions themselves. Examination of the productions described in this paper and in the other publications cited provides cogent grounds for considering them to be of essentially the same character as dreams occurring during sleep.

First, the productions described are hallucinatory experiences occurring during a state of altered consciousness in nonpsychotic individuals. Second, they have been shown to be produced below the level of awareness. Third, they make revelations about the personality of the subject in the same way that sleep-dreams do. Fourth, they can express these revelations in symbolic language. Fifth, they contain distortions similar to those which Freud described for sleep-dreams (Freud, 1931*b*, 1938, 1953). Displacement by allusion was found in a number of the dreams cited. Thus, the statement, "Pick up a bigger bat. That's what you need to hit it with," in Dream 5 is an allusion to the size of the subject's penis. A similar allusion occurs in Dream 7. In two other dreams a subject alluded to his mother by dreaming of being punished in school for having dirty hands in one case and for having lice in his hair in the other. Both allusions referred to the person who should have protected him from these occurrences. Examples of plastic word representation are found in Dreams 26 and 27, and of causality being represented by temporal sequence in Dreams 1, 12, 13, 18, 19, 20. Condensation is not found, simply because the stimuli were single units and so could hardly be further condensed.

While it is likely that the hypnotic dream is not a precise duplicate of the night dream, either in structure or function, the data of this study indicate that the differences are quantitative rather than qualitative. There are, for example, spontaneous night dreams which are simple and undistorted, while some hypnotic dreams have the symbolization and richness of imagery one customarily associates with night dreams. It is likely that simple undistorted night dreams are more common than is commonly believed since they are less likely because of their prosaic quality either to be reported by patients or to be mentioned in the literature than are dreams of vivid imagery and bizarreness. The question of the relation of hypnotic dreams to night dreams and conscious daydreams, which Brenman (1949) reasonably raises, can only be answered by a systematic comparison of the spontaneous and hypnotically induced dreams of a series of subjects.

The study provided no evidence that dream material could have a source outside of the living experience of the dreamer. There was, in fact, evidence that the educational and cultural experiences of the dreamer determine the symbols used in his dreams and that these are often highly specific. Dream symbols common to a number of dreamers were rare, and the same dreamer might use different symbols for the same function, person, or emotion upon different occasions. Despite the variety of symbols used by a subject for a particular function, person, or emotion, the subject's attitude toward the latent content of his dreams showed remarkable consistency.

These experiments suggest means by which the hypnotic dream may be used effectively in the course of psychoanalysis. Kanzer (1945) has reported their use in short term therapy. Since the therapist can choose the stimulus—the latent content in miniature—he may be able to discover a subject's feelings toward the person, thing, function, or emotion he has asked him to dream about. During periods in therapy when the nature of the transference situation is unclear, a dream elicited to the stimulus "have a dream about you and me," or the like, may prove clarifying.

Since the hypnotic dream appears to reveal unconscious attitudes in the same manner that dreams during sleep do, it may offer an experimental method for securing such material. Once the subject has been trained in the method, 10 or 12 hypnotic dreams can be obtained within the space of an hour. The use of this method for validating projective tests is, also, suggested as a possibility.

Though psychoanalysts are largely interested in the latent content of the dream and use the manifest content usually as a means of reaching the latent dream, some of the data of this study suggest that the nature of the manifest content itself—that is, the type of symbols chosen—may also make significant revelations about the dreamer's character structure.

Commentary

In the article, I listed five characteristics of dreams to which, I suggested on the basis of the data presented, the hypnotic dream also adhered. I concluded that the evidence cited provides, "cogent ground for considering them to be of essentially the same character as dreams occurring during sleep." In the next paragraph I did make the disclaimer that it was likely that the hypnotic dream is not a precise duplicate of the night dream either in structure or function, but that I thought that the differences were quantitative rather than qualitative.

If I were rewriting the article at this time, I think I would state the issues in pragmatic form. I would say, for example, that if one were interested in the hypnotic dream as an expression of a patient's personality, then from the point of view of its usefulness it was the same as the night dream. Again, if one were interested in the hypnotic dream in order to study symbolism and dream distortion, then, too, the hypnotic dream conforms to the night dream. In short, I think the question as to whether the two are identical or not is meaningless until one approaches the specific areas of one's interest.

It is quite possible, of course, that one might in a detailed description of the night dream find certain characteristics to which the hypnotic dream does not conform. At the moment, aside from the fact that the night dream occurs during sleep, I cannot think of any characteristics of the night dream which the hypnotic dream may not duplicate.

I have not published or done any other studies on that subject. I often wonder why I did not follow up the original investigation. As I recall, I had begun psychoanalysis and training and later became involved in teaching. The demands of psychoanalytic practice seem to take most of my time. I suspect, though, that there is another reason. I found that the analytic process had changed me so that, first, I was less interested in hypnosis and, second, I began to find myself much less effective in the induction process. I became quite aware when I tried to use hypnosis in my therapeutic work that I felt much less certain about my ability to induce hypnosis than I had when I was a resident physician. Perhaps as a consequence I also became much less effective at it.

MILTON MAZER

Edgartown, Massachusetts
1966

An Experimental Investigation of the Hypnotic Dream

BY ANDERS SWEETLAND AND HERBERT QUAY

At first glance the hypnotically induced dream would seem to be an excellent method for the experimental exploration of the normal sleeping dream. As Luria (1932) has amply demonstrated, hypnosis can provide an *in vito* approach which obviates many of the controls necessary in *in vivo* experiments. The experimenter, using hypnosis, can frequently circumvent many of the problems of uncontrolled variables which plague clinical research. The method is consequently tempting. However, phenotypes must be presumed until genotypes can be demonstrated. And, until this, the hypnotic dream must be studied for itself and generalization beyond the data must be reserved.

The present paper is an exploratory study of the hypnotic dream per se. It is essentially an extension of the works of Klein (1930) and Farber and Fisher (1943), which were more demonstrative than experimental. It is an attempt to relate the response to two variables: the organismic and the stimulus. The questions asked are: how are reaction time, dream duration, recall, and dream alteration related to ego-involving stimuli; and does any relationship exist between response variables and organismic factors such as social-emotional adjustment and intelligence.

PROCEDURE

Prior to the experiment, 16 psychologically naïve college students were taught to dream under hypnosis. During practice they were encouraged to "dream the same as you do at night." The experiment was begun when subjects (Ss) could no longer distinguish between their hypnotic dreams and their normal sleeping dreams.

The Ss were randomly selected only to the extent that volunteers for such an experiment are random. Test results showed that ranges of intelligence and emotional adjustment were large, including the lowest and highest deciles.

The stimuli were 50 statements of an ego-involving nature: *You overhear*

SOURCE. Reprinted by permission from *The Journal of Abnormal and Social Psychology*, **47** (3), 678–682 (July, 1952).

This study was made possible by a grant from the Research Council, Florida State University.

somebody say that he wishes he had your personality. You are accused of being a social climber, etc. These were obtained by having each member of a class in psychology list several items following a discussion of ego-involvement.

The items were edited, to make them generally applicable, and then given to 40 college students (20 males and 20 females) to rank on a seven-point scale. The ranking yielded 20 items paired in dispersion and distance from either side of a zero point. These 20 were paraphrased and ten neutral items added: *You have fish for Friday dinner, etc.* The result was 50 items fairly equally balanced around a neutral point. Immediately prior to experimentation, each S ranked this final set of stimuli on a seven-point scale.

To determine the effects of ego-involvement, the rankings were divided into three groups. Rankings one and two (markedly ego-enhancing) were called "plus." Rankings six and seven (markedly ego-assaulting) were called "minus," the remaining rankings "neutral." This division, while arbitrary, was supported by the fact that the extreme rankings tended to be stable: items thus ranked would be ranked similarly by all Ss. Although there was some shift of items in the neutral range, only rarely would a neutral item be ranked in the extremes.

Farber and Fisher indicate that the characteristics of a dream may be influenced by a change in the people present. We attempted to control this by having the same people present for each S. For males this was either (or both) of the experimenters. Each female, however, was requested to bring a "chaperone." She was asked to bring someone towards whom she had no intense emotional feelings, either attraction or dislike. This generally was the girl's roommate. All experimentation was conducted in a soundproof room. Dreams were timed by having the S raise his hand when he began each dream and lower it on its completion.

After dreaming to the 50 items (an average of three one-hour sessions) the Ss were randomly divided into an experimental and a control group. The control group immediately repeated the 50 stimuli. The experimental group was given a discussion of the theory of dream symbolization including dream work, the censor, and manifest and latent content. The experimental group then repeated the 50 items, again keeping the same people present.

The results of this repetition are not included in the present experiment, which is restricted to quantitative findings. When possible, however, we have repeated the statistical computations on this second group of data as a check on the first. The data (obtained from the repetition) may be found in parentheses.

RESULTS

Reaction Time and Dream Duration. The reaction times and duration of dreams were compared by the mean variation method (Lind-

TABLE 1

Reaction time and duration of dreams to three types of ego-involving stimuli

	Plus	Neutral	Minus
Reaction M_w	14.51	12.34	14.27
	(15.81)	(13.07)	(14.55)
S_m^2	7.59	5.79	6.30
	(12.97)	(8.75)	(10.57)
Duration M_w	13.71	13.85	15.14
	(12.23)	(13.01)	(14.12)
S_m^2	5.99	4.49	6.70
	(3.08)	(3.15)	(5.10)
	PN	PM	NM
Reaction t*	0.59	0.06	0.55
	(0.59)	(0.26)	(0.34)
Duration t*	0.04	0.23	0.23
	(0.24)	(0.66)	(0.26)

* For 15 df, t must be at least 2.131 to be reliable at the 5 per cent level. The numbers in parentheses are obtained from the repeated experiment. See text.

quist, 1940, p. 67). The results show no reliable differences suggesting that ego-involvement has no influence on either. The data are summarized in Table 1. There is also no apparent relationship between dream duration and reaction time: rho = 0.196 ± 0.26.

The data in Table 1 tend to conceal a marked personal equation. Inspection of the protocols showed that each S had his own speed of reaction and dream duration, generally consistent within a few seconds. This personal equation was also evidenced in the narratives. Music majors tended to dream about music; the journalism student dreamed about newswriting; the camera fan dreamed about photography. One male S dreamed repeatedly of nude females. We tactfully made no inquiry.

The data may give some indication of the answer to the classical question: how long does a dream last. The length of the average hypnotic dream is ten to fifteen seconds. The range of individual dream duration is large: one second to five minutes.

The Relation of Alteration to Stimulus Tone. The main consideration of the experiment was the behavior of the "dream work": the alteration (symbolization) of the stimulus material. A dream was classified as being either an alteration or a repetition of the stimulus. Dreams which were essentially a reduplication or a continuation of the stimulus (or, frequently, both) were classified as "repeat." Dreams which contained definite elements of typical dream distortion were classified as "alteration." The term *alteration* was used to distinguish the phenomenon from symbolization as conventionally used.

Two examples of "repeat" to the stimulus "You are accused of being a social climber," are: "I was walking down the hall when I heard these two girls say this. I was furious and asked them what they meant. . . ." "When I heard this I made up my mind that I would try to find out why they said this and do something about it."

Examples of "alteration" (same stimulus) are: "I was climbing up a ladder. There were people all around. They seemed to be mad at me, but I kept climbing." "It seems that my roommate said this. I don't exactly remember, but I remember that the room was all in white. I had a white bed, and a white dresser, and white walls. This was very strange to me because I knew it wasn't like that. Then I ran out of the room."

The dreams were scored independently by the two experimenters. Most samples of 50 dreams showed 100 per cent agreement. Lowest agreement was 92 per cent. An occasional dream would be classified as "repeat" by one scorer and "alteration" by the other. If discussion did not resolve the disagreement, the classification was assigned randomly. This happened in less than 1 per cent of the judgments.

Because of the close agreement between judges, no reliability coefficients were computed. It is believed that the agreement well exceeds that necessary for making group comparisons.

The first consideration was whether the distribution of alteration in each of the stimulus categories (plus, minus, and neutral) was the result of stimulus tone or chance. To determine this a chi square was obtained between the observed and expected frequencies. The expected frequency in this, and subsequent cases, was obtained from the proportional number of dreams in each category. In a strict sense, our use of chi square may not be defensible as there is some question of cell independence. It is felt, however, that the conclusions are not influenced by the choice of statistic.

A chi square of 5.21 (p between 5 and 10 per cent) was obtained. This is probably a chance variation as a similar chi square from the second group of data had a probability at the 60 per cent level of confidence. The results indicate no tendency to alter any particular type of stimulus used in this experiment.

The Relation of Dream Alteration to Emotional Adjustment and Intelligence. The unexpected findings of the experiment were the relations between dream alteration and personality adjustment. Personality adjustment was measured by two tests: The Social Security-Insecurity Test (SI) by Maslow et al. (1945) and the Minnesota Multiphasic Personality Inventory (MMPI) of Hathaway and McKinley (1943).

The SI is a 75-item inventory, designed to measure adjustment in the area of social security. The MMPI is a 560-item inventory. It has separate scales for Hypochondriasis (*Hs*), Depression (*D*), Hysteria (*Hy*), Psychopathic Deviate (*Pd*), Masculinity-feminity (*Mf*), Paranoia (*Pa*), Psychasthenia (*Pt*), Schizophrenia (*Sc*), and Hypomania (*Ma*). It also has several validating scales. Two of these were used, *F* and *K*. The *F* scale, originally designed to check sorting and clerical errors, has been found to correlate with adjustment. The *K* scale was designed to control the effects of the attitude of the person taking the test.

We had originally designed the experiment to include only *S*s of average social-emotional adjustment. To check this, each *S* was given the SI. On scoring several of these it became apparent that there was a relationship between the amount of dream alteration and the adjustment scores. To check this further, the MMPI was given. The relation between the number of alterations and the scores on the SI and the MMPI may be found in Table 2.

The results given in Table 2 indicate a definite relation between hypnotic dream alteration and test scores. This relationship may be stated: the better the adjustment of the individual, the greater the amount of alteration he produces. The correlation between SI scores and alteration is reliable at the 5 per cent level (Fisher's *z*). Although

TABLE 2
Correlations between dream alteration
and adjustment scores

SI	0.574	(0.564)
MMPI		
F	—0.028	(—0.024)
K	0.720	(0.571)
Hs	—0.004	(0.003)
D	—0.235	(—0.338)
Hy	—0.211	(—0.236)
Pa	—0.341	(—0.522)
Pt	—0.288	(—0.243)
Sc	—0.088	(—0.099)
Ma	—0.151	(—0.079)

none of the correlations with the MMPI (except that with the K scale) is reliable, the chance of obtaining eight negative correlations, assuming zero correlation, is 1 in 256.

To check the relationship further, correlations were computed between intelligence and alteration and intelligence and adjustment. The measure of intelligence was the American Council on Education Psychological Examination (ACE). This test has three subscales: Quantitative (Q), Linguistic (L), and a Total Score (T). We found small correlations between the ACE and SI scores. This was partialled out. The original correlations and the partialled correlations may be found in Table 3.

TABLE 3

Correlation between adjustment scores (SI),
intelligence scores (Q, L, and T) and
alteration (Sy)*

Product moment correlations

r	Q	L	T
SI	0.327	0.307	0.343
Sy	0.367	0.339	0.382
r_{sisy}		0.574	

Partial correlations

SySI.Q	0.515
SySI.L	0.520
SySI.T	0.510
SyQ.SI	0.231
SyL.SI	0.334
SyT.SI	0.240

* Correlations exceeding 0.482 are reliable at the 5 per cent level.

The results shown in Table 3 support the thesis that there is a real relationship between dream alteration and adjustment. The data also suggest a slight relationship between alteration and intelligence.

Rejections. Occasionally no dream followed the presentation of the stimulus. We have called this a rejection. There was no stimulus that all Ss rejected; some Ss rejected none. Feeling that rejections might have some significance, we determined the number of rejections from plus, minus, and neutral stimuli and computed the chi square between this and the expected frequency. The expected frequency was determined from the total number of dreams in each category.

The chi square obtained was 2.63. For 2 *df*, this is between the 20 and 10 per cent levels. It indicates that this variation can be attributable to chance factors. This is further supported by the chi square obtained from the second group, which was between the 70 and 50 per cent levels. Evidently rejections are not related to ego-involvement.

Inquiry indicated that some of the rejections resulted when Ss felt the stimulus inapplicable or implausible. The subject who didn't smoke, for example, tended to reject the stimulus "You find that you are out of cigarettes and purchase a package immediately."

Memory of Dreams. Two aspects were considered: the relationship of recall to stimulus tone and the relationship of recall to primacy and recency in an hour's dreams.

We awakened each S at the end of each experimental session and asked him to recall as many dreams as he could. We then compared the number of dreams recalled in each of the categories (plus, minus, and neutral) with the expected number (determined from the proportional number of dreams in each category). A chi square of 2.61 (*p*, 25 per cent) was obtained. Recall is evidently not related to stimulus tone. It should be remembered that this is based on stimulus tone, not response tone.

The effect of primacy and recency on recall was determined by dividing each session's dreams into chronological fifths. The frequency of remembered dreams was tabulated for these fifths. A chi square was computed between this frequency and the expected frequency, assuming that recall would be equally distributed. The chi square of 21.48 was significant of the 1 per cent level (4 *df*). Inspection of the computations showed that over two-thirds of the chi square (14.51) came from the large frequency in the last quintile.

To check this, the last quintile was removed and the chi square computed for the remaining data. This chi square (4.35) was reliable at the 25 per cent level (*3df*). The indication is that the last dreams tend to be remembered most.

DISCUSSION

The problem most interesting, and as yet unresolved, is the relationship of the hypnotic dream to the normal sleeping dream. Sirna (1945), in a study using the electroencephalogram, concluded that the hypnotic dream is psychologically, but not physiologically, the same. His Ss reported that their hypnotic dreams were indistinguishable from the sleeping dreams. He based his physiological differences on the difference in brain waves in sleep and in the hypnotic state. Farber and Fisher similarly report that their Ss could not distinguish between the hypnotic and the sleeping dream.

Klein reports that his Ss unanimously agree that the hypnotic dreams can legitimately be called dreams. The only differences seemed to arise from the fact that the dreams were produced in the hypnotic state. He concludes that discrepancies were the result of the setting and not the dream process.

Our Ss did not begin experimentation until they could distinguish no appreciable difference between the sleeping dream and the hypnotic dream. Similarly to Klein, we found that differences were a confusion of the situation and not of the dream per se. Further research on the problem is indicated before any definite statement can be made. We are however, impressed by the similarity and are endeavoring research in this area.

Some observations did not lend themselves to quantification. Because of their theoretical implications we have included them in the following.

Klein, using sensory stimuli (touch, smell, sound, etc.) found that some Ss had the same or similar dreams when the stimulus was repeated. Our stimuli differ: they are more conceptual in nature. On repeating them, we found very few repeated dreams: less than five in 800 repetitions. This is despite the fact that the stimuli were repeated in an identical setting and identical sequence. It would seem that the occurrence of the repeated hypnotic dream is more closely related to "peripheral" than to "central" stimuli.

It was also observed that the Ss tended to "pretty up" the dream content. Although their dreams were not altered, ego-assaulting stimuli were made to "come out all right in the end." It is our plan to quantify this in later research.

Some Ss persistently yielded dreams which had no apparent relationship to the stimulus, even when the stimulus was available for comparison. There were three protocols in which it was impossible to locate a dream from the stimulus by any method other than counting down the list.

An illustration of this remoteness of relationship between the dream and its stimulus is given in the following response: "I saw two men walking down the street talking to each other. One was walking forward and the other backward. They were gesticulating wildly and I remember they walked past a pawnshop." The stimulus was: "You have fish for Friday dinner." Other dreams were even more remotely associated with the stimulus, involving geometrical light formations, abstract designs which flowed into shapes and again into abstractions, and personifications of the dreamer into lines of poetry, notes from a song, etc.

The dreams which were remote from the stimuli were invariably dreamed by Ss having excellent adjustment scores on the personality tests. As adjustment scores dropped, the dreams became more and more reduplications of the stimuli, the poorest adjusted S showing the most trite reduplication.

The hypnotic dream seems to be closely related to organismic factors and remotely (if at all) related to stimulus factors. We should like to caution against generalizing beyond the materials used in this experiment as the use of more intense stimuli might yield different results. Although we are impressed with the similarity of the hypnotic dream to the sleeping dream, it is our feeling that interpretations made from one to the other should be held in abeyance until further research is available.

We feel that the hypnotic dream is an imaginative phenomenon and, as such, is sensitive to emotional adjustment. This interpretation tends to classify lack of alteration more in the category of the psychological deficit as described by Hunt (Hunt and Cofer, 1944). This idea is advanced tentatively. Again, further research is indicated.

SUMMARY

Sixteen psychologically naïve college students were taught to dream under hypnosis. Fifty stimuli of an ego-involving nature were twice administered. It was found that:

1. Ego-involvement showed no effect on reaction time, dream duration, dream alteration ("symbolization") and stimulus rejection.

2. Dream alteration is closely related to emotional adjustment; the best adjusted subject symbolizes most.

3. Recall is a function of recency and is independent of stimulus tone.

4. Repeated dreams occur rarely when "conceptual" (as opposed to sensory) stimuli are used.

Commentary

I would characterize the investigation as "reasonably rigorous." There was a two-year exploratory investigation that preceded the final series. (Incidentally, unlike the original Farber and Fisher studies, we found our subjects no more proficient at interpreting dreams in the final series. Nor did we have much luck at introducing nocturnal dreams via suggestion.)

We developed, naturally, a number of attitudes (biases) during the investigation. Among them was the definite feeling that dreams are not "the royal road to the unconscious": both of us discarded dream exploration as a psychotherapeutic aid. These attitudes are best encapsulated in the statement that was deleted, at the editor's request, from the original report to the effect that the findings offer little to support and much to refute conventional psychoanalytic theory. Ten years later, we still feel this to be true.

ANDERS SWEETLAND

Santa Monica, California
1966

The Experimental Situation as
a Determinant of Hypnotic Dreams:
A Contribution to the Experimental Use of Hypnosis

BY RICHARD NEWMAN,* JAY KATZ,†

AND ROBERT RUBENSTEIN‡

This paper presents our finding that in an experimental situation using hypnosis the hypnotic relationship influences the data obtained. We came to this conclusion in the course of an investigation of thought processes in different states of consciousness, in which we compared spontaneously reported dreams with hypnotic dreams.

By hypnotic dreams, we refer to dreams obtained following the suggestion of the hypnotist; that is, the experimenter tells the hypnotized subject that he will have a dream, either immediately, while under hypnosis, or afterward, during the night. The experimenter may or may not suggest what the content of the dream will be. The majority of subjects respond to the suggestion, and subsequently report dreams to the experimenter (Rubenstein et al., 1957), which may

SOURCE. Reprinted by permission from *Psychiatry: Journal for the Study of Interpersonal Processes,* **23** (1), 63–73 (February, 1960).

This research is supported by a grant to the Department of Psychiatry, Yale University School of Medicine, from the National Institute of Mental Health of the U.S. Public Health Service. This paper was read before the American Psychoanalytic Association, May, 1957.

* B.S. Harvard 26; M.D. Johns Hopkins 30; Intern, New Haven Hosp. 30–32; Voluntary Asst., Burghölzli, Zürich 33–34; Clin. Clerk, Queen Square, London 34; Res., Psychiatry 34–35, Clin. Instr. and Prof. 36–, Yale School of Med.; Lt. Cmdr. USNR 44–46. Graduate N.Y. Psychoanalytic Inst. 52.

† A.B. Univ. of Vermont 44; M.D. Harvard Med. School 49; rotating internship, Mt. Sinai Hosp., N.Y. 49–50; Asst. Res. Psychiatry, VA and Long Island Coll. of Med. 50–51; 1st Lt. USAF 51–52, Capt. and Chief of Psychiatry, Maxwell AFB Hosp. 52–53; Res., Psychiatry 53–55, Instr. 55–57, Asst. Prof. 57–58, Dept. of Psychiatry, Yale Univ. School of Med.; Exec. Officer, Psychiatric Clinic, Grace-New Haven Hosp. 55–58; Asst. Prof. Psychiatry and Law, Yale Univ. 58–; Clin. Assoc. Western New England Institute for Psychoanalysis.

‡ A.B. Stanford Univ. 47; U.S. Army 45–46; M.D. Stanford Univ. School of Med. 52; rotating internship, Stanford Univ. San Francisco Hosp. 51–52; Res., Psychiatry 52–55, Instr. 55–58, Asst. Prof. 58–, Dept. of Psychiatry, Yale Univ. School of Med.; Asst. Med. Director, Yale Psychiatric Inst. 57–; Clin. Assoc. Western New England Institute for Psychoanalysis.

differ considerably from spontaneous night dreams.[1] Moreover, immediate hypnotic dreams and posthypnotic night dreams may differ; the
experiment reported in this paper was designed to bring out these
differences. In the material we present here, however, we wish to
stress another aspect of our findings. In studying our data, we were
unable to understand or account for many aspects of the dreams until
we became aware of the importance of the hypnotic situation itself
as a dream stimulus. It is this aspect of our findings which we wish
to present.

It should be emphasized that the work here reported was experimental and not therapeutic. We assumed that the therapeutic relationship between patient and doctor and the doctor's therapeutic intent
would interfere with research interests. We were not aware, when
we undertook the experiments, of the degree to which the hypnotic
relationship would influence the data obtained.

PROCEDURE

The data presented below are from one subject of a group of six
who were each offered two artificial complexes as stimuli for hypnotic
dreams. An artificial complex is an account of a conflictual past event
presented as if it were an experience in the subject's own life. After
the artificial complex was suggested to the subject, he was told, "Your
feelings, your thoughts, and your behavior are involved in this experience which I have just described to you. You are a part of this experience. It is very meaningful to you." It was then suggested that the
subject would "continue to feel very strongly about this experience,"
but that he would "no longer remember the experience itself." Following this suggested amnesia for the complex, the subject was told,
"Shortly you will have a dream." After the production of the dream,
associations to it were obtained, while the subject was still under
hypnosis.

The subject was then told, "Tonight you will have a dream which
will deal with the experience you had and which you can no longer
remember, but about which you continue to feel very strongly. In
the morning, after you wake up, you will write down the dream."
In some instances, the order was reversed, and a night dream was
obtained first, after which the artificial complex was repeated and
an immediate dream obtained.

[1] Margaret Brenman has described varieties of hypnotic dreams and their relation
to spontaneous night dreams (Brenman, 1949). See also Farber and Fisher (1943).

Tape recordings of the experimental sessions and transcripts prepared from them, as well as some notes made by an observer behind a one-way mirror, provided us with an unusual opportunity to study the behavior of subjects and experimenters.

In setting up this series of experiments, we were not concerned with the unconscious meanings which the artificial complexes had for the subjects, but with the more formal aspects of immediate hypnotic dreams as compared with posthypnotic night dreams. However, as we have stated before, what we shall present here is another finding—not what the experiment was designed to test.

DREAM SERIES OF SUBJECT A

First Artificial Complex. In the first session, after the subject, a medical student, was in a deep hypnosis, the experimenter suggested the following artificial complex: "Now I want you to go back in time to when you were eight years old. You wanted to buy some candy and toys. You had no money. You took money from your mother's purse and bought the candy and toys you wanted." After suggesting amnesia for the complex, the experimenter asked the subject how he felt.

"I can't understand why I'd do it. Why I should do such a thing—I'm wondering whether I'm supposed to actually picture myself doing this, or you're just telling me you want to[2]—me to feel how I would react in a case like this?"

The hypnotist did not reply to the subject's questions about the procedure, but instead repeated the artificial complex with greater emphasis, again suggested amnesia for it, and once more asked the subject how he felt.

Subject A said, "I don't know—something's wrong—something's gonna happen, I don't know what. I'm anxious. I dunno what—something's gonna happen, I don't know—" He then spontaneously related the following dream.

(1) Immediate Hypnotic Dream.—Well [sighs], it's the middle of the afternoon and I'm playing in a dirt pile, I guess it is, sand pile, with a friend of mine. I guess we're playing at—ah—we're—ah—construction engineers or something. I've got a little toy steam shovel, not so little, but—and then we're building something in the—in the dirt. This is out in the fields, away from every—no, not very far away. It's away from my house though. And we're building some kind of a house, I guess it is. And it's getting late in the afternoon. Finally its time to go in.

---

[2] This slip suggests: "This is what you want, not how I feel."

So I pick up my stuff and we go home. She lives right across the street from where I do. I bring my stuff inside. Go in and show it to my mother. She was inside getting dinner ready. She asks me where I get it—where I got this steam shovel. [Softly.] Mm—no, there's something more. Someone—somehow it winds up that—ah—my allowance is to be docked to pay for this thing, but—and that's the end of the dream.

Associating to the dream while no longer under hypnosis, the subject recalled taking a drive with his family as a young child. They stopped to watch a steam shovel operating in a stone quarry, and he was fascinated. As they drove off, he continued to stare after it, hoping to be able to operate a large steam shovel himself some day.

He was puzzled about why he felt uncomfortable—"Why I should worry so much about this one thing, actually it isn't very big and I shouldn't worry about it much. Even before I showed it to her I was a little bit worried, during the afternoon, but not now. I'm not worried about this one item, it's just that I can't seem to remember why I was worried in—in the afternoon—I don't remember ever having a little steam shovel like that before—it's got a movable shovel, and you can actually pick up some dirt with it—it isn't very big. [Half-laugh.] I don't know why I'm worried about it so much." Asked how he felt at the end of the dream, he said, "Mm, I guess I was sorta relieved."

There seems to be a clear relationship between the suggested artificial complex and the manifest content of the dream. Associating to it, the subject recalls a childhood experience, is puzzled about why he feels ill at ease, and states that at the end of the dream he felt relieved and more comfortable. It seems that the artificial complex has elicited a conflict which is relieved by the dream, and the dream in turn uses the artificial complex as a theme upon which to weave some of the subject's unconscious wishes and anxieties. It is also possible that some of the subject's relief may be due to his having complied with the hypnotist's suggestion.[3]

The subject, still under hypnosis, was then told that he would have a dream about the same complex during the night. The next day he described having slept fitfully and having been awakened from the following dream by the alarm clock.

(2) *Posthypnotic Night Dream.*—I was wandering in a hall, seemed like it was in high school. There was no one around. It was on the second floor. I was supposed to have some sort of exam—a physical exam, but

[3] Another possible way in which this dream may express the subject's preoccupation with the hypnotic situation is discussed later.

I didn't know where I was supposed to go. I was worried that I was late. I saw an open door with light coming through. Everything else was dark. I went in. There were two people there in white jackets and white trousers. One of them was standing with his back to the laboratory counter. The other one was making a smear—stupidest way of making a smear I ever saw. He was taking blood and putting it on a slide. Then he rubbed off the top with a piece of glass and then put water on the top. I dunno what the hell he was doing that for.

Next I know I'm home on vacation from college. It was Christmas vacation. The day before Christmas. Someone tells me to go out and get a piece of sliced ham. I walk down to the store and buy the sliced ham. The man behind the counter picks it up and throws it underneath some furniture in the store. I'm angry. I want to get it. I run home and get a sledge hammer which I know is in the garage. The garage doors are closed. I yank them open—it was easy because the hasp broke. I get the hammer and go back to the store. I pound the furniture under which the ham is.

The subject gave very few associations to this dream; most of them expressed his feeling that the dream and what happened in it were silly and strange. In regard to the first part of the dream, which took place in a laboratory, he said that he had no idea why they were doing such a thing, that he didn't remember ever seeing such a place, that it was an "obstruse" method of wasting time, and that "he knew enough to know that the two people were not doing the right thing." Regarding the second part of the dream he said, "How did I get there? I never saw the man before. He threw the whole thing under the counter. He tried to get me angry and succeeded." In further associating, the subject said that the man behind the counter took his wallet. Asked about a possible connection or comparison between his hypnotic dream and his night dream, he said, "There doesn't seem to be much connection; maybe there's a question of money in both dreams. I have it in both cases—someone takes it away—I have to do something to get it back."

Looking only at the manifest content, one does not readily detect elements of the artificial complex in the first part of the dream. There are, however, many obvious references to the experimental situation. He is in a school building on the second floor. He is supposed to have a bizarre examination, about which he is puzzled and critical. "It is the stupidest way of doing it I have ever seen." In actuality the experiment was carried out on the second floor of a university building, and the subject had been hypnotized by two of the experimenters. The smear and the method of making it were suggestive of two experimental procedures, namely, (1) testing his ability to have an amnesia by suggesting that he see numbers on a blackboard and then erase them from the blackboard in his mind, and (2) suggesting the artificial complex and then erasing it from his memory.

In the second part of the dream, the artificial complex seems to be represented by the store, money, buying, and taking something, but the mechanisms of reversal and denial have come into play. It is not he who steals: "Someone took it away and I am just getting it back." The hammering noise which he himself makes in the dream is perhaps reversal of the ringing of the alarm clock.

Second Artificial Complex. Eight days later in the third experimental session, another artificial complex was suggested to the subject: "Now I want you to go back in time to when you were in high school. You were badly prepared for an examination. You had an opportunity to copy from one of your neighbors. And you copied part of the answers from your neighbor." The experimenter then asked the subject how he felt. "It's done, let's forget about it. But I can't forget about it very easily. I'm worried about it. To confess it would be a sign of weakness—it would mean that I would want to get off more lightly. I don't know why I cheated—I don't like the idea of doing it or getting caught. I'm mad at myself for doing it. It's an awful stupid thing to do. It was only a grade. And what difference does it make?" Amnesia for the complex was then suggested, and he was asked how he felt. "It's hard to describe," he said, "I'm not quite comfortable. I'm anxious for some reason." He was then told that he would have a dream during the night, "which will deal with the experience you had and which you can no longer remember, but about which you continue to feel very strongly."

The next day, at the fourth session, the subject returned with an account of the dream. He said that he had dreamed it at about three or four in the morning, had awakened, and had written it down. He described having slept fitfully throughout the night, and stated that he would have forgotten the dream if he had not written it down at the suggestion of the experimenter.

(*3*) *Posthypnotic Night Dream.*—Well, it starts off when I'm home. It's winter time. Just been quite a heavy snowfall overnight. And it's middle of the morning now, very bright, the sun is shining, cold. There's two or three feet of snow on the ground. And—ah—I'm out in the driveway or in the quadrangle, so to speak, at home. And I'm worried about the depth of snow on the shed roof. I don't know whether it'll be strong enough to stand up under it. And we've got a tractor and a grain drill under the shed, and don't want it to cave in on them. [Pauses.]

And I can't quite remember what's going on next. I might've awakened at this time and gone back to sleep again. I just don't know. But the next thing I remember is that—ah—it's very early morning. And I'm walking down the street that's behind the—ah—Institute here. And—ah—and also been a—a—a little bit of snow on the ground, maybe four or five inches deep. And the sky is cloudy. It's fairly dark. It's early in the morning before the sun's come up. Somebody coming off the street that's—comes up to me when I'm walking. He's the only one in sight. And he asked me if—if I can give him some morphine. I've never seen the man before. He isn't dressed very well, is kind of poorly dressed. Got what looks like an old army officer's short khaki jacket—ah—short overcoat and dark brown trousers. An—ah—very worn-out—worn-out brown shoes. Can't seem to place his face. It doesn't look familiar. But it doesn't look—looks kind of ill-bred. And he wants some morphine. He doesn't say what for. And for some reason or other I've got a—I've got some pills in my pocket in a little glass plastic vial. I don't know whether morphine comes in that shape, but that's the only [half-laugh] kind I had. And so I—ah—count out two of 'em. Give 'em to him. And for some reason or other I have to make sure and count the rest of 'em, to make sure that I've got the right number. And—ah—seems like it's an obsessive, that's a compulsive reaction, for some reason or other. I have to count those things, make sure I've got the right number. And then the fellow goes away. I didn't—I don't see him again.

And I go to—come to the New Haven Hospital. I don't know how I get inside. That part is uncertain. But once I get inside I'm in a series of rooms that are interconnected, and they all open onto one hall, but they've got doors from one to the other and they're finished in dark green, and got this old-fashioned glass—leaded glass windows. And—ah—the walls are lined with bookcases. They've got something that looks like conference tables in the center and around were chairs. Floor was covered by a—a dark brown rug. And I wander from one room to the other—ah—through the interconnecting doors. They're—I don't go out in the hallway. And I don't know just quite where I am. I don't fe—can't picture any place in New Haven Hospital that's like that, but it seems to me that I'm certain that it is New Haven Hospital. I mean it's not in Sterling Hall and it's not in the dormitory or anything. And then I, for some reason or other, I just fall asleep in one of the rooms. And—ah—I wake up and that's the end of the dream.

The subject felt that this was a "stupid" or "strange" dream. Most of his associations revolved around numbers: "I am worried about the number of the pills—did I count them right?—I gave him two and had eight left. I was worried about the right amount. I had to make sure I had the right number. I kept eight and gave him two, I did that a couple of times—oh, no, I didn't give him two a couple of times, but I gave him the two. First of all I counted them and made sure I had—knew how many I had, then I gave him two and then recounted the rest remaining one or two times—it's the numbers there that puzzle me and I had to figure them out."

In connection with morphine, the subject thought of codeine and then told of having been hospitalized six months before and of his dissatisfaction with that experience. No diagnosis was made, and he received no treatment. He was puzzled and annoyed and felt that he had lost time and had been kept in the hospital a week longer than he should have been. He was not informed of the purposes or results of the tests which were administered, and he felt that they had served the purposes of his doctors and not himself—but, typically, he said that "it didn't bother" him. With regard to morphine, he spoke of being accosted by men in the hospital neighborhood who would ask him for ten cents. He disliked this experience, did not know what to do, and said, "I can't predict what I'm going to do."

In regard to snow, he said, "I can't see any connection between the two dreams, but I just was worried—about a couple of feet of snow on the roof. I didn't want the roof to cave in; actually I had seen a roof cave in—not on our farm, but someone else had a shed roof, but that was three or four years ago and I didn't remember it particularly at the time. That part of it was fragmentary. I just don't see the connection between the first part of the dream and the second part."

In seeking indirect expression of the artificial complex, one may relate the giving of narcotics to a stranger to cheating (again a reversal: instead of taking he gives). But one does not have to seek the subject's preoccupation with the experimental situation, for it is clearly present. In the first part of the dream he is "worried about the depth of snow on the shed roof." Depth of snow may refer to both the depth of hypnosis and to sleep, and it may also mean that he is giving the experimenter a "snow job."[4] In the second part of the dream, the subject is walking early in the morning behind the building in which these experiments were conducted. He is approached by an ill-bred man who asks him for some morphine—a representation of the experimenter, who makes similarly questionable demands upon him, one of which is being fulfilled by the very fact of his having this dream

---

[4] While this sounds like a metaphorical interpretation, it probably reflects the subject's feelings during the induction of hypnosis. We have no record of how this subject felt during induction; however, for data about another subject see Gill and Brenman (1959).

at an early hour in the morning. He gives this man two pills, just as he presents the experimenter with two dreams. In discussing the dream, the subject wondered if he had told the hypnotist all of his dreams or had kept something back. (He really was "cheating"—cheating the hypnotist, as we found later, by not telling, or forgetting, another dream.)[5] He said that he was not aware of having any narcotics in his possession "until this fellow asked me for it." He also said that he would have forgotten the dream if he had not written it down at the experimenter's request.

Asked about the location of the dream, the subject said, "I've never seen one exactly like that before in the New Haven Hospital." He tried to find a similarity to some region in the hospital but was unable to do so, and finally dismissed it by saying, "It seems to be a rather silly dream." Actually the last part of the dream describes in exact detail the rooms in which the interviews were conducted. He failed to relate the dream to the room in which he was sitting and talking at the time, although the dream included a detailed description of the room's furnishings, the hallway leading to it, the bookshelves, and the colors of the walls and rug. The dream ends with his falling asleep in one of the rooms and then waking up. This parallels his behavior in each of the sessions: coming into the interview room, experiencing a sleeplike hypnosis, and then awakening. And morphine is a means of relieving pain and producing sleep.

His description of his hospitalization and the way in which he was treated may also express how he felt as a research subject in the present experiment. He was carefully observed but was not informed of the purpose of the procedure, which served the interest of the experimenters rather than his own.

In the same session, after these associations had been obtained, the same artificial complex—copying on an examination—was again suggested to him in hypnosis. To the question, "How do you feel?," the subject said, "Well, I'm glad it's over with, the test. I don't think I did too well on it. I never did like mathematics anyway, algebra and arithmetic. I'm a little bit remorseful, I guess you'd call it, because, oh, I looked over, I got one of the answers from the fellow in front of me. What the heck, I don't know why I did it." Amnesia for the complex was suggested, and he was told that he would have a dream.

[5] This acting out of the content of the suggested conflict—cheating—reminds one of Fisher's patient who brought him, instead of a dream, a chocolate Easter egg. See Fisher (1953).

(4) *Immediate Hypnotic Dream.*—I didn't—seemed to me I was outside a classroom and we were talking about—we were talking about an exam that we just had, a friend of mine and I. And—ah—I guess he—yeah—a friend of mine and I—we just—I don't know what we were particularly discussing, talking about questions and answers outside in the hall. And he was coughing, and so I told him that I had some cough drops in my locker. And we went, just went—the locker was right around the hall from it. And then I went out and—with him to my locker and gave him a couple of cough drops. And that's all. We were continue—we were talking about this exam.

Asked about the dream while still under hypnosis, the subject said, "It seemed like a perfectly normal thing to do, to talk over the exam afterwards, and a friend's coughing and you have some cough drops, and you give him a couple. The dream seemed very real. I'm glad the exam was over. I wasn't too happy about it. I didn't do too well, and matter of fact I had to take one answer from the guy who sat in front of me. Actually the guy I got the answer from was sitting adjacent to me over on the aisle on—over to my left side." To the cough drops, the subject associated codeine, which suppresses the cough reflex; and "the fellow in the dream coughed once in a while"— enough for him to notice; and "cough drops are something you'd take when you have a tickle in your throat."

In the manifest content of this hypnotic dream, the age of the dreamer and the setting and activity follow the suggested artificial complex. It becomes even more directly related to the complex by the subject's adding, as he talked about the dream, that in it he had copied from someone else—presumably his coughing friend. It would seem that the artificial complex is expressed with little distortion, except reversal: he gives to his friend instead of taking. The dream also contains elements which appear related to the earlier posthypnotic night dream: he gives his friend "a couple" of cough drops, just as he gave the stranger two morphine pills.

The subject felt uncomfortable and remembered having a tickle in his throat before the experiment. The friend from whom he copied the answer was identified as ". . . the guy—adjacent to me—over to my left," and this is where the hypnotist was sitting. Perhaps the subject was saying that he cheated by taking an answer from the hypnotist, and made up for it by giving the hypnotist two things.

The hypnotist, after obtaining this dream and associations, suggested that the subject would continue to feel strongly about this experience and that he would shortly have another dream about it. The hypnotist then briefly left the room. On his return he asked the subject what he had been doing and the subject said, ". . . thinking—working out a problem of energies—of ballistic energies—involving a bullet weighing 250 grams—the difficulty is the denominator—is 400, let's see, it's 450, 204, 240—and I get no further with it." The hypnotist then said, "You will have a dream," and the subject said:

(5) *Immediate Hypnotic Dream.*—Well, we're in algebra class. And ah—well, that's just an ordinary class, nothing in particular is going on, we review our homework and all that kind of stuff. And then the teacher hands out ah—this is at the end of the class—the teacher hands out ah—a series of papers, set of papers, the test we took the day before. This teacher is very peculiar in that he always passes out the, the ahm—the grades, the highest mark comes first, and he just goes on down the list that way. And ah—a little bit apprehensive. Don't know just what I did. I don't think I did too well. But as it turns out, I did pass it, not because I did so well, but [half-laugh] because everyone else did so poorly, not everyone else, but there were one or two people who did more poorly than I. And as I recall I got a 72, and that's just passing—passing is 70. That's all there is to it. I was greatly relieved at that.

Associating to the dream, the subject said that he disliked algebra, wondered about numbers and grades, puzzled about "the follow who announced the exam," and didn't usually dream "about this kind of thing."

The hypnotist then brought the subject out of hypnosis and asked him about the dream. The subject's associations clearly indicated connections between his dream and the hypnotic situation. For example, "The teacher was sitting as close to me as I am to you." He repeatedly suggested that he might have had another dream but forgot it—that is, that he had not told it to the hypnotist, or had cheated. The numbers 4, 5, and 2, which appeared in the ballistic problem, were numbers he had selected in the first session in the course of testing his amnesia. His feelings about the whole procedure may have been summed up by his thinking about a "problem of ballistics"—that is, about shooting the experimenter.

Feelings about the experiment and the hypnotist are probably the major stimulus of this dream, and the artificial complex can be conveniently used to screen them. The teacher who hands out tasks and reviews homework is the hypnotist, and the previous day's suggestion to dream was a test, as the whole experiment is—and as the hospitalization was; the teacher is peculiar to do the things he does, and all of it is "stupid." The concern and worry about the "right" numbers reveal their relation to the hypnotic situation when the numbers them-selves are examined. In these experiments, we induced hypnosis by counting from 1 to 10, induced amnesia by counting from 1 to 4, and, in testing amnesia in the first session, asked the subject first to see the numbers 4, 5, and 2. Moreover, the subject and the hypnotist were two (a pair), the subject had seen two hypnotists, there were two artificial complexes, and the subject was told to have two dreams about each.

The dreams obtained in our experiment expressed many of the ele-ments which occur in all dreams—for example, the expression of cur-rent life problems and anxieties, and unconscious wishes and fears, and such processes as symbolization, displacement, and condensation. Moreover, feelings aroused by the latent and manifest content of the artificial complex, which acted as a day residue, were expressed. But in addition to these elements, the hypnotic situation itself—its outer trappings as well as its emotional implications—appeared as a powerful stimulus and a major determinant of the hypnotic dreams.

Why is this stimulus so powerful? We believe that it derives its strength from the motivations and expectations which the subject brings into the experimental hypnotic situation.

In therapy employing hypnosis, the patient is seeking help from the hypnotist, who explicitly offers or promises to help if the patient will comply with his suggestions. The experimental subject volunteers to take part in an experiment in return for money; frequently states that he is curious about hypnosis; less frequently says that he hopes it may improve some mental function, such as memory; and, in our experience, only very rarely, perhaps after considerable contact with us in a long series of interviews, is aware that he is seeking psychiatric help. We believe that calling work with hypnosis "an experiment" often cloaks or conceals from both participants the fact that the subject seeks therapy. Until we know more about the psychology of the "good hypnotic subject," and his motives and expectations in volunteering for experimental work, we must regard as superficial for the subject differences between the therapeutic and the experimental hypnotic situations. We believe that our subjects are all motivated, often without awareness, by a need for help, which they hope will somehow be gratified through this relationship. This produces a conflict which seems to be present in all our subjects—namely, a conflict between their unverbalized expectations and what is explicitly offered by the experimenters. We offer them money to take part in an experiment, but they expect something else, don't know what, are disappointed and angry, and don't know why. Subject A, for instance, makes it quite clear that he went to the hospital for help and didn't get it. Most subjects believe that they come for other reasons, and only after many interviews does one begin to understand something of their motivation.

In hypnosis the "good" subject puts himself in another's hands, turning over certain critical faculties to him, doing what he suggests but retaining some control—that is, relinquishing certain ego functions, retaining others. Moreover, hypnosis itself is readily used in the service of defense. For example, hypnosis provides a way for the subject to do certain things without being aware of what he is doing, or to get someone else to command him to do something which is forbidden. Also, he not only can defend himself by submission and passivity, but is encouraged and praised when he does. He is invited to relinquish ego control to the hypnotist and told that he is a good subject if he does—a good subject when he can, or appears to, comply with the hypnotist and regresses at his suggestion or demand.

The hypnotist, with varying degrees of awareness, and varying degrees of emotional involvement, offers himself as an object for the subject's fantasies, actions, and acting out, for the expression of the subject's conscious and unconscious strivings. The hypnotist is often not aware of the unconscious meanings and imports of what is taking place. Generally the hypnotist feels that he is controlling the relationship, but actually what control he is able to exert depends upon how aware he is of what is going on at the time. This control often consists only of confining his and the subject's conscious behavior within certain boundaries Kanzer (1953). When one person hypnotizes another, who responsively carries out the hypnotist's instructions, it is easy for the hypnotist to believe that he is in complete control, that the subject is carrying out his intentions.

In studying our data and in listening to our colleagues, we have often been impressed with what we could speak of almost as control exerted by the subject—for example, to obtain a sought-after gratification. This sometimes becomes strikingly apparent when one asks a therapist why he decided to use hypnosis instead of some other procedure with a particular patient. One might state this another way in relation to the conflict between the experimenter's purposes and those of the subject: there is a great difference in the mind of the experimenter and in the mind of the person being hypnotized as to the meaning of the experimental situation.

Our subject, his behavior, and his hypnotic dreams reflect his feelings about the hypnotist and the experiment. They express conflict. On the one hand, he volunteers for this experiment because he is seeking something; on the other hand, in many ways he belittles and condemns the experiment because he does not get what he seeks. The course of this conflict is in part governed by the framework offered by the hypnotist and in part by the personality of the subject. Thus, in the first session, the hypnotist attempts to induce hypnosis, and then tells the subject that he has done something forbidden, and that he will have a dream about it. In the face of these demands, the subject at first objects and then complies by going into hypnosis and having a dream, or dream equivalent. By the evening of the first session, however, the dream mirrors an internal conflict in his feelings about the hypnotic situation and the hypnotist—a conflict which finally, in the fourth session, becomes much more explicit in the ballistic fantasy. The final immediate hypnotic dream, about passing the test given by the peculiar teacher, represents a resolution of the conflict by formal compliance, at the same time screening the combined criticism and rejection of the hypnotist and what he demands. Incidentally, in a series of dreams from a subject, later dreams often throw light upon earlier ones. We suspect that in this subject's first dream the experimental situation is a determinant of "we're playing at . . . construction engineers . . . building . . . in the dirt."

One has to consider that in this experiment we used artificial complexes which aroused anxiety in our subject, and earlier we thought that some of the subject's anger might be in response to the artificial complex. However, in later experiments in which we did not use artificial complexes but simply instructed our subjects to dream, we found that the dreams still expressed obvious and intense ambivalent feelings about the hypnotist and the hypnotic situation. Therefore we doubt that the artificial complex is a decisive determinant of these feelings, and believe rather that it is used to screen feelings about the hypnotist and the experimental hypnotic situation. It is possible for an experimenter to overlook the role of the actual situation as a dream stimulus because its meaning for the subject is lost sight of when the experimenter looks at the experiment only from his own point of view, or, to use another term, only from *his design.*

The importance of the hypnotic situation as a dream stimulus cannot be confirmed in all hypnotic dreams because associations to the dreams are sometimes meagre, particularly regarding feelings about the experiment. In such instances one can only show with certainty how the hypnotic situation is a day residue. For example, several subjects dreamed of the interview room and its furnishings. In many experiments reported in the literature, associations were not elicited, and expressions of feelings about the hypnotist may have been actively discouraged. Despite the absence of associations, however, some of the dreams are striking by their focus upon and intensity of feeling about the hypnotic situation. To be sure, each subject focuses upon certain, personally meaningful, aspects of the hypnotic situation to express his involvement. Subject A, for instance, focused on numbers.

Another subject, working with a different hypnotist, dreamed that he was out in a field where a friend was flying a model airplane. The plane was spinning around the subject's head. He tried unsuccessfully to fly it, and the dream ended with the plane flying around him, unpleasantly close. One can connect playing with a toy to the artificial complex, but the subject, in associating to the airplane, told of having a spinning sensation in his head as he went into hypnosis, and then remembered that in an earlier hypnotic session, when tested for amnesia, he had felt the same spinning sensation in his head. He went on to describe the discomfort of having this airplane pressing against him and trying to push him somewhere.

Another subject, with still another hypnotist, began her first dream with, "I was in a hospital and there were many patients there, and they were in bed, sick. It was—this is in a mental institution. And all the people that were caring for them didn't seem to—didn't seem to really care." The building in which we do our experimental work houses a mental hospital, and we are all members of the psychiatric department.

The meaning of the experimental situation for the subject has been overlooked in much hypnotic work. It may be of minor importance if the experimenter is interested, for example, only in demonstrating that thoughts may be translated into symbols; but it is of major importance if one studies larger areas of behavior. Thus it is imperative to take cognizance of the feelings and thoughts which have brought the subject to volunteer for the experiment, and all his feelings and thoughts about what is going on. We have learned that one begins to know something of all this by talking extensively with the subject before the experiment, during the induction of hypnosis, and during hypnosis itself, and by eliciting associations to the dream and talking over the experiment with him after it is over.

In his readiness to be hypnotized, the subject expresses conscious and unconscious expectations of repeating past experiences in which libidinal as well as aggressive strivings and wishes were gratified or frustrated. He carries these expectations into the hypnotic situation and there partly expresses them or enacts them in ways comparable to what would be called the transference in analysis. For this reason so many relatively neutral procedures carried out by the hypnotist appear in the dream as day residues. They screen intense feelings about the hypnotist and the hypnotic situation. While the psychoanalyst is alert to the expression of transference feelings in the analytic situation, in the analysand's behavior, and in his dreams, many experimenters have neglected to take account of the existence of transference feelings because they experience such feelings as a complication or an obstacle.

Schroetter (1911) and Roffenstein (1924) centering their interest on symbolism, report hypnotic dreams which, when restudied, suggest many relationships to the experimental situation. Farber and Fisher (1943) note the influence of the sex of the hypnotist, or the presence of a third person in the room, upon the dreams they obtained. Mazer mentions the influence of the hypnotic relationship and suggests a technique for studying it—namely, suggesting that the subject dream about "me" or about the "hypnotic relationship"—and he reports several dreams so obtained (Mazer, 1951). Other investigators have also felt that only through some alteration of the procedure does the influence of the experimental situation become evident in hypnotic dreams. Exceptions are Fisher (1953a, 1953b, 1954a, 1954b) and Kubie and Margolin (1944). Fisher had observed what we here present in detail—the importance of the experimental situation and surroundings as dream stimuli and day residues. Kubie and Margolin discuss the conscious and unconscious attitudes arising between the hypnotist and the subject, and state: "When the hypnotic state is fully achieved, an extensive carryover occurs from this pre-hypnotic state comparable precisely to the carry-over into the content of any dream of the residues from the emotionally incomplete experiences of the preceding day (the so-called 'day residue')." Schafer (1954) has described similar factors in Rorschach testing.

In our own work, we have come to three main conclusions concerning the importance of the hypnotic situation as a major dream stimulus. First, if this is overlooked, hypnotic dreams are more difficult to understand—or, more important, may be misunderstood in the service of a particular hypothesis which the experimenter is trying to test. That is, failure to understand a dream is less likely to produce errors in experimental or clinical work than is the assumption that the dream bears a one-to-one relationship to some known experimental stimulus, such as a word, idea, or artificial complex. It is accepted in clinical practice that dreams are overdetermined. The probability of overdetermination, however, is likely to be overlooked in experimental work by an experimenter who is looking for certain things. In our experiments, the hypnotic situation as a determinant came to our attention only because of the comparison of data from a series of subjects working with different hypnotists.

Second, the hypnotic situation must be carefully scrutinized in all experimental work utilizing hypnosis; such scrutiny may add considerably to the understanding of the behavior observed and the results obtained. Such a scrutiny by Freud of the analytic situation made that situation a standard one, from which general deductions could be drawn and validated. To what extent such a scrutiny can be carried out in a hypnotic setting remains an unsolved problem. Certainly there are many obstacles.

Third, our work highlights the importance of a careful appraisal of the experimental situation in *all* research work involving people. In nonhypnotic and nonanalytic research the necessity for such an appraisal may be overlooked because the relationship between experimenter and subject is less intense.

In general, hypnotic dreams express the subject's personal problems. They also express his feelings about being a research subject; about volunteering for research, but actually seeking something else, and the conflict over this; about being interviewed in the service of the experimenter's research interests and not his own; about being hypnotized, with all the possible intoxicating, assaultive, and gratifying characteristics of hypnosis; and about the suggestions and instructions given in the experiments to do something, to feel something, to regress, to experience a suggested artificial conflict, and to remember and tell the experimenter, or to forget. They portray the physical setting in which the experiment takes place: the room and its surroundings, the observation and recording, and the presence of assistants and helpers. They are also the fulfillment of the essential contract made between the experimenter and the subject, representing both compliance with what the experimenter requests and defenses against this compliance. The hypnotic dream attempts to communicate all of this to the experimenter.

Experimental Paradigms for the
Hypnotic Investigation of Dream Symbolism

BY C. SCOTT MOSS

The process of symbolization has been both the most intriguing and controversial aspect of the rich fabric of theory advanced by psychoanalysis and, unfortunately, the most resistant to scientific exploration. This paper will outline a variety of experimental approaches to the investigation of dream symbolism through innovations in hypnotic technique. The value of hypnosis in dream research is that it seemingly provides access to the symbol-translating mechanism. For instance, recall of forgotten dream elements can be facilitated, some subjects are able to "dream" upon command, and others demonstrate an increased capacity to interpret symbolic materials (Erickson and Kubie, 1938, 1940; Farber and Fisher, 1943; Rapaport, 1951; Moss, 1957c). The principal measuring instrument employed throughout these studies was the semantic differential, a method specifically designed to provide an objective measurement of the connotative (feeling) aspects of meaning.[1]

SOURCE. Reprinted by permission from *International Journal of Clinical and Experimental Hypnosis,* 9 (3), 105–117 (July, 1961).

Presented at the XVI International Congress of Psychology, Bonn, Germany, August, 1960. Awarded the Certificate of Merit as the Best Research Paper on Hypnosis in 1961 by The Society for Clinical and Experimental Hypnosis.

[1] The semantic differential is not a particular test but rather a highly generalizable operation of measurement which can be adapted to specific research problems. Its originators postulate a geometrical model in the form of a semantic space defined by logical opposites. Factor analysis was used to identify the independent dimensions of this space, representing the ways human beings make meaning judgments. The generality of this factor structure was further tested by varying subject populations, concepts judged, type of judgmental situation and the factoring method used in analyzing data.

The measuring operation or semantic differential can be described as follows: Adjectives were identified as representative of the major dimensions along with meaningful processes vary; these have a high coverage of meaning on one factor and a negligible amount on the others. These logical opposites are used to define the ends of seven point scales. In practice, an individual judges a particular concept against a set of these scales. Judgments result in the successive allocation of a concept to a point in multidimensional space. In this manner, change in the meaning of a concept over time, the subtle differences between two or more concepts, and individual differences in the meaning of a single concept may be quantitatively represented. (Refer to Moss, 1960b, for a resume of current research with the semantic differential.)

In an early experiment (Moss, 1957b), an attempt was made to test the psychoanalytic idea of dream symbol disguise, by translating it into the operationally defined concept of *semantic distance*. Ordinarily choice of a symbol should be determined by the similarity of mediational processes between a potential symbol and the latent content to be represented. However, according to Freud, anxiety-stimulating latent content results in the choice of symbols that are semantically distant; a symbol that is semantically distant from the latent content becomes unintelligible and may be said to be disguised.

Seventy-six dreams of a single patient in psychotherapy over a year period were intensively studied. A form of the semantic differential was used to measure the distance between symbol and latent content when the covert content was anxiety-arousing and when it was not. In operational terms, disguise would be indicated by a relative increase in semantic distance coincident with anxiety.

Identification of the meaning of dream symbols used by the patient-subject was a primary problem, and reliance upon conventional methods of interpretation was supplemented by training the patient to interpret his own dreams under hypnosis. The patient free-associated to the dream elements, first in the waking and then in the hypnotic state, in order to identify the latent content. Associative material obtained in hypnosis was invariably centrally related to the meaning of the dream.

The following dream demonstrates the highly meaningful nature of the patient's dreams and his facility in dream interpretation.

The patient and his wife are going on an ocean voyage. They find the gangplank steep and lined with girls. On deck the captain inquires whether the patient has a newspaper. When the patient replies that he does not, the captain assures him that he'll find one in his cabin. The patient next travels slowly down a spiral slide and finds himself seated in the dining room. There he refuses an offer of hamburgers. He is suddenly ashore again, standing beside a convertible. A voice says, "Tell your uncle he is holding up the works."

Waking associations. The dream was essentially without meaning to the patient. The predominate emotion was apprehension. The significant associations were as follows. *Water:* the patient had long suffered a mild aquaphobia. *Voyage:* his only sea voyage was in military service. *Hamburgers:* the patient was surprised at his refusal since he liked hamburgers. *Uncle:* a favorite with the patient.

Hypnotic reconstruction. The patient's first association was to *ocean voyage.* "The phrase 'going from the old to the new' enters my mind." He then drew the analogy that therapy was a means of exchanging an old, unsatisfactory adjustment for a new mode, and in this sense is like a journey. "I also find myself thinking of the voyage I took in service and how frightened I was." Therapy is therefore initially perceived as "a voyage on dangerous waters." (Later it became apparent that the patient unconsciously associated the awesome, cruel, overpowering quality of water with intense hostile impulses threatening his control and self-esteem.) The next association was to *gangplank:* "I remember how very steep it seemed—it was hard getting aboard. My *wife* being with me meant that this is *our* problem—she's the main reason I'm here." The *line of girls* momentarily thwarted recognition, but the patient then stated quite positively they represented different aspects of the relationship with his wife. To *ship captain* he associated, "Men who are strong and strict, but just—it makes me think of in here, of you, that you will help channel my thoughts into the right direction, also that it will not be an easy job, either." The *newspaper* was explained as a reference to the dreams he had been told to report, i.e., "both are a chronical of events." "I remember telling you I didn't dream very often and you said 'don't worry about it.' 'Below decks,' makes me think of 'below the surface'—dreams come from below the surface when one sleeps, in the cabin or bedroom." The patient interpreted the *slide* as, "a roundabout way of reaching a goal," meaning his old inadequate mode of adjustment. "I'm afraid that when the going gets tough, I'll slide back into the old way of thinking." "*Hamburgers* make me think of 'food for thought'—they represent the things we're talking about here, things that are distasteful and I don't want to face or swallow." The *return to shore*, was interpreted by the patient as another expression of ambivalence towards therapy, that is, his fear that the content discussed would be unpleasant and he would want to escape. The *convertible*, like the slide, was translated as an old and established but "unsafe" (neurotic) mode of goal attainment. The verbal reference to the *uncle* stimulated recall of a recent statement by the uncle to the effect that the primary defect of the patient was a lack of self-confidence. This remark sensitized the patient to his tendency to withdraw from problem situations and it made it difficult for him to retreat from therapy, i.e., "This remark keeps me from using the convertible." The three component parts of the dream are thus: ambivalence towards therapy, rejection of the situation, but inability to return to the old adjustment.

When the patient presented such a dream, one or more symbols were selected, and he was asked to rate these in-the-dream context on the differential. The patient would associate to the dream, first in the waking and then in the hypnotic state, in order to establish the latent meaning. Subsequently, in the waking state with complete recall for his dream analysis, the patient rated the identified latent content.

No adequate measure of the anxiety associated with a specific dream symbol was available; however, independent measures (psychological tests and staff ratings) indicated progressive patient improvement over a year's time. In addition, five clinicians agreed in classifying 13 of the patient's dreams as highly anxious ("nightmares"), 11 of which occurred in the first half of therapy. Contrary to psychoanalytic theory, the semantic distances between the mediational processes of dream symbols and things symbolized, as reflected on the differential, were not significantly greater for the first half as compared with the second half of therapy. Thus the hypothesis that dream symbols acquire a disguise function under the impetus of anxiety was not substantiated.

Mature consideration, however, led to the recognition that the semantic differential had definite limitations in detecting the effect of a dream censorship process. While many competent therapists seem agreed that the affective qualities of the dream are usually not subject to distortion, this is the aspect of meaning primarily measured by the differential. Needed was the development of a denotative differential.[2] Since the relationship between symbol and latent content is typically quite tenuous, such a measuring instrument would also have to be extremely sensitive to relatively minute and highly individual aspects of meaning, rather than measuring the common variance among groups of subjects.

A second study used a form of the differential composed of scales designed to measure physical qualities (e.g., large-small, wet-dry, long-short, angular-rounded, etc.); subjects were also instructed to respond to the "physical" rather than the "feeling" characteristics of symbols and things symbolized. Instead of spontaneous night dreams, data this time consisted of hypnotically induced "dreams."

Three normal, psychologically naïve subjects were first intensively studied through interview and projective techniques in order to identify areas of personal conflict. They were then induced to "dream" under hypnosis about both pleasant and unpleasant, or anxiety-arousing, personal content. The hypnotic products were typically similar to the autosymbolic phenomena experienced in the transitional hypna-

---

[2] Dreams reported during psychotherapy reveal many examples of denotative distortion. One illustration is that of a 34-year-old female patient who reported that at age 8, she had experienced a particularly vivid, recurring dream of being terrified at the pursuit of a tiny white dog. Hypnosis facilitated understanding that the dog had represented her recent discovery of death. As a child she had conceived of death as large, black, cold, ugly and threatening, and had attempted to neutralize this fear by representing it in her dream as a small, white, warm, cuddly puppy. Thus the denotative qualities were distorted to the extreme, that is, representation by a diametrically opposite symbol, but the affect remained appropriate to the latent content of the dream. The resistances which maintain repression are nicely illustrated through employment of hypno-projective dream analysis (cf. Moss et al., 1962)

gogic state between waking and sleep; while symbols were employed, they appeared relatively poor in multiple meaning.

A female subject's concern regarding a dependency conflict is depicted in this brief, representative "dream."

I am hit by a big truck which comes to rest on me. It is very heavy. I appeal to my parents to remove it but they ignore me. I struggle very hard and finally succeed in pushing it off.

In every instance the subject was instructed to be amnesic for the dream suggestion. At the conclusion of a dream the subject rated selected dream symbols on the differential (e.g.: *truck*). She was next asked to associate to the dream in the waking and hypnotic states in order to clarify and confirm the meaning of the latent content and to rate this content on the differential (e.g.: *guilt related to my struggle for independence*).

Ratings of 42 symbols and the corresponding latent content were obtained from 31 anxiety provoking dreams, while 34 such measurements were obtained from 22 dreams with pleasant content. The average semantic distance under the two conditions for each of the three subjects, did not differ significantly. These investigations again failed to support the hypothesized effect of a censorship mechanism; the results of both studies suggest that the dream work is simply a translation, representing what a person thinks while asleep. An unanswered question was the exact nature of the relationship between spontaneous and hypnotic dreams, and whether censorship could be expected to manifest itself in the latter.[3]

---

[3] Authorities are not agreed as to the exact relationship between hypnotic and spontaneous night dreams. M. Brenman (1949) states, "It is curious that investigators appear to have taken it for granted that the hypnotic suggestion to 'dream' issues in a dream." She argues that hypnotic dreams are relatively oversimplified, less influenced by unconscious thought processes, and are basically motivated by the desire to preserve the relationship with the hypnotist, rather than preservation of sleep. However, this argument is greatly weakened by her admission that spontaneous night dreams are by no means homogeneous in their expressive form and like the hypnotically induced dream, may range from an embellished reminiscence to a highly elaborated, symbolized product. In contrast, M. Mazer (1951) states that a dream should be defined by the nature of the production not by the circumstances of its occurrence, and that the hypnotic dream possesses all of the distortions characteristic of the regular night dream. It seems agreed that the hypnotically induced dream varies greatly, but that a general, unstructured posthypnotic suggestion to be carried out during regular sleep results in a product very similar to a spontaneous night dream. Present experiments are based on the assumption that hypnotic and spontaneous dreams are sufficiently similar in the employment of symbolism to allow cross-generalization.

Hypnosis provides a unique opportunity of studying the dynamic interaction involved in the acquisition and modification of the significance of signs and symbols, and a third study focused attention on the mode of symbolic transformation per se.

Four hospitalized, neurotic patients were again trained to produce hypnotic dreams, a procedure providing the opportunity to observe the transformation of a suggested content into its symbolic equivalent. An important innovation was the training of subjects to project *static* symbolic images on an imagined movie screen, such that a single symbol would depict a suggested content. Freud recognized that dream symbols are typically overdetermined, and this mechanism of condensation (in combination with displacement) was accorded primary responsibility for the unintelligibility of dreams. It is also a factor which greatly complicates precise semantic measurement. The present approach was an attempt to partially control the effect of condensation while studying displacement or symbolization. In addition, suggestions were restricted to the symbolization of simple, concrete sexual anatomy and activities. Abstract latent content is often difficult to rate against a denotative differential (just as a connotative differential was not applicable to many varieties of concrete manifest content). It was hoped to tailor both content levels for use with the denotative differential. This emphasis on sexual content was consistent with the psychoanalytic penchant for assigning sexual significance to dream symbols.[4]

Sometimes subjects responded with a single symbolization; they also responded with series of symbols, each representing the suggested content. For instance, one female subject was unhappily married, and possessed an intense fear, dislike, and envy of men. When asked to symbolize the male organ, she perceived in rapid succession: "A knife, a bull with tremendous horns, an enema bulb." Her hypnotic associations revealed that she thought of men as aggressively assaulting women. She also produced a vivid memory of impotent rage towards her mother who frequently "violated me" with enemas as a child. Her symbolizations of the female organ were also revealing of highly personal attitudes: "An outhouse, a pedestrian traffic-tunnel (where men urinate), a door on which hung a sign 'No Peddlers or Agents,' and

---

[4] A characteristic suggestion given subjects was as follows: "In a moment you will fall deeply asleep. When you do, a dream will form. You will find yourself seated in a movie theater looking at a blank screen. You will then clearly see (a suggested sexual content) followed immediately by a second picture or series of pictures which represent or stand for the same thing; just as you might have experienced it in a dream."

a new green car parked beside a pile of breadcrusts." The last represented her envy of male prerogatives. This approach allowed objective
measurement, and identification of the elements of meaning common
to a variety of symbolizations of a single latent content.

The possible methodological variations provided by hypnosis in the
study of the symbolic process in action are practically unlimited, and
several additional approaches are suggested in the following examples.
Subjects were instructed to project a series of static symbols, each
of which would become increasingly transparent in meaning, until
the latent content was directly represented (a desymbolizing process).
For example, when a second single, female subject was given a suggestion to symbolize the male genitalia, she responded:

"I see a couple of small peanuts. They are moving about, they won't
stand still. Now they have spots like potatoes. Sprouts are growing out
of the spots—they are changing, curving. It looks like a unicorn with
a horn on its nose. I just see the head. There are circular lines around
the horn. The head is changing again, into a sac—it is wrinkled. Oh!
testicles and penis!"

A second type, detailed experiment with the same subject will demonstrate the potentialities inherent in another variation, that of directly
suggesting the symbols a subject should use to depict a specified
content.

1. The subject rated three sexual concepts on the differential, *penis,
vagina, intercourse,* interspersed among a dozen irrelevant (nonsexual)
concepts. Hypnosis was then induced and she was instructed to fall
deeply asleep and to have a dream of being seated in a movie theater
looking at a blank screen. She was instructed to perceive the male
sex organ on the screen, and that it would be followed immediately
by a second picture which represented or stood for the same thing,
"just as you might experience it in your dreams."

2. The patient signaled the beginning and termination of a dream.
Still under hypnosis she reported having seen "a man with no clothes
on—the lower part of his body. *It* looked big and hard and bony.
It gave me a funny feeling in my stomach." She reported that this
image was then replaced by a "necktie with a tight knot in the end
of it." The patient was told that when she awakened she would be
amnesic for this episode until a given signal, whereupon she would
remember *only* the necktie (not its covert meaning).

3. The patient awoke, smiled, and apologized, saying that she must
have dozed off. Questioning elicited no apparent memory for what
had transpired. She was then asked to rate the general concept "neck-

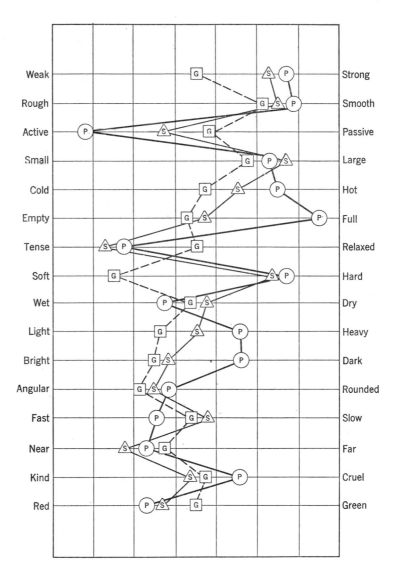

Figure 1. Comparison of three concepts: *penis* ⓟ, rated prior to experiment; *necktie* △, as an unconscious symbol for penis, rated in dream context; necktie ⑤, general or nonsymbol, rated later out of the dream context. Quantitative relationship (D statistic): penis versus necktie-nonsymbol = 7.68; penis versus necktie-symbol = 4.80; necktie-nonsymbol versus necktie-symbol = 5.48. (The smaller the number the closer the relationship.)

tie" on the differential. Next she was asked her associations to the concept. "An article of men's wearing apparel. I think of them as being attractive. They are so versatile and come in so many different shapes colors, sizes, and designs. I also think of them as reflecting the personalities of the men who wear them."

4. At the pre-arranged signal she instantly and with seeming surprise, recalled the necktie she perceived on the screen (but not its association with the male organ). She was asked to visualize the scene as vividly as possible, and then to rate this specific necktie on the differential (refer to Figure 1).

5. The patient entered a second hypnotic trance, and was again told to perceive the movie screen and upon it the now familiar necktie, but that this time the necktie would depict the female genitalia.[5] She was again requested to be amnesic for the suggestion. Upon indication that the "dream" had ceased, she awoke and stated that she had again seen the necktie but that this time it was a "red necktie, just about the reddest necktie you can imagine; it had a crease down the center of it and seemed quite curved."

6. She rated this new necktie on the differential. Asked to associate to the new tie, she replied, "The red makes me think of something that is very bright and active, something which is very stimulating, it is definitely more feminine than most colors that men will wear." (Refer to Figure 2.)

7. The subject was placed in a third hypnotic state and was instructed that this time she would briefly witness herself having intercourse, and that this scene would then be replaced by another picture representing the same thing to her; she was told to remember only the latter scene.

After signalling completion of the dream," the subject reported that she had seen, "A hotdog between two slices of bun. It was an extremely large hotdog, pointing straight upwards, and also there was a large slice of onion between it and the bun." She was instructed to be amnesic for the entire experience.

8. Upon awakening the subject was asked to rate "hotdog" on the differential. By a pre-arranged signal she next remembered the hotdog seen on the screen (but not the immediately preceding scene or latent content) and was asked to rate it.

---

[5] Another test of a prevalent psychoanalytic belief suggests itself here. To paraphrase Jones (1948, p. 98), an individual is free to choose his dream symbols or to make new ones, what he cannot do is to give a regular (universal) symbol a different meaning.

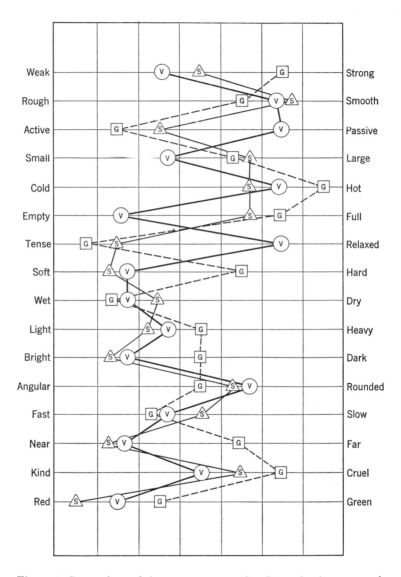

Figure 2. Comparison of three concepts: *vagina* Ⓥ rated prior to experiment; *necktie* △, a male symbol which subject was required to use as a female symbol, rated in the dream context; *necktie* ◻, nonsymbol, rated out of the dream context. (Quantitative relationships: vagina versus necktie-female symbol – 7.28; vagina versus penis = 11.22; intercourse versus necktie-female symbol = 6.56; vagina versus necktie-nonsymbol = 6.40; intercourse versus necktie-nonsymbol = 7.81.)

9. The patient was returned to a hypnotic state, and was asked to associate to each of the symbols she had used and to attempt an interpretation of their meaning.

First necktie—"As I said before, an article of men's clothing, something intimately related to a man, something definitely masculine. The straightness of it makes me think maybe it is starched or stiff. The knot in the end looks like, well, like a man's organ."

Second necktie—"That reminds me of a man's organ, too, but it's different somehow. The curve reminds me of the curve of a woman's body. The red makes me think of something that is very much alive; it makes me think of the vagina. I connect the idea of redness with the act of menstruation. I feel afraid of the penis though I know it would not really hurt me, but I am afraid it would make me pregnant. The vagina is not pregnant when it menstruates. The crease down the front of the tie is actually the opening of the woman's organ, and the curve is the shape of the vagina, too. Actually, this necktie is both male and female, but the female seems to predominate. The first necktie was only the penis. Both of them are stimulating, but the second is more so. It sort of makes me think of a penis being in a vagina, that is, of sexual intercourse."

Hotdog—"Well, the hotdog is the penis, too. It is very pointed and it is slanted—it is slanting away from me. This causes the thought that I mustn't touch it because it would make me pregnant. The bun is the vagina, and the fact that it is holding the weiner indicates that sexual intercourse is taking place. The whiteness of the onion indicates purity to me—the need to avoid having intercourse so that pregnancy will not occur. It, and the slant of the hotdog, and the redness of the necktie all represent the same thing—the need to avoid sexual contact."

10. The patient was obviously distressed at this point and was solicited to talk further about her feelings. She responded that the hotdog had brought up a "forgotten" subject to her, "Something that I had put out of my mind and refused to even think about anymore." She then related that six months previous she had gone on a picnic with her boy friend and they had experienced intercourse for the first time. She spontaneously recalled a specific memory of lying wrapped in the blanket with him after having completed the act, and glancing up over his shoulder and seeing a half-eaten, shriveled hotdog. She laughed and commented that it looked like his "hotdog." Thus, the choice of the symbol produced in the experimental situation was apparently determined by this repressed but dynamically active experience. She further volunteered that later she had experienced several nightmares in which she was choking on a hotdog, and that in the past six months for reasons until now unknown to her, hotdogs had become completely unappetizing.

It is of considerable interest to note that the subject is not merely symbolizing automaton, but responds with symbolic productions which graphically depict personal needs and problems. Rich potentialities for the clinical employment of this technique as a projective method for personality exploration have only recently been explored (Watkins, 1956). Here the suggestion activated a very real conflict situation for the subject, reflecting both sensitivity of the method and the precautions that must be observed in its experimental application.

The remainder of the paper will deal with one specific application of the demonstrated methods, the study of the process of cognitive interaction involved in meaning formation and change which Osgood et al. refer to as the principle of congruity (Osgood, 1957, p. 200). Briefly, this principle states that whenever two signs having different meanings (different mediation processes and different profiles against the semantic differential) are related, the meaning of each shifts toward agreement with the other, the magnitude of the shift being *inversely proportional to the intensity* (degree of polarization, as reflected on the differential) of the interacting reactions. Two signs are said to be congruent to the extent that their mediating reactions are equally intense, either in the same (compatible) direction, or in the opposite direction. Results obtained in the reported investigations suggest several features concerning the process of dream symbol acquisition and modification.

1. At the moment of symbol selection a situation exists in which the latent impulse "scans" a pool of potential symbols which share one or more physionomic qualities with the content to be represented (e.g., the similarity in shape between hotdog and penis). Logically, the analogy may be quite tenuous, of course. Differences are largely disregarded, with two important exceptions: (*a*) Each dream has a general theme or setting [e.g., psychotherapy = a dangerous ocean voyage], determined by the predominant affect and the selection of one or two key symbols. The remaining symbols will tend to be consistent [e.g., gangplank = resistance, ship captain = therapist, cabin = sleep, etc.]. This gives the dream its theatrical quality. (*b*) The *preinteraction* location of the potential symbol in relation to the latent content cannot be highly incongruent with respect to the emotional aspects of meaning. This would appear to account for seeming preference for symbols which, in their own right (independent of the dream context), are often innocuous or affectively neutral.

2. The fact that the latent content has, typically, powerful associated affective and cognitive processes, which in combination with the affec-

tivity neutral (or possibly congruent) potential symbol, determines the flow of significance from the primary sign (A) to the secondary idea or symbol (B). These observations are completely predictable from the principle of congruity. The more polarized one sign is, relative to the other, the less change it undergoes. Where one member of an assertion is neutral, *all* the shift in meaning is concentrated on this concept.

3. Insofar as B receives its meaning from identification with A, it functions as its symbolic equivalent. In the dream a momentary situation obtains in which the interaction is maximized, that is, the meaning of each sign is shifted totally to the point of mutual congruence. At this moment the dreamer is completely credulous: He accepts the symbol as reality! However, the tendency is, after such cognitive interaction, for the meanings of related signs to "bounce" back to their original locus, and the whole phenomena has a mercurial quality which defies direct measurement, although the employment of hypnotic techniques allows almost immediate access to and reproducibility of this symbol-making process. When the dreamer awakens, there will be a reduction in the congruity effect both as a function of time and an altered state of consciousness (the semantic distance between latent and manifest content increases to the point where dream symbols become largely unintelligible).

It should be noted that when the affect associated with the primary idea is too intense (as in the last case example), an individual continues to experience a continuing, disturbing, logically incomprehensible identity of signs (hotdog = intercourse) resulting in a phobic reaction, or in the extreme case, a psychotic delusion or hallucination.

SUMMARY

Several forms of Osgood's Semantic Differential were employed in the study of spontaneous and hypnotically induced dreams. While the use of hypnosis to investigate symbolization is not original with these studies, the feasibility of objectification of this elusive psychological phenomenon has been demonstrated, including a step towards identification of the psychological laws underlying the acquisition and modification of sign significance. The primary intent of the paper is to stimulate and provoke experimentation in an important area of human behavior long resistant (resisted) to scientific investigation.

The Ability of Hypnotic Subjects to Interpret Symbols

BY C. SCOTT MOSS AND JAMES G. STACHOWIAK

INTRODUCTION

The long association of hypnosis with the sensational, magical and supernatural has led to the widespread belief that the hypnotized subject possesses abilities which clearly transcend normal volitional limits. This paper is concerned with one aspect of the hypnotized subject's reputed increase in mental prowess, his ability to intuit the meaning of symbolic phenomena.

Numerous investigators, beginning with Schroetter (1911), Roffenstein (1924), and Nachmansohn (1925), reported the ability of hypnotized individuals to "dream" in response to suggestion. Farber and Fisher (1943) confirmed these observations, and in addition found that approximately 20 per cent of their hypnotic subjects were adept at translating a variety of symbolic content, including their own dreams and those of others. However, Farber and Fisher essentially negate this latter premise by attributing the generally sexualized interpretations of their subjects to the nature of the hypnotic relationship. Perhaps the clearest statement of the affirmative position is provided by Erickson and Kubie (1940) who, in an article based on the ability of one hypnotized subject to translate the cryptic automatic writing of another conclude:

> The main event of this unplanned and unexpected experience is in itself worthy of record for it is an arresting fact that one human being while in a dissociated trance-like condition can accurately decipher the automatic writing of another—writing which neither of the two subjects was able to decipher while in states of normal consciousness. The observation stresses from a new angle a fact that has often been emphasized by those who have studied unconscious processes but which remains none the less mysterious—namely, that underneath the diversified nature of the consciously organized aspects of the personality, the unconscious talks in a language which has laws so constant that the unconscious of one individual is better

SOURCE. Reprinted by permission from *Journal of Projective Techniques,* **27** (1), 92–97 (1963).

equipped to understand the unconscious of another than the conscious aspect of the personality of either (pp. 61–62).

In view of the provocative nature of assertions such as these, it is rather surprising that so little experimentation has been undertaken in this area.

EXPERIMENTAL DATA

Three test items were used to evaluate the ability of hypnotized subjects to interpret the meaning of symbolic productions. These included a fairy tale (Little Red Riding Hood), a brief Rorschach protocol, and a dream. The fairy tale was taken from Fromm's *The Forgotten Language* (1951), and his interpretation was used as the determinant of correctness; the meaning of the Rorschach protocol, chosen from a paper by Moss (1957a), had been consensually validated by three schizophrenic patients, while the dream had been produced and interpreted by a patient possessed of singular and impressive skill in interpreting his own dreams under hypnosis (Moss, 1961). In a few instances, time permitting and where a subject showed exceptional promise of interpretative ability, two additional items were administered, a Biblical excerpt (Jonah and the Whale, also chosen from Fromm), and a detailed example of cryptic automatic writing reported in the aforementioned article by Erickson and Kubie. These items were chosen deliberately to represent a wide range of difficulty and a variety of validating criteria. Each item was treated separately in the analysis of results, and responses were judged on the basis of (*a*) over-all agreement with the criterion variable, and (*b*) the specific interpretation of seven or eight of the most prominent symbols appearing in each test item. Data were also scrutinized for communality of interpretation among subjects, regardless of "objective" correctness.

A frequent criticism of investigations involving hypnosis is that they lack necessary controls (Orne, 1959). In a preliminary phase of this study, the three standard items were presented to 22 waking subjects for interpretation. To insure serious motivation, these volunteer college subjects were told that recent research had conclusively demonstrated that symbolism was a highly meaningful language, and that many people had an unsuspected or latent ability to understand this form of communication. They were also instructed to avoid approaching the task in an intellectual or logical manner; instead, they were asked to relax, free associate, and to await spontaneous insight. While a modest range of individual differences obtained, there was no evidence that any subject possessed impressive ability at symbol translation.

A sizeable group of college students were next screened on the basis of the Friedlander-Sarbin Scale of Hypnotic Suggestibility (1938), and 15 hypnotizable subjects were selected (eight of whom were full somnambules). Each subject was utilized as his own control, since all test items were first presented in the waking and then in the hypnotic state for interpretation. This was a very time-consuming procedure, of course, requiring 4–5 hours per subject. Subjects were requested under both conditions to free associate to the item as a whole and then to selected symbols. A method designed to facilitate imaginal associations was also used. Subjects were asked to imagine a movie screen and on it the symbol in question. They were then told that at a given signal the symbol would be automatically replaced by a second image, representative of the underlying, covert content (Moss, 1961).

Results were disappointingly negative in terms of agreement with the external validating criteria; nor did subjects demonstrate any appreciable agreement among themselves. There were occasional insights, usually attributable to the transparency of the symbolized content and the applicability of conventional social stereotypes; for example, many subjects interpreted "wolf" as meaning a predatory male, or interpreted the flight of Jonah as an attempt to escape the wrath of God.[1]

The chief differences in the waking and hypnotic interpretations were that the latter showed greater embellishments, the items became more personally meaningful, and the interpretations were reported with a feeling of greater subjective "certainty." The need for "cognitive congruence" was nicely illustrated in numerous subjects who offered related interpretations of different test items. Several even stated the belief that because of the perceived similarity all items must have been produced by the same person, thus exemplifying the existence of a central theme which preoccupied them to the extent that it sought expression regardless of the specific stimulus content. A final striking difference was that as the investigators pressed subjects for interpretive significance in hypnosis, sudden closures were often effected, though the responses were obviously of a highly personalized nature.

Table 1 depicts the waking and hypnotic interpretations of one

---

[1] In his investigations Hall (1953a) concluded that "many persons have real talent for dream interpretation," and attributed this ability to their familiarity with colloquial speech (slang), which has many parallel expressions to the symbols employed in dreams.

subject of Little Red Riding Hood. This was one of the most encouraging single responses and represents a promise unfulfilled by other subjects, or even with this subject on most other test items. Most instructive and typical, however, was the degree of blatant projection stimulated by hypnosis.

TABLE 1

A subject's waking and hypnotic interpretation of Little Red Riding Hood

Symbol	Waking interpretation	Hypnotic interpretation
Cape of red velvet	A covering or protection.	Potential for maternity. Femininity. I see the female sex symbol used in biology. I also see a red "A," meaning a scarlet letter or adultery. She has sex to use wisely or unwisely.
Don't run off the path (mother's prohibition).	Don't deviate from what is safe or expected.	Don't use the potentiality for motherhood unwisely.
Don't fall and break bottle (also mother's prohibition).	Might run into danger.	Her virginity—like the basket of food—she might ruin her capacity for motherhood.
Going deeper into the woods.	Straying from safety, becoming more involved in temptation.	Attracted to use of herself in a purely sexual way.
The wolf.	The end result of deviation, danger.	Any man who would violate her.
Swallowing of grandmother and the girl.	The final undoing of both due to the behavior of Red Riding Hood.	This all suddenly applies to me personally—my indecision about vocational plans and goals. (She goes on in great detail regarding her conflict between elevated educational goals, i.e., medicine and her wish to be a wife and to have children.)
The woodsman.	A second chance a redeemer.	

(*Continued*)

TABLE 1 (*Continued*)

Symbol	Waking interpretation	Hypnotic interpretation
Filling the wolf's belly with stones.	A substitution in an attempt to distract the danger.	Pride replaced by humility. (This again led into a highly personalized discussion in which she questions whether she has been blinded by an ambition and conceit. Despite the projected nature of these responses being pointed out by E, the subject was quite unable to resume normal emotional distance, repeatedly returning to highly personal themes.)
General interpretation:	It is very easy to trod a forbidden path, since the grass is always greener on the other side and so inviting. But a second chance is usually available for first offenders.	The path to any worthwhile goal is treacherous—there are constant temptations. Marriage is a threat to my plans. (She elaborates on the conflict between playing the conventional role of a woman and that of becoming a doctor, a man's goal.) By going into this field I am afraid I will lose my femininity. (Continued effort to objectify her interpretations at the insistence of E finally brings partial recovery and this interpretation. "Grandmother is motherhood, the red cap is the potential for maturity, the bottle of wine and basket of food is the girl's youth, energy and sexual attractiveness. Deviation from path means indulging in lustful, sexual pleasure. The wolf is a husband whose intentions seem fine but is primarily animal in his desires. Only the help of a priest can pull them from their lust, and aid the girl's desire for motherhood and love on a higher plane. Renewed intentions on the part of the girl is too much for the lust of the wolf and it is killed.")

In some instances, information was revealed about the nature of the hypnotic relationship as experienced by the subject. This was illustrated in a case where responses to the three items reflected an autonomy-dependency conflict and the subject stressed the dissatisfaction of the central figure at being unable to gain support from an omnipotent authority figure. Subsequent investigation revealed that he had volunteered for the experiment with the hope that it might provide him a therapeutic relationship. Such results constitute additional confirmation for the contention of Newman, Katz, and Rubenstein (1960) and other authors that the hypnotic relationship invariably intrudes into subject performance.

DISCUSSION

The results of the present investigation did not substantiate the assertion that hypnosis can facilitate the latent capacity of subjects for the understanding of symbolic language. They do support the findings of an unpublished study by Finzer, Kaywin, and Hilger, reported by Gill and Brenman (1959). None of the subjects in that study demonstrated an ability to translate the dreams of other people. As in that study results did suggest, however, that the hypnotized subjects "were in closer touch with their own unconscious conflicts and unsolved problems than in the normal state" (page 350).

These results were also consistent with an earlier report by the senior author (Moss, 1957b) on a patient-subject with a phenomenal ability to interpret his own dreams while hypnotized. The patient's unusual talent was employed as a facilitant to psychotherapy and in addition, the data he provided were used to test the psychoanalytic hypothesis of the disguise function of dream symbols. A feature of the case not hitherto reported was a test made of the patient's ability to interpret symbolic phenomena derived from other sources, i.e., dreams supplied by other patients, paintings with symbolic implications, myths and fairy tales. In every instance his responses were obvious projections and he provided no evidence of valid interpretive ability.

It is of interest that in the current study subject interpretations were essentially non-sexual and thus dissimilar to those obtained by Farber and Fisher, in the only comparable published study. This difference is possibly attributable to the relatively simple, suggestive test items used in that first experiment, some undefined variation in the hypnotic relationship (the majority of subjects in this study were males), or the stronger psychoanalytic orientation of the earlier investigators. Another interesting difference is that Farber and Fisher reported that their subjects were unable to "make any sense" out of the symbolic content presented to them in the waking state, either before or after they were hypnotized. In this study subjects *always* inferred some meaning. This difference is possibly attributable to the "set" established by the instructions; namely, that subjects in this study were consistently encouraged to demonstrate such an ability in both states. It should be further pointed out that Farber and Fisher's employment of suggested posthypnotic amnesia would be directly equivalent to an implanted prohibition against interpretation, and, therefore, failure of interpretation under these circumstances should be anticipated. Failure to employ posthypnotic amnesia should result (and did) in spontaneous recall for the majority of subjects and a performance level at least equal to that of the hypnotic state.

If it is assumed that a hypnotic subject is anxious to please the hypnotist and will generally do whatever he is directed to the best of his abilities, the present experimental procedure should have constituted a rigorous test of his capacity to engage in symbol interpretation. The high quantity of the subjects' productiveness indicates this motive was functioning; therefore, it is of considerable significance that they failed to confirm the experimenters' very positive expectations. So certain were the investigators of finding one or two subjects talented in symbol interpretation that the procedure reported here was initially considered only as the introductory step in an effort to identify the distinguishing personality characteristics of such subjects.

The authors concur with other psychologists that because of minimal reality commitments, dreams constitute a relatively pure form of projection. For example, Hall (1948) compared dreams to projective test material, and concluded that his studies indicated that dreams expressed the more socially unacceptable content; he suggested that both dreams and projective tests should be used in personality studies. The symbolic and therefore essentially ambiguous nature of dreams dictates that the act of interpretation becomes projective in turn. That is, when subjects (or therapists) are requested to interpret the symbolic productions of others for the ostensible purpose of discerning the latent content, this situation is well designed to elicit projective responses by virtue of both the ambiguous nature of the stimulus and the misdirection of attention involved. When the dream to be interpreted emanates from a subject's own sleep consciousness, the resulting product is a near perfect projective stimulus, specifically tailored as-it-were to the individual subject. (A perfect projective situation might consist of a self-produced and interpreted dream, if it were possible to eliminate the subject's awareness of the source of the symbolic stimulus.) The introduction of hypnosis into this situation further enhances the projective qualities of the performance, since the hypnotherapeutic relationship is ordinarily characterized by feelings of comfort and confidence which allow the subject to reduce his defensive operations, and the subject can be encouraged to direct his attention inwardly, resulting in a blurred distinction between internal and external reality and an increase in ego-centricity and frank projection.

The hypnotically produced and self-interpreted dream would thus appear to provide one highly flexible approach to the "custom-built projective method" (Forer et al., 1961). Watkins (1956) and Moss (1957c) have reported on the use of the hypnoprojective fantasy in psychotherapy as a possible variation of such an approach. This is a manner of investigation and treatment that combines tactics drawn from psychoanalytic dream interpretation, hypnosis and projective techniques of personality appraisal. The hypnotized subject is stimulated to involve himself in an ongoing, self-directed, dream-like fantasy—his participation is subjectively most real at the moment—and the therapist encourages him to continually develop the fantasy while avoiding direction and structure.

In conclusion it is recognized that failure to verify the original intent of this investigation may reflect inadequacies of the hypnotic technique employed, for instance, insufficient time allotted for subjects to develop the required performance. Another possible limitation relates to subject selection: The occasional dramatic cases reported in the literature may be based on the fortuitous occurrence of an exceptionally gifted subject whose impressive behavior defies replication in the experimental situation. Early in his career, Freud believed that the capacity for symbol interpretation was diagnostic of schizophrenia, but later concluded that ". . . it is simply a question of a personal gift without perceptible pathological significance (1960)." The possibility exists that some unsophisticated persons have a capacity for symbol-translation, and this remains a contaminating variable in any experiment of this nature. Nevertheless, the firmest conclusion derivable from this study is that no evidence was obtained that hypnosis endows the ordinary subject with a propensity for symbol interpretation in any objective sense. In the absence of objective criteria it is a moot point to ask what any unconsciously produced symbol *really* means. However, it can be stated with certainty that the interpretation of symbolic content, especially one's own dreams, particularly under hypnosis, is a projective method of considerable value in soliciting covert personality dynamics.

Night Dreams and Hypnotic Dreams:
Is There Evidence That They Are Different?

BY BILL DOMHOFF

Abstract: The evidence against equating night dreams and hypnotic dreams is reviewed in the light of two developments in dream research—Dement and Kleitman's (1957a; 1957b) physiological and behavioral indicators of dreaming and Hall's (1951; 1963) quantitative studies of dream content.

It is concluded that the equivalence of the EEG patterns of the hypnotic trance and the "dream" stage of sleep (Stage I) cannot be ruled out. It is further concluded that the psychologically important question of content differences between night and hypnotic dreams has never been examined in a controlled, quantitative manner.

The method of free association is an important technique for the scientific study of dream content, but it is not a powerful enough method to win widespread acceptance for Freud's ideas. Nor is it very successful with typical dream symbols (Freud, 1960). What is needed is an experimental technique, a method for controlling dream content and for producing and translating dream symbolism. Such a potential technique, viewed by many with great promise despite its checkered history, is hypnosis. Since 1911, when Karl Schroetter reported that he had obtained symbolic hypnotic dreams from three different Ss, it has been hoped that hypnosis might become the experimental technique capable of spearheading a systematic study of dream content.[1]

Today, however, the hopes for the hypnotic dream as the experimental key to night dream interpretation have never been dimmer. EEG studies seem to concur in finding no physiological justification for equating sleep and hypnotic trance (e.g., Diamant, Dufek, Hoskovec, Krištof, Pekárek, Roth, and Velek, 1960; Schiff, Bunney, and Freedman, 1961), and the more important possibility of psychological equivalence between night and hypnotic dream is seemingly ruled out by significant content differences (e.g., Brenman, 1949; Gill and Brenman, 1959).

SOURCE. Reprinted by permission from *The International Journal of Clinical and Experimental Hypnosis*, **12** (3), 159–168 (1964).
[1] Cf. Moss (1961) for recent suggestions.

In the face of such evidence, it may seem unrealistic to cling to the idea that hypnosis could become an important experimental adjunct to dream research. However, it is submitted that two developments in physiological and quantitative dream research expose the weaknesses of negative evidence concerning the hypnotic dream. It is further suggested that these two developments necessitate a reconsideration of the entire question.

SLEEP, HYPNOSIS, AND THE EEG

It is often stated that the EEG patterns of sleep and hypnosis are two different matters. Some authors gloss over the unsettled nature of the question. For example: "The lack of EEG changes is a usual finding in this and other laboratories." The reference which is cited as corroborating evidence by Schiff et al. (1961) actually contains many reports of slow alpha waves and theta waves during hypnosis (Chertok and Kramarz, 1959). Schiff et al. (1961) showed, in the study quoted above, that the rapid eye movements now known to be indicative of night dreams were also present in the hypnotic dreams of their only experimental S. But they failed to consider the possibility that methodology and/or personality variables might account for the subtle, small-frequency differences between the pattern correlated with dreaming (4–6 cps, but sometimes faster), theta rhythms (5–7 cps), and slow alpha (8–9 cps). Their judgment on the matter is accepted by Barber (1962) in his critique of the hypnotically induced dream. Barber cites the Schiff et al. (1961) findings on one S as evidence for his contention that the posthypnotically suggested night dreams of his own Ss may have taken place after the Ss awakened during the night.[2] Barber also refers the reader to Sirna (1945). Sirna's report will be singularly disappointing as it contains no EEG data, only the conclusion that the sleep EEG and the hypnotic EEG are different. Sirna does not state his criterion for a sleep EEG (nor did he himself even obtain such data), but he does note in passing that there were slight changes in the alpha rhythm during hypnosis.

---

[2] Stoyva (1961) has recently shown that posthypnotic suggestions do in fact appear in the dream content from Stage I sleep: "The present study confirmed the findings of earlier investigators that subjects could be made to dream on the night following a hypnotic trance about topics suggested by the experimenter during the trance. Furthermore, through the use of the physiological approach first described by Aserinsky and Kleitman (1955) it was established that when instructed to do so, certain subjects will dream about the suggested topic in every dream of the night" (p. 4).

At this point the now well-known physiological and behavioral indicators of dreaming should be discussed in more detail for they raise a fundamental question about the "sleep EEG" used as a criterion in previous studies comparing brain wave patterns during sleep and hypnosis. The correlation between rapid eye movements (REM) and dream reports was first published by Aserinsky and Kleitman (1953), and was spelled out more completely (with the added brain wave correlate) by Dement and Kleitman (1957*a*; 1957*b*): Dement and Kleitman noted a characteristic sleep cycle: as the *S* dropped off to sleep his EEG pattern was one of low voltage, fast frequencies, ranging from the drowsy-waking 10 cps to the 4 cps frequency.[3] No rapid eye movements were seen during this initial Stage I, dreams were not reported when the *S* was awakened (the *S* often maintained he was still awake), and muscular tension was apparent from eye leads. The shift to slower, higher voltage frequencies was usually signaled by the appearance of sleep spindles (14–16 cps) against a low voltage background (Stage II). Following this, the *S* moved into the slow, high voltage frequencies classically associated with sleep (Stages III and IV). About 60 minutes after falling asleep, the *S* reversed the sequence and returned to a low voltage, nonspindling, fast frequency sleep pattern. Although similar in brain wave characteristics to the Stage I of falling asleep, there were several differences. Auditory waking thresholds were higher, discrete bursts of REM's appeared, there was no muscle tension from eye leads, and dreams were usually reported upon awakening. (These differences between initial Stage I and later Stage I—termed "emergent" Stage I—may be important considerations for future studies comparing sleep and hypnotic trance.) This cycle—from Stage I down to Stage IV and back to Stage I—is repeated 4–6 times during the night, with less time in the classical slow wave sleep as the night progresses. The details of this general picture, as well as the necessary qualifications due to individual differences, can be found in Dement and Kleitman (1957*a*; 1957*b*), Kamiya (1961), and Kleitman (1960; 1963).[4]

[3] "Stage I. The essential characteristic was *an absolute lack of spindle activity*. In general, a low voltage, relatively fast pattern corresponding to the 'B' stage of Loomis et al., The 'Drowsy' stage of Gibbs, and including what the Loomis group called the 'A' or interrupted alpha stage. Thus, any EEG pattern between full wakefulness and the appearance of spindles was included in Stage I" (Dement and Kleitman, 1957*a*, p. 674).

[4] It is true that some investigators have reported mentation upon awakening from other stages of sleep (Foulkes, 1962; Kamiya, 1961; Rechtschaffen, Verdone, and Wheaton, 1961). However, as both the Foulkes (1962) and the Rechtschaffen et al. (1961) studies point out, such mentation is quantitatively less and qualitatively different from that of Stage I. Further, methodological controls for

Because of the time and expense involved, most EEG studies of sleep have only sampled brain wave patterns during the night. In fact, it was only after Dement decided to run the EEG all night, in order to clear up discrepancies between his data and that of Aserinsky and Kleitman, that the sleep cycle was discovered. It is therefore submitted that all pre-Dement and Kleitman studies comparing sleep and hypnosis must be reconsidered. It is suspected that most past investigators used sleep spindles and/or large, slow waves as their criteria of sleep, and thereby failed to consider the possibility that the hypnotic EEG may be similar to that of Stage I, the very stage of sleep associated with dreaming.[5] It is further suggested that many early investigators ignored or played down seemingly-minor changes in the hypnotic EEG as a mere "slowing of the alpha frequency" because they were not aware of the importance of Stage I sleep. These considerations, plus the several studies that have noted "theta rhythms" during the hypnotic trance (Chertok and Kramarz, 1959), hint that the crucial equivalence—between the hypnotic trance and Stage I sleep—may well be present.[6] That the two are not greatly different also can be seen from this account of Stage I:

The Stage I EEG persisting throughout the eye movement periods showed considerable variation within this classification. Generally a low voltage, irregular pattern, there were also many bursts or trains of regular 7–10 cps waves in the occipital leads, and 18–25 or 5–7 cps waves in the frontals. Although all these variations were usually seen in every subject, the occipital regular waves were more common in subjects with a prominent waking alpha rhythm and were characteristically 1–2 cps slower than the waking frequency (Dement and Kleitman, 1957a, p. 678).

An objection can be raised that the aforementioned criticisms do not apply to the study by Schiff et al. (1961), which actually dealt

---

subject bias, as introduced by Kremen (1962), suggest that some of the mentation from other stages may be methodological artifact and/or hypnopompic imagery. Finally, the close relation between Stage I content and eye movements, and the several physiological concomitants of Stage I (Roffwarg, Dement, Muzio, and Fisher, 1962), suggest that the verbal equation of Stage I, REM, and dream should be retained, at least for the time being.

[5] This is clearly the case with the classic study of Loomis, Harvey, and Hobart (1936, p. 276). For those who might want to re-examine the scores of conflicting studies in the light of these comments, cf. the bibliography in Kleitman (1963).

[6] Solovey and Milechnin (1960) report spontaneous rapid eye movement after 10 minutes of hypnotic trance in some Ss: "In fact, when we made these subjects pass into a lighter hypnotic state after they had been having eye movements for some minutes, and asked them to tell us their recent experience, the subjects gave us material of an oneiroid type, which appeared to have no difference from natural dreams" (p. 132).

with the work of Dement and Kleitman. This objection can be met with reports from other post-Dement and Kleitman investigating teams, whose results suggest that EEG changes are obtained during the hypnotic trance with slight changes in the experimental interaction. Borlone, Dittborn, and Palestini (1960) found that the alpha pattern is present when the S answers during the trance state, but that it largely disappears, to be replaced by theta rhythms, when the S is not communicating with the investigator. Similarly, Fujisawa and Obonai (1960) found that when rapport was maintained with their three Ss the EEG resembled waking alpha, while it was closer to that of classical sleep when rapport was not maintained. While neither of these investigations was concerned with hypnotic dreams, their findings underline the importance of considering methodology in evaluating the contradictory evidence on the EEG of sleep and the hypnotic trance.

The theoretical ideas of Kleitman (1963) are also relevant at this point. Taking his cue from the discovery of the near-alpha frequency associated with dreaming, Kleitman hypothesizes that alpha frequency may be an index of consciousness, of the level of analytical functioning. Kleitman points to the slower alpha of the young, the old, the bored, the alcoholic, and the dreamer as evidence for his contention, and in a personal communication adds that the hypnotized S may often be added to this continuum.[7] If in fact small changes in alpha frequency are shown to be indicative of significant changes in mental functioning, this would strengthen the argument that a hypnotic trance with an EEG similar to that of Stage I would be useful in studying "dreamwork" (Freud, 1960) and symbol formation.[8]

The conclusion to be drawn, it is suggested, is not that of Schiff et al. (1961) or Barber (1962), but that of still another investigating team conversant with the work of Dement and Kleitman:

So far, then, the EEG findings allow us to say with certainty only that hypnosis is not deep sleep. We do not have the right to say that hypnosis is the same as the ordinary waking state: first, there is some evidence—shaky, it is true—that the EEG of hypnosis will be shown to differ from the EEG of the alert waking state; and second, an individual who seems to be asleep may show EEG patterns ordinarily associated

[7] Taking the cue from their studies of sleep learning, Simon and Emmons (1956) also suggest alpha changes as an index of change in consciousness.
[8] Kleitman (1963) emphasizes the considerable individual differences in alpha frequency. Individual differences plus the importance of establishing even 1–2 cps changes in frequency show how important it is to have the same Ss in both sleep and hypnotic trance conditions in future studies.

with wakefulness (the change during stimulation of the sleeper who does not awake, and during dreaming). As far as the EEG is concerned, it is still possible to call the hypnotized subject a dreamer (Gill and Brenman, 1959, p. 226).

THE CONTENT OF NIGHT DREAMS AND HYPNOTIC DREAMS

Since the first studies by Schroetter (1911), it has been found that some hypnotic dreams are very prosaic, while others are very similar to the traditional stereotype of the night dream—bizarre and "symbolic." Further, as is shown by the work of Barber (1962) and Gill and Brenman (1959), the positive (often remarkable) results of Schroetter (1912), Roffenstein (1959), Farber and Fisher (1943), and Mazer (1951) have not been regularly repeatable. For those interested in hypnosis as an experimental technique, it would be important to understand these contradictory findings in terms of methodological and/or personality variables. For example, the aforementioned Dittborn et al. study (1960) suggests the importance of the S's expectations as determined by prehypnotic instructions, while the Fujisawa and Obonai study (1960) emphasizes the importance of distinguishing between hypnotic states where rapport is maintained with the hypnotist and where it is not maintained. The Solovey and Milechnin study (1960) suggests that the hypnotic dream may not occur immediately, which in turn points to the possibility of shifts in the depth of hypnotic trance. Then, too, differences could perhaps be expected between states produced by passive and active methods of induction, and between states accompanied by passive suggestions (such as deepening procedures) and active suggestions (such as dreaming). Further, many investigators have stressed the central importance of the particular psychodynamics underlying each hypnotist-subject relationship (e.g., Farber and Fisher, 1943; Newman, Katz, and Rubenstein, 1960; Rubenstein, Katz, and Newman, 1957). On the question of subject variation there is the interesting study by Hilgard (1963), which shows that "good" Ss may do very poorly on specific tasks. For example, those who do well on "positive hallucinations" may do poorly on "negative hallucinations" or "dreams." This profile approach to subject selection should assure that future studies do not disagree because "good" Ss were picked by criteria irrelevant to success in hypnotic dreaming.

The studies most often referred to in discounting the possibility of similarities of night and hypnotic dream content are those by Brenman (1949) and Gill and Brenman (1959). These investigators placed the hypnotic responses to the instructions "to dream" in four categories—"embellished reminiscence," "static pictorial image," "quasi-allegory," and "quasi-dream"—and gave examples of each type. The distinction between the hypnotic dream categories and night dreams, as epitomized by the examples, may not be entirely convincing to those who have read through the dream series of normal Ss, nor perhaps to those who are familiar with quantitative studies of dream content. Gill and Brenman (1959) present no quantitative comparisons of samples of night and hypnotic dreams to buttress their claims, and a search of the literature shows that no one has made such a quantitative comparison. Until a properly controlled, quantitative study is made, preferably using the same Ss in both hypnotic and sleep conditions, the statement that there are differences between the content of night and hypnotic dreams cannot be accepted without reservation.

Actually, these investigators agree that there may be a great deal of overlap between night dreams and hypnotic dreams. Brenman (1949) quotes Freud with approval in suggesting that it is still an open question as to whether even all night dreams have precisely the same structure, formal qualities, and kinds of distortion:

A dream without condensation, distortion, dramatization, above all, without wish fulfillment, surely hardly deserves the name. You will remind me that, if so, there are other mental products in sleep to which the right to be called "dreams" would have to be refused. Actual experiences of the day are known to be simply repeated in sleep; reproductions of traumatic scenes in "dreams" have led us only lately to revise the theory of dreams. There are dreams which by certain special qualities are to be distinguished from the usual type, which are, properly speaking, nothing but night fantasies, not having undergone additions or alterations of any kind, and in all other ways similar to the well-known daydreams. It would be awkward, certainly, to exclude these imaginings from the realm of "dreams" (Freud, 1959, p. 421).

The "actual experiences," "traumatic scenes," and "night fantasies" which Freud would find awkward to exclude from the realm of dreams are qualitatively difficult to distinguish from "embellished reminiscences," "static pictorial images," and "quasi-allegories."

A second recent development in dream research—quantitative studies of dream content—is relevant at this point. Beginning in the mid-1940's Hall (1951; 1953b) started collecting dreams from normal adults, college students, children, and neurotics. With a sample of nearly 10,000 dreams, he has developed manuals for classifying and quantifying every element in the dream narrative—e.g., characters, settings, objects, activities, interpersonal relations, and emotions (Hall, 1962a; Hall, 1962b; Hall, 1962c; Hall, 1962d). Early results of this research are summarized in Hall (1956), and recent findings are now being published (Hall and Domhoff, 1963*a*; Hall and Domhoff, 1963*b*; Hall and Domhoff, in press).

The application of Hall's content categories to samples of night and hypnotic dreams would make possible a quantitative comparison of significant content variables, a first step in the attempt to demonstrate what is the crucial equivalence from the point of view of the present paper—psychological equivalence. If it is objected that the night and hypnotic dreams might differ in latent content, it is equally possible to quantify the verbalizations by which latent content is uncovered—the free associations (Hall and Domhoff, 1962). Hall's (1963) equation of male stranger = father has demonstrated the usefulness of quantitative techniques with night dreams and their attendant free associations. Further, Moss (1961) is the most recent to comment on the fact that hypnotized *S*s often do very well at interpreting their own dreams. Thus, an ideal study of latent content would compare, quantitatively, free associations (waking and/or under hypnosis) to night and hypnotic dreams. Also, the similarity of the dreamwork in night and hypnotic dreams could be demonstrated by obtaining manifest content predictable from psychoanalytic experience with the representations of specific wishes and fears (cf. Farber and Fisher, 1943). Finally, for whatever a subjective criterion may be worth, several of Klein's (1930) *S*s reported that they felt there was no difference between night dreaming and hypnotic dreaming. Perhaps the combination of variables leading to such a statement would also produce hypnotic dream content similar to that of night dreams.

CONCLUSIONS

The sleep EEG pattern correlated with dream reports is very similar to that sometimes obtained during hypnosis. It is concluded that there is as yet no adequate evidence for claiming that the hypnotic EEG is different from that associated with dreaming (Stage I). On the other hand, while REM's have been shown to be associated with hypnotic dreaming, it is not claimed that evidence permits identification of Stage I with hypnotic trance. Suggestions are made for empirical studies of this problem.

A search of the literature on hypnotic dream content reveals that there never has been a quantitative comparison of the content of samples of night dreams and hypnotic dreams. It is concluded that until such studies are made there is not adequate evidence to accept the statement that there are significant differences between night and hypnotic dreams. Suggestions are made for quantitative comparison of both the manifest and latent content of the two types of productions.

Toward a Theory of "Hypnotic" Behavior:
The "Hypnotically Induced Dream"

BY THEODORE X. BARBER[1]

Schroetter (1911), Mazer (1951), Schneck (1953a), and other investigators (Farber and Fisher, 1943; Nachmansohn, 1925; Roffenstein,
1924; Wolberg, 1945) have presented data to support the contention
that "hypnotically induced dreams" include symbolizations, distortions,
and other characteristics of the "dream-work" and are in general indistinguishable from spontaneous night dreams. Along related lines, Farber and Fisher (1943) interpreted experimental findings as indicating
that under "hypnosis" unsophisticated individuals are able to understand the "meaning" of dreams. The present paper critically reviews
these and other investigations, focusing on the following questions:
(1) Is the "hypnotic dream" a spontaneous production related to the
nocturnal dream or is it a purposefully contrived product—a "made-up
dream"? (2) Are suggestions given under "hypnosis" more effective
than suggestions given under normal waking conditions in eliciting
dream-like material? (3) Can "meaningful" dream interpretations be
more effectively elicited under hypnotic than under non-hypnotic
conditions?

THE TYPICAL "HYPNOTIC DREAM"

In operational terms, the "hypnotically induced dream" refers to
the product resulting from the suggestion, given to a "hypnotized"
person, "to dream" either (1) during the hypnotic session itself or
(2) during the following night. Specific instructions used to elicit
the former, henceforth termed the "hypnotic dream," and the latter,
henceforth termed the "posthypnotic dream" vary widely; e.g., the

SOURCE. Reprinted by permission from *The Journal of Nervous and Mental
Disease*, 135 (3), 206–221 (September, 1962).
[1] Research Department, Medfield State Hospital, Medfield, Mass.; and the Division
of Psychiatry, Boston University School of Medicine. The writing of this paper
was made possible by research grants (MY3253 and MY4825) from the National
Institute of Mental Health, U.S. Public Health Service. The author wishes to
express his appreciation to the following persons who critically read a preliminary
draft of the manuscript: Paul D. Parker, M.A.; W. Dennis Engels, M.D.; and
Arje Latz, M.A.

"hypnotized" subject may be given only the bare suggestion "to dream," he may be given partial or complete specification of the dream content, he may be told to continue dreaming where a former night dream terminated, he may be instructed to dream and then presented with an external stimulus designed to trigger the dreaming process. D. B. Klein's (1930) investigation is paradigmatic of these studies:

Eight subjects (Ss) were "hypnotized" by means of visual fixation and verbal suggestions. The "genuineness of the hypnotic state" was tested by suggesting inability to open the eyes and to pry the clasped hands apart. S was then instructed to sleep for a few minutes. After one or two minutes, he was asked to sit up but to continue sleeping, and told: "I want you to watch carefully for any dreams you may have and as soon as the dream is over tell me all about it." While S waited for a dream to appear, an external stimulus was introduced. Immediately following the stimulus presentation, the "hypnotized" Ss reported imaginative productions which they termed "dreams." The author presented the following illustrative examples:

(1) Stimulus: Right hand stroked with cotton for a few seconds. Dream report: "A cow licked me on the hand." Hypnotist: "Is that all you can tell me?" S: "Yes."

(2) Stimulus: Bottle of asafetida held to nose for ten seconds. Dream report: "Smelled something dead—a horse—a dead horse." Hypnotist: "What else?" S: "He was just dead."

All "dreams" presented by Klein's "hypnotized" Ss were similar to the above, seemingly consisting of brief and unelaborated thoughts and images. However, Ss agreed that the experiences could be termed "dreams," and the author concluded that since "hypnotic dreams" deal with events that subjects regard as "really" taking place at the time of the experience, they belong "in the same category of mental processes as the ordinary night dream."

The "hypnotic dreams" presented in the above study are not atypical; the majority of "hypnotic dreams" reported in the literature seem to consist of brief, unadorned products which are difficult to differentiate from verbal or imaginal associations to the suggested dream topic. Erle (1958), for example, instructed "hypnotized" Ss to dream to unstructured verbal stimuli such as to the phrase "he loves": in response, Ss typically reported such "hypnotic dreams" as: "I thought of my mother, just saw her head, a blurred vision of her face"; and, "I seemed to imagine a man embracing a woman." Similarly, in an extensive analysis of 405 "hypnotic dreams" produced by 16 "psychologically naïve" college students, Quay (1952) found that in 84 per cent of the cases the "dreams" could be classified as verbal or imaginal associations to the suggested dream topic. Other workers (Brenman, 1949; Moss, 1960a; Regardie, 1950) have also noted that in many instances "hypnotic dreams" consist of a single static image.[2]

THE "HYPNOTIC DREAM" AS A REMINISCENCE

Although most "hypnotic dreams" appear to consist of static imagery or verbal associations to the dream stimulus, some "hypnotic dreams" seem to consist of the recall of former nocturnal dreams or the recall of former events. Barber (Unpubl.) found that of 12 highly selected "deep trance" Ss instructed to dream about their fathers, only one presented a dream which appeared to resemble a nocturnal dream in pictorial character and bizarre features. Although this S at first referred to the production as having been "dreamt" under "hypnosis," she stated during the post-experimental interview that it was actually a former night dream which had been recalled but not dreamt during "hypnosis." Three of the remaining Ss presented "hypnotic dreams" which they defined in post-experimental interviews as consisting of recent experiences with their fathers. Other workers (Brenman, 1949; Farber and Fisher, 1943) have similarly observed that some "hypnotic dreams" are "embellished reminiscences" or unaltered recollections of previous

---

[2] Some nocturnal dreams may be as lacking in characteristics of the "dream-work" (symbolization, condensation, displacement, substitution, etc.) as the typical "hypnotic dreams" described above. In a recent study Goodenough et al. (1959) awakened 16 Ss when electroencephalographic (EEG) recordings and eye movements indicative of dreaming were present (Aserinsky and Kleitman, 1955; Dement and Kleitman, 1957a, 1957b). "A large number" of nocturnal dreams reported under these conditions were unembellished, internally consistent, and lacking in bizarre features. Polster (1950) presented similar findings: of 1080 night dreams reported the next day by four groups of Ss (children, adolescents, normal adults, and hospitalized neurotics), nearly half (in each of the four groups) could be classified as straightforward narratives with a very high degree of likelihood that the events depicted in the dream could occur in everyday life. However, since Polster found, as had earlier investigators (Freud, 1953, 1960), that more than half of the reported nocturnal dreams included some degree of reality-distortion, it appears likely that typical nocturnal dreams are more elaborated and more illogical than typical "hypnotic dreams." Also, since the majority of "hypnotic dreams" seem to span a time interval varying from about 10 seconds to two minutes (Farber and Fisher, 1943; Klein, 1930; Moss, 1960a; Sweetland and Quay, 1952; Welch, 1956), they appear to be of much briefer duration than most night dreams (Dement and Kleitman, 1957a, 1957b).

happenings. Additional experiments are needed to specify more precisely the proportion of "hypnotic dreams" which consist of the recall of past events or of former night dreams.

EXPERIMENTAL CONTROLS AND THE "HYPNOTIC DREAM"

Most investigations in this area (e.g., Beigel, 1959; Brenman, 1949; Moss, 1960a; Pierce, 1957; Regardie, 1950) lack a necessary control: non-hypnotized persons were not instructed "to dream." This control, however, was included in Klein's study (1930). The control group consisted of three non-hypnotized persons. One of these had been previously rejected as a "poor" hypnotic subject. Ss were instructed to close their eyes and to report any dreams experienced. As in the hypnotic sessions, an external stimulus—e.g., an odorous substance—was introduced while S waited for a dream to appear. Although the results of the control sessions are not presented in detail, it appears that in some instances the non-hypnotized controls reported imaginative productions which more or less resembled the "dreams" they or others had produced under "hypnosis." However, the control group denied that the productions were dreams. In contrast, in the hypnotic sessions, all Ss had agreed that their experiences could be categorized as "dreams." This control study is open to criticism:

(1) One of the three controls had previously shown that he was a "poor" hypnotic S. This introduces a bias into the experiment. A series of recent studies, summarized elsewhere (Barber, 1962b), strongly suggests that (prior to participation in hypnotic experiments) potentially "poor" hypnotic Ss characteristically tend to inhibit daydreaming, fantasy, and other behavior involving imagination or imagery. If "poor" hypnotic Ss are assigned to the control group, an experimenter may thus be in danger of confounding the control treatment with the controls' unwillingness to indulge in imaginative activities.

(2) When an experimental S is given the suggestion "to dream" in a situation defined as "hypnosis" and explicitly or implicitly defined as a situation involving a sleeplike state, it appears unlikely that he views the suggestions as incongruous with the situation. In contradistinction, when a control S is told "to dream" in a situation defined explicitly or implicitly as involving normal waking behavior, he may perceive the instructions as incongruous with the normal waking situation and may find it difficult to categorize his imaginative productions

as "dreams." However, recent studies[3] indicate that a series of overt behaviors *and subjective reports* that have been considered as characteristic of "deep hypnosis"—e.g., "hypnotic color-blindness," "hypnotic analgesia," "hypnotic age-regression," "hypnotic hallucinations," "hypnotic amnesia"—can be elicited from non-hypnotic controls, provided that disbeliefs concerning the possibility of experiencing these phenomena have been minimized and provided that the non-hypnotic controls are ego-involved in the test situation and motivated to perform well on the criterion tasks. These investigations suggest an experiment as follows: the situation should be defined to the controls as one in which it is appropriate "to dream," and they should be motivated to visualize and to imagine vividly but no attempt should be made to induce either sleep or "hypnosis." It may be possible to accomplish this as follows: the controls could be told by an authoritative figure that "scientific studies with the electroencephalogram demonstrate that it is possible to experience dreams immediately after closing the eyes without actually being asleep"; they should then be motivated vividly to visualize scenes or actions concerned with assigned "dream" topics. It can be hypothesized that under these conditions a non-hypnotized control group will report imaginal productions indistinguishable from "hypnotic dreams" and will also define the productions as "dreams."

THE "SYMBOLIC HYPNOTIC DREAM"

Although most "hypnotic dreams" appear to be prosaic products containing very few if any distortions or symbolizations, a number of investigators have reported "hypnotic dreams" which symbolically represented the suggested dream topic.

In 1911 Schroetter (1911) presented 13 "symbolic hypnotic dreams" produced by three relatively sophisticated Ss (a medical student, a graduate student in philosophy and a pharmacist). Three of the dreams were produced in response to suggestions to disguise or to symbolize the dream topic; the others were produced without such suggestions. Examples of the latter are as follows:

(1) A "hypnotized" female S, suffering from a stubborn headache, was told to dream of her headache vanishing. She reported: "I stroll on the Ring [the main avenue of Vienna] with a giant hat on; the

---

[3] Barber, 1957c, 1959a, 1959b, 1959c, 1960b, 1961a, 1961b, 1961c, 1962a, 1962c, 1962d, **Barber** and Calverley, in press; Barber and Deeley, 1961; Barber and Glass, 1962; Barber and Hahn, 1962; Glass and Barber, 1961.

wind flutters it, threatening to carry it off. I hold it, but it flies off and everyone stares at me."

(2) A "hypnotized" woman was instructed to dream the following night of homosexual relations with her girl friend. She presented a "posthypnotic dream" in which she saw her girl friend carrying a suitcase which contained a label that read: "For ladies only." The friend said to her: "Don't you want to come with me? I am on my way home."

Since Schroetter's account contained 13 dreams of which the majority seemed to represent the suggested dream topic symbolically, and since explicit suggestions to symbolize were given in only three instances, it has been quoted (Mazer, 1951; Wolberg, 1945) in support of the contention that some "hypnotic dreams" are essentially the same as nocturnal dreams. The following arguments, however, suggest caution in accepting this conclusion:

(1) It appears possible that the Ss had some familiarity with Freudian dream theory. Such awareness could have come from their graduate studies, from membership in intellectual circles in Freud's Vienna or from their interactions with the experimenter, who was versed in psychoanalytic theory.

(2) It appears that Schroetter published only his successful cases. Although the report states that the dreams presented were selected from a larger sample, it does not state how many Ss were tested, how many experiments were conducted with each S, and how many experiments yielded negative results.

(3) Although in most of the experiments which are reported explicit instructions were not given to symbolize, it appears that such instructions may have been given in earlier sessions and may have carried over to the reported sessions.

Experiments subsequently carried out by Dattner and by Schilder did not confirm Schroetter's findings. In these investigations, as reported by Roffenstein (1924), Ss either did not dream at all (although they were considered excellent hypnotic subjects) or a nonsymbolic dream was produced when symbolization was directly suggested. In his own investigations, Roffenstein (1924) was unable to elicit symbolic dreams from an unspecified number of "hypnotized" Ss but finally succeeded with a 28-year-old uneducated domestic worker. This subject was given the following suggestions under "hypnosis": "You will dream of (masturbation, rape, intercourse, etc.) but you must dream this so, distort the dream so, hide its contents so, that the dream will seem entirely innocuous . . . ." Upon energetic repetition and reiterated explanation of these suggestions, she produced "symbolic hypnotic dreams" such as the following: when given the suggestion to dream of rape, she reported a dream in which she was attacked by a dog which tore at her throat; when given the suggestion to dream of masturbation, she reported dreaming of eating candy in bed. Roffenstein does not spell out the nature of his relationship with this S: it is not clear, for example, if she was in therapy with him. However, his report does state that S had participated in an unspecified number of prior hypnotic experiments in which she produced only non-symbolic "hypnotic dreams."

Nachmansohn (1925) subsequently succeeded in eliciting "symbolic posthypnotic dreams" from three women undergoing hypnotic therapy for neurotic disorders. Under "deep hypnosis" the suggestion was given to dream the following night on a selected topic and to record the dream in the morning upon awakening. In some experiments instructions were given to represent the dream topic symbolically; in other instances the instructions were to dream without symbolizing; and in still other instances instructions to symbolize were implied but not stated explicitly. Although all three patients seemed to be "in deep hypnosis" when given the suggestions, each responded differently; one consistently produced "symbolic hypnotic dreams," one consistently dreamt without symbolic alterations and one reported dreams which apparently varied in accordance with the instructions. Since the report appears to indicate that all three Ss had a close relationship with the physician-hypnotist and that all were "good" hypnotic Ss, the differential responsiveness may have been due to (1) personality differences or (2) differences with respect to familiarity with dream theory or dream symbols. Nachmansohn favored the first possibility, writing that "the extent of distortion is proportional to the complexity of the personality." That the second possibility should not be dismissed, however, is indicated by the statement that one patient "knew that the snake is supposed to represent sexual drive," thus appearing to have had more than average familiarity with Freudian symbolism.

"Symbolic hypnotic dreams" have also been elicited in more recent studies. Working with 25 college students, Farber and Fisher (1943) found that at first all Ss presented "hypnotic dreams" which were paraphrases of or associations to the suggested dream topic even when suggestions were given to symbolize. After an unstated number of unsuccessful sessions, however, five of the 25 Ss (25 per cent) began to report "hypnotic dreams" which at times indirectly represented suggested sexual material. Mazer (1951) reported comparable findings with 26 "hypnotized" Ss who were given suggestions to dream symbolically. After an unspecified number of hypnotic sessions in which only non-symbolic "dreams" were produced, ten of the 26 (38 per cent) began to report "hypnotic dreams" containing symbolic representations; e.g., when instructed to dream symbolically about the female breast, one S "dreamt" of a young boy walking barefoot over a very soft feather quilt.

Why did some "hypnotized" persons participating in the above experiments succeed and others fail to symbolize? Mazer contends that the production of "symbolic hypnotic dreams" is largely determined by "the depth of trance." However, since Mazer defines "the depth of trance" in terms of the number and difficulty of the suggestions to which S has previously responded, this contention appears difficult to differentiate from the tautology that a "suggestible" person (that is, a person who has responded positively to a number of "difficult" suggestions) is "suggestible" (that is, responds positively to the suggestion to symbolize). A more fruitful approach to differential responsiveness to "suggestions" appears to lie in the assessment of two interrelated variables: (1) the interpersonal relationship between S and experimenter; and (2) the personality characteristics of S.[4] Farber and Fisher emphasized personality factors, noting that in their study the 20 "hypnotized" persons who could not be induced to dream symbolically were rigid and inhibited as compared to the five who produced "symbolic dreams." Sweetland and Quay (1952) have presented comparable data. Working with 16 college students, they found a significant positive correlation ($r = 0.57$) between personality adjustment, as indicated by the Social Security-Insecurity Test, and degree of symbolization in the "hypnotic dream."

THE "SYMBOLIC HYPNOTIC DREAM" AND THE "AUTOSYMBOLIC PHENOMENON"

Some investigators (e.g., Moss, 1960a) are of the opinion that "hypnotic dreams" which symbolically represent the suggested dream material involve similar processes as found in Silberer's "autosymbolic phenomenon." In 1909 Silberer (1909) reported that he had succeeded in observing the transformation of his abstract thoughts into concrete perceptual images. His first such experience occurred inadvertently while resting on a couch; although extremely sleepy, he forced himself to think about a problem in philosophy. Having fixed one philosophical

[4] Barber, 1956, 1957b, 1958a, 1958b, 1960a, 1961b; Barber and Glass, 1962.

theory in mind, he turned to an alternative theory; when he then tried to recall the first theory, it was gone and seemed beyond recovery. The futile effort to recall suddenly represented itself to him as a concrete symbolic image: he saw himself asking a morose secretary for information but the secretary gave him an unfriendly and rejecting look. Silberer writes that the vividness and appropriateness of the sudden imagery surprised him. Henceforth, forcing himself when drowsy to think of theoretical problems, he succeeded in observing other instances of the "autosymbolic phenomenon"; e.g., while thinking of improving a rough passage in an essay, he suddenly became aware that he was visualizing himself planing a piece of wood.

Silberer did not minimize the difficulties in observing the "autosymbolic phenomenon," emphasizing that to observe the conversion of thoughts into symbolic imagery it is necessary to maintain a "labile condition" between sleep and waking. That the observation of such phenomena is indeed difficult is attested by the apparent paucity of confirming studies reported during the half-century which has intervened since Silberer's publication. In searching the literature, the present writer was able to find only one comparable report published within recent years (Munroe, 1955, p. 50).[5]

Although "symbolic hypnotic dreams" and the "autosymbolic phenomenon" may possess some common characteristics, a recent study appears to indicate that they may also differ in basic aspects. In the "autosymbolic phenomenon," as described by Silberer, abstract thoughts are converted into concrete symbolic images spontaneously, unexpectedly, and without volition. In contradistinction, Barber (unpubl.) has presented experimental evidence indicating that at least some "symbolic hypnotic dreams" may be non-spontaneous productions which are purposively constructed or "made up" by S in order to comply with the desires and expectations of the hypnotist. In this experiment four "deeply hypnotized" women students were given the suggestion "to dream symbolically, hiding, distorting, disguising the dream topic." A control group consisting of ten non-hypnotized

[5] A number of investigations, summarized by McKellar (1957), have been concerned with "hypnagogic imagery," a phenomenon which ostensibly resembles the "autosymbolic phenomenon" in that the subject observes his own imagery under conditions bordering between sleep and waking. However, "hypnagogic imagery" and the "autosymbolic phenomenon" appear to differ in essential respects. In the "autosymbolic phenomenon" S observes the conversion of abstract thoughts into concrete symbolic images; in contradistinction, subjects reporting "hypnagogic imagery" state that the imagery is unrelated to ongoing thought processes.

women students was instructed *"to imagine dreaming* symbolically—hiding the dream topic." Five dream topics were presented to both groups; e.g., "You are giving birth to a baby." The students interpreted their own "dreams." Two of the four Ss in the Hypnotic group and four of the ten in the Control group presented at least two "dreams" which appeared to symbolically represent the suggested dream material; e.g., a "dream" produced in response to the suggestion to dream of giving birth was: "I was picking cherries off a tree and standing on a ladder and the ladder fell down." In response to questionnaire items, given post-experimentally, both the Hypnotic Ss and the Controls who had produced "symbolic dreams" stated explicitly or implicitly that they had purposefully created or "made up" the symbolic material; e.g., "I had to think up symbols and make a real effort to have them."

In summary, a number of investigators have published "hypnotic dreams" and "posthypnotic dreams" which symbolically represented suggested dream topics. Although these "dreams" have been compared with nocturnal dreams and with the "autosymbolic phenomenon," a recent study suggests the following hypotheses: (1) Similar if not identical products can be elicited from non-hypnotized persons by instructions to make up symbolic dream-like material. (2) The "symbolic hypnotic dream" differs from the nocturnal dream and from the "autosymbolic phenomenon" in that it does not appear spontaneously; the "hypnotized" S purposively creates, "makes us," or tries to think of symbols which indirectly represent the suggested dream topic. Carefully controlled experiments are needed to confirm or disprove these hypotheses.

"HYPNOTIC DREAMS" WITH "BIZARRE FEATURES"

In the experiments reported by Roffenstein, Nachmansohn, Mazer, Farber and Fisher, Barber and others, discussed above, the "hypnotized" Ss responded positively to suggestions to dream *symbolically* about *specified* topics. This type of "symbolic hypnotic dream" should be distinguished from an apparently related type of "hypnotic dream" which is rich in pictorial character and contains some bizarre features but does not symbolically represent a specifically-suggested dream topic.

Schneck (1953a, 1954) has presented a series of such "dreams" produced by a patient in analysis; these elaborate productions at times included bizarre features with sudden changes in locus, cast of actors and types of action. The author compared the patient's "hypnotic dreams," "self-hypnotic dreams," and nocturnal dreams and concluded that the three types were indistinguishable with respect to degree of activity, extent of embellishment, and nature of symbolizations. However, he also noted that the "hypnotic dreams," in contrast to the nocturnal dreams, typically included lengthy conversational situations during which the patient spoke for herself or projected onto others various points of view concerning her immediate problems. Wolberg (1945) and Kanzer (1945, 1953) have also presented "hypnotic dreams," rich in pictorial character, which were produced by patients in analysis.

Both Schneck and Wolberg imply that these elaborate "hypnotic dreams" which contain bizarre features are essentially the same as spontaneous night dreams. However, the possibility has not been excluded that similar imaginative productions can be elicited from non-hypnotized patients by instructions to imagine or to visualize certain events or situations. Ferenczi (1926) found that instructions to visualize a scene were sufficient, without "hypnosis," to evoke embellished dream-like fantasies from some psychoanalytic patients. Adler (1948) has presented in detail a number of bizarre fantasies elicited from non-hypnotized patients by instructions to visualize significant events or situations. He writes that "in the case of most people, with the expenditure of a little time and practice, these situations, or, as we might more aptly term them, these mental images, show a certain autonomous life and movement; they develop and acquire added characters" (p. 57).

In brief, although a small number of "hypnotized" psychoanalytic patients have reported "hypnotic dreams" which appeared to resemble nocturnal dreams in pictorial character and bizarre features, carefully controlled experiments are lacking to exclude the possibility that similar imaginative productions can be elicited from some non-hypnotized psychoanalytic patients by instructions vividly to imagine or to visualize certain events or situations.

THE "POSTHYPNOTIC DREAM"

The above considerations are applicable to the "hypnotic dream" which is produced in an interpersonal setting; somewhat different factors may be relevant to the "posthypnotic dream" produced after the hypnotic session, usually during the following night. Two questions should be answered with respect to "posthypnotic dreams": (1) Is the suggestion to dream at night on a selected topic more effective

when given to a "hypnotized" person than when given to a non-hypnotized person? (2) Is the "posthypnotic dream" more akin to the spontaneous night dream or to the "made-up dream"?

Fisher (1953a) has presented data which bear on the first question.
This investigator observed that some psychoanalytic patients who were
able to attain only a "very light hypnotic trance" responded positively
to suggestions to dream at night on selected topics. Since Fisher
doubted that his patients were "hypnotized" when they received the
dream suggestions, he hypothesized that "characteristics of the therapeutic relationship, other than the presumptive hypnotic state, might
account for the acceptance of suggestions to dream, and that such
acceptance might occur even if the hypnotic state were eliminated"
(Fisher, 1953a, p. 223). To test this hypothesis an experiment was
performed as follows: (1) Suggestions to dream at night on selected
topics were given under waking conditions to six patients undergoing
psychoanalysis. The patients received a total of 95 dream suggestions,
each given at the end of an analytic hour. (2) Five personal friends
of the experimenter were given a total of six dream suggestions in
.a non-experimental setting (under ordinary conditions of social intercourse). (3) A "good" hypnotic subject was given similar dream suggestions in 21 hypnotic sessions. (4) As a control, the six psychoanalytic patients were not given dream suggestions in 60 sessions but
a note was made of the specific dream suggestion that would have
been used if this were to be an experimental day. The suggested dream
topic was included in the manifest contents of: (1) 12 per cent (11
of 95) of the dreams presented the following day by the patients
in analysis; (2) 33 per cent (two of six) of the dreams presented
by the personal friends; and (3) 14 per cent (three of 21) of the
dreams presented by the hypnotic subject. In contrast, (4) three per
cent (two of 60) of the dreams presented on control days by the
psychoanalytic group included the might-have-been-suggested dream
topic in the manifest contents. Analysis of the dreams in terms of
the presumed latent contents appeared to indicate that 53, 33, and
57 per cent of the dreams presented by the psychoanalytic patients,
personal friends, and hypnotic subject, respectively, included the suggested topic, as compared to ten per cent of the dreams presented
on control days by the psychoanalytic group. Fisher interpreted these
findings as supporting the original hypothesis that the interpersonal
relationship between subject and experimenter, not the presence or
absence of "hypnotic trance," determines response to dream suggestions. However, the findings can be taken only as suggestive since
the experiment was not performed in a rigorous manner; e.g., only

one hypnotic subject was used, the suggested dream topic varied with each presentation, and the data were not treated statistically.

Barber and Calverley (in press) subsequently presented a more rigorous study. The Hypnotic group consisted of six women college students pre-selected as meeting criteria of "deep trance." This group was given the suggestion, under "hypnosis," to dream the following night on a selected topic ("riding a bicycle") and to record the dream upon awakening in the morning. The Control group consisted of 11 women students who were not selected for hypnotic susceptibility. To structure the experiment as a formal test-situation, this group was first given items from five Wechsler-Bellevue Intelligence Scale sub-tests for a period of 15 minutes with periodic verbal reinforcement of their responses ("that's very good," "that's fine"). Immediately after the Intelligence Test, the Controls were told that the next part of the experiment consisted of a dream study; the suggestion was then given to dream the following night about "riding a bicycle" and to record the dream upon awakening. (To rule out the possibility that dreams concerned with "riding a bicycle" might occur if such dreams were not suggested, a third group, consisting of 35 women students, was asked to record any dreams occurring the following night; none of the dream reports presented by this group included a bicycle in the manifest contents.) On the day following, two of the six Ss in the Hypnotic group and two of the 11 in the Control group presented dream reports which revolved around the suggested topic (e.g., "I had a dream in which I was riding a bicycle; there were a lot of other people riding too and they were going up a hill"). (The other Hypnotic and Control Ss stated either that they did not dream or could not remember their dreams.) Although there appeared to be a trend toward heightened responsiveness to the dream suggestions on the part of the "hypnotized" group, the differences did not attain statistical significance. It should be noted that this experiment was deliberately designed to favor the hypnotic condition as follows: (1) The Control group consisted of unselected subjects. The Hypnotic group consisted of Ss meeting criteria for "deep trance"; this explicit criterion is difficult if not impossible to differentiate from an inter-related implicit criterion, namely, that Ss were highly responsive (with or without "hypnosis") to various types of "suggestions." (2) The Hypnotic group but not the Control group had participated in a previous (selection) experiment in which it had interacted with the experimenter and had an opportunity to form a friendly relationship with him. (3) Although the "trance induction procedure" administered to the Hypnotic group included suggestions designed to produce positive motivation or ego-involvement in the test-situation, no attempt was made to motivate the Control group to perform maximally on the suggested task. Additional experiments are required which control these factors. Hypnotic and control Ss should be randomly selected from a homogeneous group of "good" hypnotic subjects or from a homogeneous group of unrated subjects (Barber, 1962b; Sutcliffe, 1960). Both groups should have a comparable amount of prior contacts with the experimenter. Both groups should be given motivating instructions prior to the administration of the dream suggestion. The results of the Barber and Calverley experiment appear to indicate that if S variables, interpersonal factors, and motivational variables are controlled, the null hypothesis, that "hypnotized" and control Ss do not differ in response to dream suggestions, may be difficult to reject.

THE "POSTHYPNOTIC DREAM" AND THE "DAY RESIDUES"

It appears possible that some dreams occurring during the night following the hypnotic experiment may be influenced by a significant event from the preceding day—namely, the hypnotic session itself—in the same way as many nocturnal dreams are influenced by other "day residues." Such dreams would belong to a large class of natural dreams which Freud (1953, p. 250) discusses as follows:

The residue from the previous day which gives rise to dreams is a residue from the great interests of waking life. If the physician's words and the stimuli which he gives have become of importance to the patient they can enter into whatever constitutes the residue and can act as mental stimuli for dream-formation, just like other interests of affective value roused on the preceding day which have not subsided; they operate in the same way as bodily stimuli which affect the sleeper during sleep. Like these other factors inciting dreams, the trains of thought roused by the physician can appear in the manifest dream-contents or be revealed in the latent thoughts.

In a recent experimental study of nocturnal dreaming, Trosman et al. (1960) found that the experimental situation itself significantly influenced the dream contents. Two Ss slept at night in a laboratory while continuous recordings were made of EEG and eye movements. At various times during the night, whenever EEG and eye movements indicative of dreaming were present (Aserinsky and Kleitman, 1955; Dement and Kleitman, 1957a, 1957b), Ss were awakened and asked to report their dreams. A total of 106 dreams were thus obtained over 32 experimental nights. The experimental situation was found to be a major determinant of the dream contents. In some dreams the experimenter appeared as an actor; in other dreams Ss' pre-occupation with research was evident. The authors write that in general "the subject appeared to utilize the experimental situation as a screen for the projection of transference reactions which were characteristic of his personality."

Somewhat along similar lines, Newman et al. (1960; cf. Rubenstein et al., 1957) presented data indicating that some "posthypnotic dreams" include elements of the hypnotic experimental session in the manifest contents. In this study "artificial complexes" involving cheating in an examination and stealing money were induced in a "deeply hypnotized" S. S, still under "hypnosis," was then given the suggestion to dream about cheating or stealing during the following night. The dreams presented the next day were influenced by the hypnotic experimental situation but the authors are not certain if the suggested dream topic was included in either the manifest or latent contents, writing as follows concerning the suggestion to dream about cheating: "In seeking indirect expression of the artificial complex, one may relate the giving of narcotics to a stranger to cheating (again a reversal: instead of taking he gives). But one does not have to seek S's preoccupation with the experimental situation, for it is clearly present." Not only did the figure of the hypnotist intrude into the dream narratives but the physical setting of the experiment—the research building, the arrangement of furniture in the experimental room—was also directly represented. Furthermore, S's feelings about being in a research project, about being used in the service of the experimenter's interests and not his own, appeared to find representation in the dreams.

Although the dreams presented in the Newman et al. study appear to have been influenced by a significant "day residue"—the hypnotic experiment itself—they may not have been "posthypnotic dreams," i.e., dreams produced in response to "posthypnotic suggestions" to dream at night on a selected topic. An experiment as follows is in order: A group of "deeply hypnotized" Ss should be given the suggestion to dream at night on a certain topic. A second group should also be "deeply hypnotized" but *not* given dream suggestions. A third group should undergo an experimental treatment which Ss find interesting but which does *not* involve "hypnosis" or dream suggestions. The next day all groups should be asked to recall any dreams occurring during the night. It can be hypothesized that some persons in each group will present dreams containing features from the experimental situation in the manifest contents. It would be of interest to determine if the dreams reported by the first group which was given the "posthypnotic suggestion" to dream on a selected topic differ from the dreams presented by the latter groups which were not given suggestions to dream.

THE "POSTHYPNOTIC DREAM" AND THE "MADE-UP DREAM"

Recent studies suggest the possibility that "posthypnotic dreams" which include the specifically suggested dream topic may be purposively constructed or "made up" by S when awake at night, while he strives to comply with the wishes or expectations of the hypnotist. Fisher (1953a, p. 230) observed that some Ss (psychoanalytic patients and one hypnotic subject) who were given suggestions to dream at night on selected themes "had strong conscious desires to dream, would remind themselves of the suggestion during the day and before falling asleep, would awaken frequently during the night, think of the suggestion and make efforts to remember any dreams that they had." Barber and Calverley (in press) obtained comparable findings in the experiment, summarized above, which included six hypnotic Ss and 11 controls. On the day following the suggestion to dream at night about "riding a bicycle," four Ss (two in the Hypnosis group and two in the Control group) presented "dreams" on the suggested topic. In response to post-experimental questionnaire items, three of the four stated that they had not slept normally during the night (e.g., "I kept waking up all through the night and kept thinking I would have to get back to sleep and dream about riding a bike"; "I'm exhausted! I have the feeling of having been awake all night"); and two (one from the Hypnosis group and one from the Control group) implied that they had purposively tried to "make" the dream appear (e.g., "When I was almost asleep I started myself thinking about it [the suggested dream topic] and then different episodes that had occurred previously came to my mind").

The data obtained in the Fisher and the Barber and Calverley experiments suggest that the hypnotic Ss and non-hypnotic controls may have executed the dream suggestion, not when they were asleep, but after they awakened at night. Schiff et al. (1961; cf. Sirna, 1945) have recently presented an electroencephalographic study in line with this possibility. These investigators monitored EEGs during "hypnotic dreaming" in a carefully selected "deep trance" S. This S's "hypnotic" and "posthypnotic dreams" were associated with a waking EEG pattern, and were distinguishable from natural nocturnal dreams which are associated with a light sleep EEG (Aserinsky and Kleitman, 1955;

Dement and Kleitman, 1957*a*, 1957*b*). Schiff et al. emphasize that when the "hypnotized" *S* is given the "posthypnotic suggestion" to dream on a selected topic during the following night while asleep, he awakens (according to EEG criteria) when he executes the suggestion.

In summary, experiments concerned with the "posthypnotic dream" appear to indicate the following:

(1) In a few instances, *S*s who were "hypnotized" during the day experienced dreams the following night which were influenced by a significant "day residue"—the hypnotic experiment itself. Although these dreams were categorized as "posthypnotic dreams" with the implication that they were produced in direct response to suggestions to dream at night on a selected topic, the possibility was not excluded that similar dreams would have occurred if *S*s had participated in experiments which they found interesting and important but which involved neither "hypnosis" nor the suggestion to dream.

(2) The suggestion to dream at night on a selected topic given under non-hypnotic conditions to psychoanalytic patients, to personal friends, and to students may be as effective as the same suggestion given to "hypnotized" persons in evoking "dreams" on the selected topic.

(3) Experimental evidence suggests the possibility that (*a*) "posthypnotic dreams" which specifically incorporate the suggested dream topic may be purposively constructed or "made up" by *S* when he awakens during the night and (*b*) the motivation for such "dream construction" may be imbedded in *S*'s desire to fulfill the wishes and expectations of the hypnotist. Additional experiments are needed to determine if "posthypnotic dreams" can be differentiated from "made-up dreams." A "deeply hypnotized" group should be given the suggestion to dream at night on a selected topic. A control group should be asked to make up a dream-like narrative on the same topic. The experiments reviewed suggest the hypothesis that both groups will present similar "dream" reports.

INTERPRETATION OF DREAMS UNDER "HYPNOSIS"

Farber and Fisher (1943) reported that individuals who could not interpret dreams under normal conditions were able to do so when "hypnotized." Twenty-five college students were told, under "hypnosis," that since they were now asleep they were capable of understanding the meaning of dreams; they were then given a series of imaginative products to interpret. Although Ss were told that the imaginative products were dreams, they were actually myths, psychotic productions, fantasies of the experimenters, and, in a few instances, dreams reported by patients in analysis. (In the few cases in which actual dreams were used, the original dreamer's associations to his dreams were not presented to Ss.) Although all hypnotic Ss claimed that they were not familiar with "the theory of dreams," five (or 20 per cent) interpreted the "dreams" in terms of sexual symbols. A dental extraction in a man was translated as castration and in a woman as giving birth to a baby. The story of Moses in the bulrushes was presented to a "hypnotized" female S; she stated that someone was going to have a baby—the bulrushes stood for pubic hair. A "hypnotized" woman was told that "a girl dreamt that she was packing her trunk when a big snake crawled into it; she was terrified and ran out of the room." S interpreted this as indicating that the girl was afraid of being seduced.

Gill and Brenman (1959, p. 348) set out to replicate this study. Eight "good" hypnotic subjects, who were not sophisticated with regard to the psychology of dreams, were selected from an original group of 60. Each one was given the same four dreams to translate under normal conditions and after the induction of "hypnosis." Instructions under both conditions were: "You have probably heard that dreams have meaning. I am going to tell you the dream of another person. I would like you to tell me what the dream means." The results did not confirm Farber and Fisher's study: in *no* case did a "hypnotized" S translate the dreams into the "expected" dream interpretation.[6]

The conflicting findings in the above investigations may be due to differences in the experimental conditions, or to S-differences such as the following:

[6] Moss and Stachowiak (1963) have also failed to confirm Farber and Fisher's findings. Although the reviewer was unable to obtain a copy of this report, as yet unpublished, the following personal communication from C. S. Moss summarizes the study: "We used 16 hypnotizable subjects and presented them with three (sometimes five) rather detailed symbolic items for interpretation. . . . The procedure was to have our subjects associate to the material first in the waking and then in the hypnotic state. The very firm conclusion derived from our investigation was that we obtained no real evidence of valid interpretative ability in either state—there was certainly no evidence that hypnosis enhanced the ability of our subjects to intuit the meaning of these materials. Equally evident was the fact that hypnosis had the effect of loosening the associative processes of our subjects with the result that they presented us with very rich and meaningful personal projections."

(1) Farber and Fisher worked with college students while Gill and Brenman used unsophisticated adults who presumably had less formal education. Although Farber and Fisher write that all of the students were "ignorant of any knowledge of the theory of dreams," this does not exclude the possibility that, during the course of their college studies, some of the student-subjects may have formed an association between the words "dream interpretation" and "sex" or between the words "psychiatry" and "sex." (The experimenters were introduced to the students as psychiatrists.)

(2) Farber and Fisher worked with 25 Ss, while Gill and Brenman used only eight. It appears possible that included in the larger but not the smaller sample were some individuals who (a) had a "talent" for dream interpretation, or (b) were sufficiently uninhibited as individuals to refer without qualms to sexual matters, or (c) had formed a sufficiently close relationship with the experimenter to speak uninhibitedly of sexual functions. These factors are discussed in more detail below.

Some individuals seem to have a "talent" for understanding the "meaning" of dreams. Freud (1960, p. 351) wrote as follows:

Advances in psycho-analytic experience have brought to our notice patients who have shown a direct understanding of dream-symbolism of this kind to a surprising extent. They were often sufferers from *dementia praecox*, so that for a time there was an inclination to suspect every dreamer who had this grasp of symbols of being a victim of that disease. But such is not the case. It is a question of a personal gift or peculiarity which has no visible pathological significance.

Working with 24 college students, Reis (1951) found that "most subjects were able without suggestions by the investigator to interpret their own dreams meaningfully," i.e., more or less in accordance with psychoanalytic dream theory. Hall (1953a) concluded from a series of investigations concerned with dreams that "many people have real talent for dream interpretation although some of these have little or no information about Freudian symbolism."[7]

Although a "talent" for dream interpretation may be helpful or

---

[7] Hall (1953a) notes that the unsophisticated person's ability to translate dream symbols may be related to the following: "People have been using a consciously contrived form of symbolism in their daily speech for centuries. It is called slang. Although there are slang expressions for many things, much of it is sexual in character . . . many of the dream symbols for the sex organs and for sexual intercourse are identical with those found in Partridge's *Dictionary of Slang and Unconventional English*."

necessary, it is questionable if it is sufficient to elicit a sexual interpretation of dream material. Additional factors which may be necessary
are: (1) a relatively uninhibited S, and (2) a close relationship between
S and experimenter. Farber and Fisher noted that the five Ss who
offered erotic interpretations of the "dream" material were the least
rigid and most uninhibited of their 25 subjects. Furthermore, these
five Ss gave sexual interpretations only when interviewed by the ex-
perimenter-hypnotist; when interviewed by another person, with
whom they presumably had not formed a close interpersonal relationship, they gave conventional nonsexual interpretations even when they
appeared to be "in the hypnotic state." Possibly related to this is Reis's
(1951) finding that the extent to which non-hypnotized persons arrived at "meaningful" interpretations of their dreams appeared to depend on the intensity of their rapport with the experimenter.

SUMMARY AND CONCLUSIONS

A series of investigations appears to indicate that the "hypnotic
dream" differs in essential respects from the nocturnal dream:

(1) The "hypnotic dream" is typically an unembellished imaginative product containing very little if any evidence of the "dreamwork." In some instances it consists of straightforward recall of previous happenings or of former night dreams; in the majority of instances,
it consists of banal verbal or imaginal associations to the suggested
dream topic.

(2) The evidence suggests that (a) "good" hypnotic subjects who
are given the suggestion *to dream* may define their imaginative productions as "dreams" in order to comply with the wishes and expectations
of the hypnotist and (b) if such "good" subjects were to be instructed
to imagine or to visualize, similar productions would result which the
subjects would *not* define as "dreams."

(3) Although most "hypnotic dreams" appear to be prosaic products
without symbolizations or distortions, a number of investigators have
published "hypnotic dreams" containing symbolic material or bizarre
features. In many of these instances Ss were told to represent the
dream topic symbolically; however, in a few instances, it appears that
patients in analysis produced "hypnotic dreams" which were rich in
pictorial character and ostensibly contained some symbolic material
when suggestions to symbolize were not given. These reports have
been interpreted as indicating that some "hypnotic dreams" are essen-

tially the same as natural night dreams; however, a series of independent investigations suggests that similar productions may be elicited from some non-hypnotized persons by instructions to "make up" symbolic dream-like material or by instructions to visualize or to imagine events or situations of personal significance.

The above considerations apply to the "dream" produced during the hypnotic session itself; related considerations appear applicable to the "posthypnotic dream" which is produced at a later time, usually at night:

(1) Some Ss, who have been "hypnotized" during the day, experience dreams during the following night which contain features of the hypnotic session in the manifest contents. These dreams have at times been categorized as "posthypnotic dreams" with the implication that they were produced in direct response to "posthypnotic suggestions." However, experimental evidence suggests that similar dreams may occur if suggestions "to dream" are *not* given during the hypnotic session. In recent investigations it was found that participation in various types of experiments, hypnotic or non-hypnotic, is at times a significant "day residue" which influences the contents of night dreams.

(2) In recent studies in which some "hypnotized" Ss *and some non-hypnotized* controls responded positively to suggestions to dream at night on specified topics, evidence was found which seemed to indicate that the "dreams" may have been purposively constructed or "made up" by persons in both groups when awake at night. Both the "hypnotized" and the non-hypnotized Ss did not sleep normally and appeared to strive during the night to produce thoughts and images which revolved around the suggested dream topic, and some implied in post-experimental interviews that the "dreams" did not appear spontaneously but were created purposively. Additional investigations are necessary to determine if "posthypnotic dreams" produced in response to a suggestion to dream at night on a selected topic can be distinguished from the productions of non-hypnotized controls who are instructed to make up a dream-like narrative on the same topic.

The contention that "hypnotized" Ss are able to understand the "meaning" of dreams is based on one experimental study which found that five of 25 "hypnotized" college students, who denied knowledge of "dream theory," interpreted "dreams" in terms of sexual symbols. This report has not been confirmed in subsequent studies. Even if it were to be confirmed, the interpretation of the findings would be equivocal since a series of investigations indicates that a certain proportion of non-hypnotized persons who state that they are unacquainted with psychoanalytic theory are able to interpret dreams in terms of Freudian symbols.

This review suggests three general conclusions: (1) it has not been demonstrated that "hypnosis" enhances the ability to interpert dreams; (2) as Brenman (1949) had suggested in a previous review, it is open to serious question if "the hypnotic dream is a psychic production which duplicates, either in function or structure, the spontaneous night dream"; and (3) it appears possible that "dreams" induced by suggestions given to "deeply hypnotized" Ss may be difficult if not impossible to differentiate from the imaginative productions of non-hypnotized controls who are instructed and appropriately motivated to imagine vividly selected scenes or situations or who are instructed to make up dream-like material.

The Hypnotic Dream: Methodological Problems and a Review of the Literature

BY CHARLES T. TART

Abstract. Investigations of the hypnotic dream have been confounded by a variety of unrecognized methodological problems, such as inadequate specification of demand characteristics, trance depth, and nature of the *E-S* relationship. Failure to recognize that *S*s have a variety of experiences in response to dream suggestions has further obscured the literature. These methodological shortcomings are discussed and the literature on hypnotic dreams is reviewed.

It has long been known that if a hypnotized subject is instructed to dream, many subjects will subsequently report an experience in response to this suggestion. This reported experience is usually called the hypnotic dream. Opinions about the nature of the hypnotic dream have ranged all the way from considering it a made-up fantasy to concluding that it is identical in all essentials to noctural dreaming in the strictest Freudian sense. Comprehensive and scientifically adequate data on the nature of the hypnotic dream are, however, quite scarce, primarily due to serious methodological shortcomings of most of the published studies in this area. As many of these methodological problems have not been adequately recognized and dealt with in the literature, this paper will discuss these problems and review the experimental literature on the hypnotic dream in general.

At this point, the crucial terms "hypnosis," "dream," and "hypnotic dream" should be precisely defined. One of the main points to be brought out in the discussion below, however, is that these terms have been used quite ambiguously in the literature, so only some rough working definitions will be given at this point.

Hypnosis will be used in the conventional manner to refer to that

SOURCE. Reprinted by permission from *Psychological Bulletin*, **63** (2), 87–99 (1965).

This paper was written during the tenure of a Postdoctoral Research Fellowship, 1-F2-MH-14, 622-01, from the National Institute of Mental Health, United States Public Health Service, to which I wish to express my appreciation, as well as to my sponsor, E. R. Hilgard, for his helpful comments on this manuscript.

psychological state generally brought about by conventional induction techniques (see, e.g., Weitzenhoffer, 1957), and characterized, among other things, by hypersuggestibility of the hypnotized subject. *Dream* will refer to a subjective experience[1] in which the subject, the dreamer, finds himself bodily "located in" another world of experience, the "dream world," which he generally does not perceive as unreal at the time he is dreaming about it. *Hypnotic dream* will refer to an experience of the hypnotized subject in response to the suggestion to dream, a definition based primarily on what the experimenter does.

The chief methodological problems will be discussed under four related headings: (*a*) the nature of the suggestion to dream; (*b*) the subject's understanding of the suggestion; (*c*) the experiential-behavioral response of the subject; and (*d*) the physiological response of the subject. In other words, these are: (*a*) what the experimenter does; (*b*) what the subject thinks the experimenter wants; (*c*) and (*d*), what the subject does. This paper will then discuss posthypnotically affected dreams, mention other criticisms applicable to many of the studies in the literature, discuss what we know about the nature of the hypnotic dream, and finally compare different types of responses to the suggestion.

SUGGESTION TO DREAM

The hypnotic suggestion to dream, given to the subject, consists of four important parts. The first is, obviously, the command to dream. The second part is a specification of content, what is to be dreamed about, and the third part is a specification of manner, how the subject is to dream. Both the second and third parts may be either implicit and/or explicit, or omitted altogether. The fourth part consists of a specification of when the dream is to occur, but since this is almost always implicitly or explicitly specified as immediately, it will be ignored until the discussion of posthypnotically affected dreams. The dream suggestion may be represented in general form, then, as "Dream (about X) (in the manner of Y)." In the simplest case, the experimenter simply suggests to the hypnotized subject that he dream, period. At the other extreme, the experimenter may suggest to the subject that, for example, he dream about masturbating (X) in the same way

---

[1] My interest is primarily in the subject's experience, not his verbal report. I make the assumption that, with normal subjects, this report is a reasonably accurate account of their experiences, subject to semantic limitations, and so this article will talk about dreams, not about subjects' reports of their dreams.

that he dreams at night (Y_1), with the further implicit instruction that night dreaming consists of disguising the suggested topic (X) in a Freudian manner (Y_2). The experimenter may or may not be aware of the implicit instructions he gives to his subjects.

These implicit instructions associated with the explicit suggestion to dream are what Orne (1959, 1962) has called the *demand characteristics* of the experiment. These demands may be communicated by the wording of the suggestions, the physical setting of the experiment, the experimenter-subject relationship, paralinguistic features of the suggestions, etc. That an experiment is being carried out in a hospital and the experimenter is identified as a psychiatrist may, for example, imply to some subjects that the experimenter "interprets" dreams, and therefore his dreams should be disguised, with a little sexual symbolism thrown in for good measure! The extensive studies of Rosenthal and his co-workers (Rosenthal, 1963, 1964) of the ways in which experimenter bias and demands can affect experimental outcomes, even with animal subjects, should be mandatory reading for all those carrying out research in this area, especially in view of the fact reported in one study (Troffer and Tart, 1964) that sophisticated experimenters who were aware of this problem nevertheless treated hypnotic subjects in a biased manner, without realizing it.

Besides falsely "proving" the experimenters' hypotheses, a further drawback of implicit demands is that as the demands become more and more implicit, they probably become more ambiguous to the subjects, with a consequent increased variability in the way the subjects comprehend and react to these demands and to the more explicit instructions. While such ambiguity may be desirable for a projective test, or may be studied in itself, it is undesirable as an uncontrolled variable in experiments on hypnotic dreams.

In surveying the literature on hypnotic dreams, one finds an almost universal lack of sufficient information about the experiments to allow one to make even a good guess about the demand characteristics. Several studies (Barber, 1962a; Farber and Fisher, 1943; Fisher, 1953a, 1953b; McCord, 1946; Mazer, 1951; Newman, Katz, and Rubenstein, 1960; Rappaport, 1951; Rubenstein, Katz, and Newman, 1957; Tart, 1964b) have pointed out that the experimenter-subject relationship affects the hypnotic dreams, but generally these authors have not applied this insight wholeheartedly to their own studies, nor to the interpretation of the hypnotic dream literature as a whole. Knowledge of these demand characteristics is particularly critical in evaluating many studies which were carried out within a psychoanalytic framework because of the rather subtle nature of the analyses made.

SUBJECT'S UNDERSTANDING OF THE SUGGESTION

The use of the word "dream" in the suggestion to the subject carries a semantically ambiguous, implicit demand with it. The implicit demand is that dream may be interpreted by a subject as, "Dream as you do at night." The related semantic problem is that the word does not have a high degree of linguistic standardization because it refers to a relatively private experience. People vary greatly in the way they experience dreaming, so to some subjects dream may mean, "See some vague poorly formed black-and-white pictures," while to others it might mean, "Have a rich, vivid, and emotionally stimulating experience in your dream world." Many studies (Eiduson, 1959; Howarth, 1962; Orlinsky, 1962; Puryear, 1962; Rychlack, 1960; Schonbar, 1961; Tart, 1962) suggest great variability of many characteristics of dream experience, probably resulting from various personality factors. Thus the very use of the word dream may create ambiguity and consequent increased variability of results.

The literature on hypnotic dreams contains no information on the effect of this semantic ambiguity. Future studies should attempt to clarify the usage of dream to their subjects, and/or sytematically study the effect of various interpretations of dream by the subjects on the resulting hypnotic dreams. It might also be possible to avoid the use of the word dream altogether by instructing the hypnotized subject that in a moment he would experience X in the manner of Y, etc.

EXPERIENTIAL–BEHAVIORAL RESPONSE OF THE SUBJECT

The subject's response to the dream suggestions is determined not only by the explicit and implicit demands and suggestions of the experimenter, but also by characteristics of his own about which we know little at present. An almost universal demand in the hypnotic dream literature is that the subject dream in the way he does at night, and the term hypnotic dream implies that these experiences are indeed similar. It has been noted, however (Barber, 1962a; Brenman, 1949; Gill and Brenman, 1959), that the hypnotic dreams reported by many subjects are not dreamlike at all. The present author's experience suggests that there are at least four rather discrete types of responses, occurring rather frequently, and distinguished by certain formal characteristics of the subjects' experiences, which, a priori, should be discriminated by questioning the subjects. We can term these: (a) *dream-*

like hypnotic experience,[2] in which the subject reports he was bodily "located within" a dream world; *(b) intense hypnotic imagery,* for vivid, usually visual hallucinations, but which are more like watching a film; *(c) hypnotic fantasy,* for daydreaming and fantasy of less than hallucinatory intensity; and *(d) hypnotic thoughts,* for simply thinking about a topic, with little or no imagery. A fifth possible response to the suggestion, discussed more fully below, is that the subjects slip into Stage 1 sleep in order to dream. Other types of responses exist,[3] but the above seem to be the most frequent and closest to the way the subjects themselves describe their experiences.

Now these are admittedly rough categories, and, at present, precise boundaries separating them cannot be specified (although subjects have little trouble making these distinctions). Nor is it known whether these are qualitative distinctions or points along a continuum. Such distinctions, even if imprecise, need to be drawn, however, for common experience indicates differences between dreaming and thinking, hallucinating and fantasying. Including all of these responses under the blanket term "hypnotic dream" again leads to increased variability of results insofar as these different responses almost certainly have

[2] The use of the adjective "hypnotic" in these terms is based upon the assumption that these phenomena would not be experienced unless the subject entered a hypnotic state. Some subjects, however, may be able to experience some of these phenomena without any prior formal induction of a hypnotic state (Barber and Calverly, 1962, 1963). Whether it is best to conceptualize these experiences as hypnotic ones occurring after the subject has spontaneously hypnotized himself, or whether to conceptualize them as phenomena which can be experienced outside a hypnotic state is unknown at present. The possibility of additional response categories if the latter alternative is valid should be kept in mind.

[3] Preliminary data collected at the Laboratory of Human Development indicate that these four types of responses (*a, b, c,* and *d*) occur approximately 13%, 26%, 15%, and 14% of the time, respectively, with "no dream" or "unable to classify" occurring 26% and 6% of the time, over a variety of experimental conditions. Some other descriptions occasionally reported by subjects are: brief, static images; vivid but momentary images, "flashes"; and images similar to the hypnagogic imagery they experience while falling asleep. Sometimes a subject reports that he responded by recalling an earlier night dream or real experience (Barber, 1962*a*), but the manner in which this recall is experienced would allow it to be placed in one of the above classifications. Gill and Brenman (1959) have also suggested some classifications of responses based on their work with patient populations and dealing with the degree of "primary process" material in the responses. These are: embellished reminiscence; static, pictorial image; quasi-allegory; and quasi-dream. As this classification is theoretically complex when we have so little basic data upon hypnotic dreams, as well as being somewhat removed from the immediate experience of the subjects, it will not be dealt with further at this time.

distinct experiential and psychological characteristics. The degree to which they have distinctive characteristics is, of course, a matter of empirical research, but unless it is shown that the differences are unimportant the hypnotic dream literature contains a great deal of confusion as a result of mixing these different responses indiscriminately.

About the only attempt to discriminate between differing responses which can be found in the hypnotic dream literature is that of asking the subjects whether their hypnotic dreams were like their sleep dreams (Farber and Fisher, 1943; Klein, 1930; Mazer, 1951; Sirna, 1945). The subjects apparently replied affirmatively, and the inquiry ended there. This rather global response by the subjects is probably of little value, however, for the (implicit) demand to dream as they did at night would tend to bias their answer, and we do not have enough information about these studies to know how strong this demand was. Tart (1964a) asked his subjects to compare their hypnotic and nocturnal dreams on a number of characteristics, and all subjects indicated that their hypnotic dreams differed from their nocturnal ones, although for a wide variety of reasons, which were not consistent from subject to subject.

The question of whether a subject will always give the same type of response to dream suggestions or will vary them can be raised. Preliminary data collected at the Laboratory of Human Development suggest that subjects are as likely to report a different type of experience in response to the hypnotic dream suggestion on a second day as they are to report the same type of experience, even though they feel just as hypnotized.

The data of one published study touch on this question to a small extent. Mazer (1951) reported that only subjects who reached a deep hypnotic state would report dreams in which the suggested content, X, had been disguised. Whether this would hold across varying degrees of the hypnotic state within a single subject is unknown. This finding is also rendered somewhat unclear, because in Mazer's studies the subjects apparently had to "learn" to dream in the disguised manner expected by the experimenter.

In summary, there are apparently a variety of experiential-behavioral responses by hypnotized subjects to the suggestion "Dream (about X) (in the manner of Y)" which should not be indiscriminately mixed, as they have been in the hypnotic dream literature. Quay's (1952) study and the present author's own data certainly cast doubt on the notion that most hypnotic dreams are very dreamlike. Future studies should not naïvely equate the hypnotic dream with the actions of the experimenter, but should question their subjects (being careful of the demands the questions create!) about the nature of their experiences in response to the dream suggestions.

PHYSIOLOGICAL RESPONSE OF THE SUBJECT

As mentioned above, one possible response to "Dream (about X) (in the manner of Y)" would be for the subject to slip into Stage 1 sleep and so dream. Many recent experiments, summarized elsewhere (Kamiya, 1961; Kleitman, 1960, 1963; Oswald, 1962; Snyder, 1963), strongly indicate that (a) what we ordinarily think of as nocturnal dreaming in which the dreamer has experiences "in" a "dream world," takes place in a particular kind of sleep,[4] called Stage 1 sleep after its characteristic electroencephalographic (EEG) pattern by Dement (1955); (b) three to five Stage 1 periods occur in fairly regular progression throughout a night of sleep, each period generally longer than the previous one, and altogether occupying between 15% and 30% of the total sleep time of normal adults; and (c) binocularly synchronous, rapid, eye movements (REMs) almost always accompany Stage 1 dreaming, and the evidence (Berger and Oswald, 1962; Dement and Kleitman, 1957a; Dement and Wolpert, 1958; Roffwarg, Dement, Muzio, and Fisher, 1962) strongly indicates that these REMs are a scanning of the imagery being experienced by the dreamer.

Studies of the EEG concomitants of the hypnotic state, on the other hand, indicate strongly that the EEG pattern of the hypnotic state is a waking EEG pattern (Barber, 1961a; Crasilneck and Hall, 1959; Gill and Brenman, 1959; Gorton, 1962) within which there are various degrees of activation. More specifically, it has been shown (Schiff, Bunney and Freedman, 1961; Sirna, 1945; Tart, 1964a) that hypnotic dreams are accompanied by a waking EEG pattern. Insofar as one would expect different psychological attributes of an experience occurring in a different neurophysiological state, the response of going into Stage 1 sleep in order to carry out the hypnotic suggestion to dream must be carefully distinguished from the other responses mentioned above.

---

[4] There is evidence (Foulkes, 1962; Goodenough, Shapiro, Holden, and Steinschriber, 1959; Rechtschaffen, Verdone, and Wheaton, 1962) indicating that some mental activity occurs in other stages of sleep than Stage 1. It appears to be qualitatively different from Stage 1 dreaming, more like a sort of "slowed down thinking." Insofar as it is only rarely recalled and little is known about it, it will not be further discussed in this paper, although it may turn out to be important for understanding hypnotic dreams.

While slipping into Stage 1 sleep in order to dream is a possibility, does it actually occur? There is no direct EEG evidence for this in the literature. However, instances of subjects falling asleep while ostensibly in hypnosis have been reported (see, e.g., Chertok and Kramarz, 1959; Crasilneck and Hall, 1959; Diamont, Dufek, Hoskovec, Kristof, Pekarek, Roth, and Velek, 1960), and some behavioral observations (Gill and Brenman, 1959; Solovey and Milechnin, 1960) also lend some support to this possibility. Arguing against this possibility is one report (Rechtschaffen, Wolpert, Dement, Mitchell, and Fisher, 1963) that under nonhypnotic conditions it is extremely rare for a normal subject to begin dreaming in Stage 1 immediately upon going to sleep.[5] Thus until we know how frequent or rare this type of response is, it would be wise to utilize EEG monitoring or some other technique[6] to distinguish this type of response.

Since hypnosis is conventionally defined as a state of hypersuggestibility, and since it appears from the above mentioned studies that if a subject shows a sleep EEG pattern during the hypnotic state he does not respond to suggestion,[7] the earlier definition of hypnosis given in this paper will now be made more restricted. In the remainder of this paper the term hypnosis refers to that psychological state, brought about by conventional induction techniques, characterized, among other things, by hypersuggestibility of the subject, and accompanied by a waking EEG pattern, which pattern may show various alterations depending on the subject's degree of activation (Malmo,

[5] An additional factor here is that Stage 1 periods which normally occur briefly at the onset of sleep, and seem to be associated with hypnagogic imagery (McKeller, 1957) may be psychologically and neurophysiologically different from the later Stage 1 dream periods of the night (Rechtschaffen et al., 1963). They are not accompanied by REMs. There is little else that can be said about this phenomenon at present, but this fact should be kept in mind, particularly as some subjects describe their hypnotic dreams as being like hypnagogic imagery.
[6] Electroencephalogram monitoring entails an expensive investment in equipment, as well as time to apply electrodes to each subject. It might be possible to develop an operant task that could be carried out by a hypnotized subject but not by a sleeping subject and use this to differentiate hypnotic and Stage 1 responses, provided the task did not interfere with the hypnotic dreaming. Using short time periods for hypnotic dreams with subjects who are not drowsy might also be a fair safeguard. Both of these methods would have to be checked against EEG monitoring eventually.
[7] One study (Krakora, 1953) known to the present author contradicts this, for it reports that hypnotized subjects can respond to suggestions while showing a sleep EEG pattern, but as Krakora is rather vague on reporting details of his procedures, it does not seem necessary to modify the above assertions at present.

1959) within the hypnotic state.[8] Thus as a response to the hypnotic suggestion to "Dream (about X) (in the manner of Y)" a subject may show any of the hypnotic responses (dreamlike, hallucination, fantasy, or thinking) discussed above, or slip into Stage 1 sleep. We may term the latter response *Stage 1 dreaming within hypnosis*. It is possible that the subjects might not be able to distinguish this latter response from a dreamlike hypnotic response in response to questioning.

In addition to the EEG, the possibility of other psychophysiological measures distinguishing various responses to "Dream (about X) (in the manner of Y)" needs to be investigated. The greatest differences would probably be found between Stage 1 responses and responses within the hypnotic state. Tart (1964*a*) found that hypnotic dreams (which seemed quite dreamlike) about emotionally charged topics were accompanied by frequent, high amplitude, nonspecific, galvanic skin responses (GSRs), while Stage 1 dreams about the same topics were never so accompanied.[9] The average level of basal skin resistance (BSR) also differentiated dreams in the two states, although on a quantitative, rather than an all-or-none basis. Insofar as there seems to be a fairly dramatic alteration of some aspects of physiological functioning in Stage 1 sleep, variables such as respiration, blood pressure, cardiac activity, and reflex activity might also prove to differentiate the two types of responses, hypnotic and Stage 1.

Whether physiological measures can differentiate the various responses to "Dream (about X) (in the manner of Y)" which occur within the hypnotic state cannot be assessed from the literature, as studies have not discriminated among these various possible responses. There are a number of reports of physiological measures associated with hypnotic dreams in general, however. Schiff et al. (1961) report

[8] This is not to imply that periods of sleep interspersed with the hypnotic state are to be ignored, but only that they should be carefully distinguished from what is ordinarily considered the hypnotic state. Indeed, these sleep periods raise some very interesting questions in their own right.

[9] As pointed out in Footnote 4, the brief Stage 1 period at the onset of sleep (often called a "drowsy" EEG pattern in earlier literature) may be physiologically and psychologically different from the later Stage 1 periods of the night, so this striking difference in nonspecific GSR activity might not hold for initial Stage 1 responses. Burch and Greiner (1960) have reported a paradoxical increase in the amplitude of GSRs to stimuli during drowsiness, and if their use of drowsiness means the brief Stage 1 as a subject goes to sleep, any stimulation a hypnotic subject received might break down the above differentiation. This paradoxical reaction might be a startle response which would not be present in many hypnotic experiments, though.

that REMs occurred in conjunction with the hypnotic dreams of one subject whom they studied intensively, and these REMs seemed to be scanning movements of the dream imagery similar to those found for Stage 1 dreams. Other investigations indicate that emotions experienced in hypnotic dreams have respiratory (Rowland, 1932, 1936), cardiovascular (Kaplan, Gottschalk, Magliocco, Rohovit, and Ross, 1961; Rowland, 1936), dermal (Rowland, 1936), and gastric (Scantelbury, Frick, and Patterson, 1942) concomitants.

POSTHYPNOTICALLY INFLUENCED DREAMS

As briefly mentioned before, the hypnotic suggestion "Dream (about X) (in the manner of Y)" has a fourth component viz., a stipulation of when the dream is to occur. In the studies of the hypnotic dream discussed so far, this component has had a constant specification, viz., "Have the dream now." It would be possible to specify this time to occur after the subject had been dehypnotized and was normally awake, although the author knows of no experimental literature in which this was done. One would guess that the subject would spontaneously reenter the hypnotic state and have a hypnotic dream, but it would be of some interest if posthypnotic suggestions to dream could bring about dreamlike experiences in a later waking state.

A number of experimenters (Barber, 1962a; Fisher, 1953a, 1953b; Moss, 1961; Nachmansohn, 1951; Newman et al., 1960; Schiff et al., 1961; Schrotter, 1951; Stoyva, 1961; Tart, 1963, 1964a) have specified this later time as the subject's sleep that night, and their subjects generally reported dreams the next day which seemed to have been affected by the posthypnotic suggestions, often quite markedly. There may have been several types of responses among these subjects, however. One response would be exactly what was assumed, viz., that the normal, nocturnal dreams (Stage 1 dreams) of the subjects were influenced by the experimental suggestions. We may term this response the *posthypnotically influenced Stage 1 dream.* It is also possible that a subject would awaken during the night, spontaneously enter a hypnotic state, have any of the various hypnotic dream responses discussed above, and go back to sleep, without realizing that his dream did not occur in normal sleep.

In surveying the literature, we simply cannot tell what types of responses occurred in most of the studies, as there was neither EEG monitoring of the subjects' sleep nor intensive questioning about these formal characteristics of their experiences. That Stage 1 dreams can be strongly influenced by posthypnotic suggestion, often to the point

TABLE 1
Studies of hypnotic dreams

Study	Type — Psychoanalytically oriented	Type — Primarily theoretical	Conditions — Types of dreams studied	Conditions — Types of subjects used	Conclusions — Recognize need for comparison	Conclusions — Assume or conclude that . . .	Criticisms — Inadequate hypnotic depth information	Criticisms — Experimenter-subject relationship unclear	Criticisms — Lack of EEG monitoring	Criticisms — Conclusions depend on experimenter's opinion
Barber (1962)	+		HD & SD	N	++	HD ≠ SD	+	+	+	
Brenman (1949)		+	HD	P	++	HD ≠ SD		+	+	+
Erle (1953)			HD	N			+	+	+	+
Farber & Fisher (1943)	+		HD	N					++	
Fisher 1953a, 1953b	+		SD	P		HD = SD	+		++	++
Gill & Brenman (1959)	++	+	HD	N			+	+	+	+
Kanzer (1953)			HD	P						
Kaplan et al. (1961)			HD	P		HD = SD	++	++	++++	++++
Klein (1930)			HD	N				++	+++	+++
McCord (1946)	+++		HD	P				+++	+++	
Mazer (1951)	+++		HD	N	+	HD = SD		++	+++	
Moss (1961)	++		HD & SD	N & P		HD = SD			+++	
Nachmansohn (1925)	+		SD	P		HD = SD	+++			++
Newman et al. (1960)	+		SD	N		HD ≠ SD	++++	+	+++	+++
Pierce (1957)			HD	N						
Quay (1952)			HD	N					++	

246

Rappaport (1951)	+	+								
Roffenstein (1924)	+		HD	N		HD = SD	+	+	+	+
Rowland (1932)			HD	N			+	+	+	
Rowland (1936)			HD	N				+	+	
Rubenstein et al. (1957)	+		HD	N			+		+	+
Scantelbury et al. (1942)			HD	N			+	+	+	
Schiff et al. (1961)			HD & SD	N	+		+	+		
Schneck (1953*a*, 1953*b*)	+		HD	P	+				+	+
Schrotter (1911)	+		HD & SD	?		HD = SD	+	+	+	+
Siebert (1934)			HD	?		HD = SD	+	+	+	+
Sirna (1945)			HD	N	+		+	+		
Solovey & Milechnin (1960)			HD & SD (?)	P		HD = SD	+	+	+	+
Stoyva (1961)			SD	N	+		+			
Sweetland & Quay (1952)			HD	N	+		+	+	+	
Tart (1963)			SD	N	+					
Tart (1964*a*)			HD & SD	N	+	HD ≠ SD				
Welch (1936)			HD	N			+	+	+	
Wolberg (1945)	+	+	HD & SD	P		HD = SD				

Note. HD = hypnotic dream, SD = sleep dream, N = normal *Ss*, P = patients, and + indicates possession of that characteristic.

of almost total control of the dream content, has recently been demonstrated (Stoyva, 1961; Tart, 1963, 1964a). Stoyva also reported that the posthypnotically suggested dream content sometimes affected the "thinking" that was going on in Nonstage 1 sleep, as well as apparently having an effect on the amount of time spent in Stage 1 dreaming. On the other hand, Schiff et al. (1961) report that their intensively studied subject had a hypnotic dream (waking EEG) when she had been instructed to dream about a specified topic in her sleep, and she did not realize that her dream was not a sleep dream. These authors further state that this was a universal finding for an unreported number of other subjects. Thus it cannot be assumed that posthypnotic suggestions influence the content of Stage 1 dreams in a particular experiment unless there is EEG confirmation.

ADDITIONAL CRITICISMS OF THE LITERATURE

In addition to the basic methodological shortcomings discussed in detail above, there are a number of other criticisms common to many studies in the hypnotic dream literature. These are: (*a*) inadequate specification of the nature of the subjects' responses; (*b*) inadequate specification of the demand characteristics, the nature of the experimenter-subject relationship, and the experimental setting; (*c*) inadequate description of the subject population, especially with respect to how much they knew about psychoanalytic dream theory and whether or not they were patients; (*d*) inadequate specification of the depth of the hypnotic state used, not only generally important to hypnosis research (Gorton, 1962; LeCron, 1956), but specifically implicated as affecting hypnotic dreams (Mazer, 1951); (*e*) a general lack of EEG monitoring; and (*f*) an almost total dependence on the experimenters' opinions for the assessment of results, an especially prominent fault of the psychoanalytically oriented studies.

Specific characteristics and shortcomings of the various studies in the hypnotic dream literature are summarized in Table 1. Because of these widespread shortcomings, most of the results cited in the discussion below should be considered as suggestions, rather than as well-established facts.

NATURE OF THE HYPNOTIC DREAM

A variety of questions about the nature of hypnotic dreams can be, and have been, asked, and will be discussed briefly. Ideally, these questions should be separately asked of each of the distinct types of

responses to the dream suggestions, but the present state of the literature does not allow this, so the following discussion must treat of
hypnotic dreams in general.

An initial question that can be asked is whether there is an "uncon-
taminated" hypnotic dream, that is, can X and Y be made perfectly
explicit, so that the resultant hypnotic dream is a function of only
the condition of hypnosis, X, Y, and the subject's own characteristics?
The experimental situation and the experimenter-subject relationship
can strongly influence the hypnotic dreams of subjects, sometimes
to an even greater extent than the formal experimental suggestions.
A comparable influence of the experimental situation and the experimenter-subject relationship has been reported for Stage 1 dreams collected in the laboratory (Offenkrantz and Rechtschaffen, 1963; Whitman, Pierce, Maas, and Baldridge, 1962; Wolpert and Trosman, 1958),
which can apparently be quite long lasting with psychiatric patients.
Dement,[10] however, has found that adaptation seems to be rapid for
normal subjects, so that after a few nights in the laboratory the experimental situation is represented in the dreams considerably less frequently than on the initial night. The question of how quickly subjects
adapt to the experimental situation, so that it is no longer a major
determinant of their hypnotic dreams, has no answer in the hypnotic
dream literature.[11]

Assuming that subjects can be adapted to the experimental situation
well enough to be able to discount implicit demands, what lawful
relationships determine how the suggested content (X) is dealt with,
or limit the mode (Y) of dreaming? In considering this question we
should note that there are five types of experimental manipulations
that can be carried out here: (a) specifying X and Y; (b) specifying
X but not Y; (c) specifying Y but not X; (d) specifying neither
X nor Y; and (e) introducing further specifications of X and/or Y
during the hypnotic dream itself. The last category includes the introduction of sensory stimuli during the hypnotic dream. The questions,
then, are what lawful relationships govern the form of hypnotic dreams
under these various conditions, and what is the nature of hypnotic
dreams that are determined primarily by the subject himself (i.e.,
when the experimenter specifies neither topic nor mode)?

[10] W. Dement, personal communication, 1963.
[11] Although it has been treated here as a "contaminating" factor, the process
of adaptation is, of course, an interesting area of study in itself, and it could
be related to such variables as the type of experimenter-subject relationship,
depth of the hypnotic state, personality characteristics of the subject (and the
experimenter), etc.

The question of how suggested dream topics (Xs) are dealt with must be considered simultaneously with the question of how specific instructions as to the mode (Y) of dreaming are dealt with, because in the hypnotic dream literature there was almost certainly a universal (implicit if not explicit) instruction to dream as you do at night, and often the further (implicit) instruction to dream in a disguised form (in accordance with Freudian theory).

An indisputable conclusion that may be taken from the literature is that the hypnotic dream may be either a direct representation of the suggested topic or a disguised representation (i.e., the dream is manifestly different from the suggested topic but supposedly related to it by a set of lawful operations of transformation). In psychoanalytic terms, which have usually been employed in the literature, the suggested topic, X, acts as the latent dream content which is then transformed into the manifest dream content by means of various dream work mechanisms (Freud, 1960). Two basic questions are immediately raised: (a) what determines whether a hypnotic dream will be a direct or disguised representation of the suggested topic; and (b) what is the nature of the process of disguise, the transformation process?

We shall deal with the latter question first. The studies carried out primarily within a psychoanalytic framework all generally take the position that disguise will occur whenever the suggested topic consists of emotionally charged material that is threatening to the subject, or if the material while seemingly bland to the experimenter, is associated by the subject with emotionally threatening problems of his own. The suggested topic is assumed to act directly as the latent content and/or as a sort of day residue which links up with preconscious or unconscious impulses. These psychoanalytic studies conclude that their findings demonstrate the existence of the dream work mechanisms (symbolization, displacement, condensation, etc.) postulated by Freud, and that these dream work mechanisms explain the process of disguise in hypnotic (as well as nocturnal) dreams.

These findings are almost entirely a matter of the experimenter's opinion, supported with selected examples of hypnotic dreams, as well as having the other faults rated in Table 1. There can be little doubt that, for these (selected) examples, at least, these studies have demonstrated that suggested dream topics can be transformed in the manner Freud described, but that this is the "natural" or invariable way in which the hypnotic dream is produced is doubtful, for these results may be almost wholly attributable to the (unknown) demand characteristics of the experimental situations. In one study (Tart, 1964a)

where there were no demands to dream in accordance with psycho-analytic theory, the experimenter reported that there were no instances of disguise of the suggested topics at all, although this is again a matter of opinion. Two studies using relatively objective assessment techniques report results at variance with those claimed by the psychoanalytically oriented studies. Sweetland and Quay (1952) found that whether a suggested dream topic was disguised or not was unrelated to the degree of its emotional impact, and that well-adjusted subjects (judged from MMPI profiles), rather than poorly adjusted subjects, showed more frequent alteration and disguise of the suggested topics. The emotional suggestions used in this study were not of the intensity used in most of the psychoanalytically oriented studies, however. But Moss (1961), using the semantic differential technique as a measure of degree of disguise, found degree of disguise to be unrelated to the emotional impact of the dream suggestions, even though the rating of impact had resulted from extensive interviewing and psychological testing of the three subjects used in order to discover areas of psychic vulner-ability and strength.

There are a number of miscellaneous results dealing with the way information is processed in hypnotic dreams. Mazer (1951) studied the "latent period," the time elapsing between the suggestion to dream and the subject's signal that he had begun to dream. He reports that this latent period was longer for dreams which showed more disguise, and also that occupying the subjects with some other task during this latent period did not affect the dream production. Although these findings are, again, largely a matter of the experimenter's opinion, the latter finding is particularly intriguing if it can be validated, for it suggests that the process of disguise takes place "outside" of con-sciousness. But Sweetland and Quay (1952) failed to replicate Mazer's finding that a longer latent period was associated with greater disguise. Current studies at the Laboratory of Human Development suggest that depth of hypnosis is positively correlated with the vividness and dreamlike quality of hypnotic dreams.

Several studies (Benussi, 1927; Klein, 1930; Siebert, 1934; Solovey and Milechnin, 1960) have reported on the effects of presenting sen-sory stimuli during the hypnotic dream, and Klein (1930) and Erle (1953) sometimes used single words as "stimuli" to evoke hypnotic dreams. They have not generally recognized, however, that this pro-cedure constitutes an implicit instruction to dream about the stimuli, and this instruction may be more important than the nature of the stimulus. Thus about all that can be definitely concluded from these studies is that sometimes such stimuli are incorporated in the content of the hypnotic dream, sometimes directly and sometimes in disguised form.

Benussi (1927) and Welch (1936) report data indicating that subject's perception of time may be condensed or dilated during a hypnotic dream, a finding which needs to be more fully investigated.

Returning now to the question of what causes a hypnotic dream to be a direct or a disguised representation of the suggested content, the best answer that can be given at present is that the dream is not disguised unless there is an explicit or implicit demand for it to be. This may not be universally true, but in all the studies which reported disguised dreams it can be strongly argued that there were demands on the subjects to produce such dreams. Indeed, in some of these studies the subjects did not realize at first that they should disguise their dreams, but they gradually "learned" to do so, perhaps as a result of the experimenters expressing more interest in disguised dreams than in direct representations of the experimental suggestions. Whether subjects would produce disguised hypnotic dreams in the absence of demands for them is currently unknown, although it is an important question.

Let us now consider the hypnotic dream in which the experimenter specifies neither content (X) nor mode (Y), either explicitly or implicitly, what we might call the "spontaneous" hypnotic dream. Are there such hypnotic dreams? Gill and Brenman (1959) have speculated that there are never spontaneous hypnotic dreams because of the strong effect of the experimenter-subject relationship. On the other hand, Solovey and Milechnin (1960) report that hypnotized subjects who were resting quietly in the hypnotic state dreamt spontaneously, something the experimenters had not expected, but provide little information beyond that bare fact. Probably subjects have not been worked with over a long enough period to allow them to completely adapt to the laboratory situation, so that there have been no spontaneous hypnotic dreams in the literature. Nor do we know for certain whether sufficient adaptation can ever occur so that we may speak of a truly spontaneous hypnotic dream. Assuming that sufficient adaptation can occur, however, there are a multitude of questions that can be asked about them. On a very basic level, what sorts of things happen in them? A content survey similar to that of Hall's (1951) on nocturnal dreams would be in order. What aspects of the subject's personality determine dream content? How does day residue enter in? What lawful relationships exist among various aspects of the hypnotic dream?

RELATIONSHIPS BETWEEN RESPONSE TYPES

A question which has been implicitly raised a number of times in the above discussion is how various features of one type of response to "Dream (about X) (in the manner of Y)" compare with features of another type of response. The particular form in which this has generally been raised in the hypnotic dream literature has been asking whether hypnotic dreams were the same phenomenon as nocturnal dreams. Many studies either assumed or concluded this was so. Others have recognized the need for a direct comparison of the two phenomena and some have speculated on possible differences between the two phenomena (Barber, 1962a; Brenman, 1949; Gill and Brenman, 1959), but only one experimental comparison of suggested dreams occurring in the two states has been reported (Tart, 1964a), and this comparison suggests important differences between the two phenomena. There are, of course, theoretical reasons to expect differences. Hypnotic dreams do not seem to arise from a "need" to dream as Stage 1 dreams may do (Dement, 1960), they are not protecting sleep as Freud (1960) postulated nocturnal dreams do, nor are they instigated by personal needs, in the Freudian sense, but by the experimenter's suggestion. In view of the methodological shortcomings of practically all the studies in the literature, then, the question of similarities and differences between dreams occurring in hypnosis and sleep is still essentially unanswered at the present time.

Similarly, the problem of differences and similarities between various hypnotic responses to dream suggestions has barely been touched, there being no literature at all on this. A further problem, raised by Barber (1962), as to the relations between various hypnotic responses to dream suggestions and conscious attempts to make up dreams is also completely unanswered at present.

SUMMARY

The present paper has attempted to present a summary of our present knowledge of the hypnotic dream. The general picture is that of a very large number of basic questions to which we have only a few suggestions rather than answers, largely because of important methodological shortcomings of much of the research which has been done in this area.

Some (but certainly not all) of the more important and basic questions have been discussed above. These questions have largely centered about the ambiguous specification of the demand characteristics of experiments and a clarification of the various responses of subjects to the hypnotic suggestions to dream. The desirability (and often the necessity) of physiological measures in distinguishing different responses has been pointed out.

There has been no discussion of theories of hypnotic dreams because theorizing seems premature with so many basic questions unanswered, but the reader may consult the pertinent literature on this (Brenman, 1949; Farber and Fisher, 1943; Fisher, 1953a, 1953b, 1954; Gill and Brenman, 1959; Kanzer, 1953; Rappaport, 1951; Solovey and Milechnin, 1960; Wolberg, 1945). Nor have the clinical diagnostic and psychotherapeutic uses of the hypnotic dream been covered (Gill and Brenman, 1959; McCord, 1946; Newman et al., 1960; Rubenstein et al., 1957; Schneck, 1953a, 1953b; Wolberg, 1945). Insofar as the literature indicates that the hypnotic dream can be a valuable diagnostic and psychotherapeutic aid, as well as helping us understand the nature of thinking, fantasy, hallucination, and dreaming, more work is warranted in this area. Methodologically sophisticated studies can answer many of the basic questions raised above, and despite the difficulties of this area of research, it should yield a rich reward to systematic investigation.

Posthypnotically Suggested Dreams and the Sleep Cycle

BY JOHANN MARTIN STOYVA

Beginning with the work of Aserinsky and Kleitman (1953), several studies have shown that the cycles of rapid conjugate eye movements appearing during sleep are reliable indicators of dream occurrence. Researchers have noted that subjects ordinarily pass through four to seven such cycles in the course of a night and, typically, it is during the stage 1 phase of sleep (low-voltage fast electroencephalographic pattern) that rapid eye movements occur and from which vivid, narrative-type dream reports are readily obtained.

The use of hypnosis to influence dream content was first investigated by Schroetter (1911), who reported that subjects could be made to dream on the night following a hypnotic trance about topics suggested by the experimenter during the trance. Schroetter's main concern was to test Freud's theory of symbol formation, and he concluded that his subjects dreamed about various topics, primarily sexual ones, in the fashion that had been predicted from psychoanalytic theory; i.e., the symbols of sexual activity chosen were ones familiar in psychoanalysis. Schroetter's work was later confirmed by Roffenstein (1924) and Nachmansohn (1925).

The initial purpose of the present inquiry was to investigate the effects of hypnosis on dreams using the newly developed techniques of dream study (Aserinsky and Kleitman, 1953; Dement and Kleitman, 1957a). It was hoped not only to replicate the earlier experiments but to extend them by answering such questions as: Does the subject dream about the suggested topic only in the first rapid eye movement (REM) period, or will he continue to do so in every REM period of the night? Does the suggested material form a separate scene, or is it contextually related to the remainder of the manifest dream content?

A further point of interest was related to current thinking about a "need-to-dream." Dement (1960) had systematically deprived subjects of their regular REM time over a series of nights by interrupting

SOURCE. Reprinted by permission from the *Archives of General Psychiatry*, **12**, 287–294 (March. 1965).

255

each REM period within a short time of its onset. On a subsequent recovery night, consisting of uninterrupted sleep, amount of REM time was significantly increased over what it had been on baseline nights. This evidence gave rise to the idea that there is, perhaps, a "need-to-dream"; i.e., a need for the sort of fantasy activity that occurs during REM periods. It was then reasoned by the present investigator that if there is a need for this type of fantasy activity, possibly the dream-like hallucinations that can be made to occur during the deep trance state (Schroetter, 1911; Farber and Fisher, 1943) could, under certain conditions, serve as a substitute for the REM type of dream.

In the process of exploring the hypothesis that trance "dreams" might substitute for rapid eye movement type dreams, it was noticed that there was a sharp reduction in time spent in REM periods on those nights when the subject had been given a posthypnotic dream suggestion. In the instance of the first subject in whom this phenomenon was observed, it was noticed upon inspecting the 16 nights for which this subject had already been run that there was a decided difference in the length of the first REM period depending upon whether or not the subject had been given a posthypnotic dream suggestion. Examination of the data showed that the mean length of REM period 1 for this subject's ten experimental nights was 5.2 minutes (range 2.0 to 9.5 minutes). The mean length of REM period 1 for the six control nights—on which no posthypnotic dream suggestions had been given—was 21.4 minutes (range 12.5 to 34.5 minutes). These 16 experimental and control nights were interspersed in a nonsystematic fashion and were spread out over a period of three months.

The "shortening effect" observed in this particular subject was of considerable interest since it was an instance of a psychological variable affecting amount of REM time. Therefore, the exploration of trance dreams was set aside in favor of investigating this new phenomenon more systematically. On the basis of the preliminary findings it was decided to carry out the research in two stages: (1) validation of the shortening effect by extending the study to a greater number of subjects; (2) inquiry as to the underlying psychological mechanism producing the shortening effect.

METHOD

1. *Subjects.* Since the preliminary study pointed to the tentative conclusion that the shortening effect occurred only when the subjects were dreaming in accordance with the suggested topics, it was decided to choose only subjects who gave signs of going into an extremely deep trance.

The selection criteria used were that the subject show complete posthypnotic amnesia for a trial trance period, and also that he be able to follow a simple posthypnotic suggestion.

Seventy-one individuals were tested, of whom 17 met the selection criteria. (One of the original group of 17 Ss had to be dropped from the sample since the trance procedure brought on symptoms of severe emotional disturbance.) All of the subjects were either present or past students at the University of Chicago. And with the exception of one individual (patient 1), the entire group consisted of males. The ages of the subjects ranged from 18 to 43—only two subjects were past the age of 30.

2. *Laboratory Procedure*. *A.* Brain waves and eye movements were recorded in the manner described by Dement and Kleitman (1957a). The following attachments of the silver disc electrodes were made: (*a*) occipital lobe versus a reference ear lobe, (*b*) parietal lobe versus a reference ear lobe, (*c*) right eye versus left eye. The eye leads were attached lateral to each eye at a distance of one half to three quarter inches from the external canthus. (*d*) One frontal lead was placed above the left eye and as close to the subject's hairline as possible. The purpose of this lead was to serve as a spare should the ear attachment work loose during the night, thus making it possible to continue getting a record without having to awaken the subject and thereby interfering with his REM time.

B. The subject was allowed to go to bed, connected to the EEG, and put into a hypnotic trance. The trance induction procedure consisted essentially of suggesting to the subject that he progressively relax his musculature, that he was becoming extremely drowsy, that he was listening only to what the experimenter was saying, and finally that he was sinking asleep. Generally, between five and ten minutes were spent for this induction phase.

C. During the trance, dream instructions were given as follows:

"Now I want you to listen carefully to what I say. You will dream in every dream tonight that you are 'climbing a tree.' You will dream of this in every dream tonight. You will dream only of this—that you are 'climbing a tree.' And you will dream of this *only* for tonight." (This last instruction was adopted after some subjects reported dreaming about the suggested topic even on some nights subsequent to serving in the laboratory.)

D. After amnesia for the entire trance period had been suggested, the subject was taken out of the trance and then allowed to lapse into a natural sleep. Length of trance—including the induction phase—was typically some 24 minutes. On their laboratory nights, subjects slept between six and seven hours.

In the course of running a particular subject, baseline and experimental nights were interspersed with one another. Also, any given subject was *not* run for consecutive nights. The reason for adopting these procedures was to minimize any effects from one night to the next, including the possibility of partial "dream deprivation" accumulating from awakenings on initial nights.

3. *Apparatus.* The EEG used was an Offner 8 channel Type R. It had been equipped with an automatic paperspeed changer which proved very useful. Its manner of operation was such that the chart paper would run for 55 seconds at slow speed (1.5 mm per second); then it would automatically speed up to 15.0 mm per second for an interval of 5.0 seconds. Two subjects were run simultaneously, one being allotted the top four channels, the other the bottom four. Each subject was quartered in a separate room. The experimenter occupied a third room, where the EEG machine was located.

Gain settings of the amplifier on the parietal and occipital leads were either 20μv or 40μv per centimeter—whichever gave the clearest reading at the time. The time constant was fixed at 0.1 seconds. As for the eye leads, one channel was set at a time constant of 1.0 second together with a gain of 0.2 mv per centimeter. The other channel was set at a very short time constant, 0.1 seconds, together with a sensitivity close to that of the EEG leads, 50μv per centimeter. The purpose of this second channel was to improve scoring reliability. When this short a time constant was used, no eye movement would register on this channel unless its frequency was faster than 0.1 second, in which case it would appear as a sharp "blip." This provided a means of rather sharply distinguishing rapid eye movements from slow eye movements. And, by comparing the two channels, it proved possible to resolve the status of doubtful eye movements with little difficulty.

RESULTS

1. *Dream Reports in Accordance With Suggestion.* Table 1 shows, for each subject, the percentage of REM awakenings where *S* reported dreaming in accordance with the suggested topic. The 16 subjects fell into three rather distinct groups. In group 1, where percentage of recall in accordance with the suggestion ranged from 71% to 100%, there were seven subjects. Group 2, where percentage of recall in accordance with the suggestion ranged from 43% to 57%, contained five subjects. Group 3, where percentage of recall in accordance with the suggestion ranged from 0% to 33%, contained four subjects.

Note should be made that for each subject the figures in Table 1 are based upon more nights than are indicated in Table 2. The reason for this is that, on a subject's first one or two nights in the

TABLE 1

Percentage of REM period awakenings where S reported dreaming
in accordance with suggestion

S	Number of awakenings	Content recall	Per cent of recall content	Recall in accord-ance with suggestion	Per cent of recall in accord-ance with suggestion
Group 1					
2	13	13	100	13	100
9	13	12	92	11	92
3	18	17	94	15	88
1	51	48	94	41.5	86
10	6	6	100	5	83
11	12	11	92	8	73
8	9	7	78	5	71
	Mean percentage		93		85
Group 2					
12	7	7	100	4	57
13	3	3	100	1.5	50
14	2	2	100	1	50
15	10	8	80	3.5	44
4	8	7	87	3	43
	Mean percentage		93		49
Group 3					
6	6	6	100	2	33
5	9	8	89	1	13
16	5	5	100	0	0
7	2	2	100	0	0
	Mean percentage		97		11

laboratory, three to six REM awakenings took place per night. Thus, while data from these initial nights were available for determining the percentage of dream reports in accordance with the suggestion, these nights could not be used in testing for the shortening effect, since REM periods had been interrupted by frequent awakenings.

Dreams were scored as being in accordance with the suggested topic if the reported content showed a clear connection with the suggestion; i.e., there were identical or very similar images present. While most

TABLE 2

Reduction in REM time shown as difference between mean control REM time and mean experimental night REM time for each subject

S	Per cent of recall per suggestion	REM times						Reduction in REM time, experimental-control night difference*
		Control nights			Experimental nights			
		Mean	Range	Number	Mean	Range	Number	
Group 1								
2	100	33.0	27–41	3	24.2	17–36	4	8.8
9	92	54.0	54	1	55.5	55.5	1	−1.5
3	88	47.3	43–52	3	40.4	31–55	5	6.9
1	86	32.6	18–44	4	19.0	12–25	10	13.6
10	83	27.0	16–38	2	19.7	12–26	3	7.3
11	73	22.3	14–29	3	11.5	3–23	3	10.8
8	71	16.2	8–23	3	15.7	2–33	6	0.5
Group 2								
12	57	15.0	9–21	2	35.3	24–50	3	−20.3
13	50	24.5	23–26	2	15.5	7–27	3	9.0
14	50	44.0	44	1	46.0	45–47	2	−2.0
15	44	44.0	44	1	38.5	36–40	3	5.5
4	43	39.5	32–47	2	36.0	36	1	3.5
Group 3								
5	13	11.0	11	1	31.0	31	1	−20.0
16	0	18.0	18	1	30.0	30	1	−12.0
			N = 29				N = 46	

* For a given subject "experimental-control night difference" refers to the mean amount of time spent in REM periods for all the control nights minus the mean amount of time spent in REM periods for all the experimental nights. All times given are in minutes. Cut-off point was 3.5 hours.

of the reports were easy to rate as being in accordance with the suggestion or not, there were a number of doubtful cases where the similarity between the suggestion and the dream report lay only in a minor detail—for example, "I dreamed that I threw a pebble into a *pool of water*," in response to the suggestion, "You will dream in every dream tonight of rowing a boat." For the purpose of determining the percentage of dreams in accordance with the suggestion, such doubtful reports were scored as half a point rather than a full point since this similarity, i.e., the reference to *water*, may have been only a chance correspondence. These doubtful reports, which came mainly from the *S*s in group 2, made up less than 10% of the total.

The seven subjects in group 1 usually reported dreaming about the same general topic throughout the night. Although there were variations on the basic theme, the original suggestion was still clearly recognizable in most of the successive reports from the same night (see example 3 below).

Below are some typical examples of the dream reports obtained and the manner in which they were classified:

Example 1: Dream report scored as being in accordance with suggestion.
Dream Suggestion. "You will dream in every dream tonight of climbing a tree."
Subject 2; awakened after 16.0 minutes in REM period 2.
"There's this old *maple* in front of our house in Philadelphia. It used to scratch against the window and, ahhh, sometimes we had to cut off the *branches*. So, I don't know, usually we just go out on the roof, but we were all *going up the tree* by the base to do it. All of us. The whole family and my grandmother—and she's been dead for about five years now. We couldn't get up it and just scratching (sic) against the windows and making scraping noises."

Example 2: Dream report scored as being in accordance with suggestion.
Dream Suggestion. "You will dream in every dream tonight that you fall from a horse."
Subject 3; awakened after 9.0 minutes in REM period 2.
"I was, it was in this field in the dark; it was at night. There was this horse, and I had a huge knife and I was chopping at it, and I was chopping at it, and I was chopping at it, attacking me (sic) and it wouldn't go away; cut it and chop at it, it's sumpin' awful! It wouldn't fall off, and a, a, attacked the horse and it wouldn't go, just wouldn't go! I hated it! I don't know why, why I dream about horses, anyway. I hate horses! I don't dare get near a horse!"

Example 3: Series of dream reports from one night. Scored as being in accordance with suggestion.
Dream Suggestion. "You will dream in every dream tonight of climbing a tree."
A. Subject 1; first awakening, after 2.5 minutes in REM period 2.
"We made a, an outing trip, and I don't know where we went; we went through the *woods*. We marched and marched and marched. Oh, it was very colorful, very much so. That's all I know. I think the dream isn't finished."

B. *Subject 1;* same night, second awakening, after 11.0 minutes in REM period 3.

"Mmmmmhhh, I'm walking, I don't know, with people. I'm going places in *woods* and then we climbed on an apple tree to pick some ripe beautiful apples.

Examiner: "Did this remind you of any place you'd ever been?"

S: "Yes, at home, you know, the apple orchards we have and the meadows where the cows are. Very picturesque."

C. *Subject 1;* same night, third and final awakening; 24.0 minutes after end of REM period 4.

"I was dreaming about; oh what was it now? (ten second pause) Egypt, my beloved Egypt! And I was taking people to a tomb in Upper Egypt. And we were looking for some shadow, shade—couldn't find any. And I took them inside to some of the king's tombs so that we could escape the strong heat.

It was a long trip along the Nile and we were thirsty and were looking for some shade—couldn't find it. *Trees* were very scarce there. So we visited some tombs in the meantime to escape the strong heat and I showed them all some beautiful paintings in the king's tombs. Oh, the dream wasn't finished."

Example 4: Dream report scored as "doubtful."

Dream Suggestion. "You will dream in every dream tonight that you are rowing a boat."

Subject 4; awakened after 13.0 minutes in REM period 4.

"I was standing by our *pool* at home. Then I decided to call up my girl-friend for a date. That's all I can remember."

Example 5: Dream report scored as failing to follow suggestion.

Dream Suggestion. "You will dream in every dream tonight that you are swimming a river."

Subject 5; awakened after 8.0 minutes in REM period 3.

"I was taking a test. It was very much like filling out the form here tonight. You were in it, too. My EEG wires were all tangled up."

2. *Reduction in REM Time.* On the basis of the preliminary observations it had been hypothesized that the subjects must be dreaming in accordance with the suggested topic in order for the reduction in REM time to occur. This formulation implied that those subjects who failed to dream in accordance with the posthypnotic suggestion would also fail to show the reduction in REM time.

For the purpose of comparing REM time on experimental nights with the amount on control nights, it was decided to consider only the first 3.5 hours of sleep (210 minutes). The reason for adopting this arbitrary cut-off point was that it had been the experimenter's practice to awaken subjects after the first two REM periods in order to determine whether S was actually dreaming in accordance with the suggestion. This meant that uninterrupted sleep time was available only prior to this "check-awakening." Moreover, a cut-off point of 3.5 hours interrupted only a few "ongoing" REM periods, since a time of 210 minutes was one which fell very close to half-way between the end of REM period 2 and the onset of REM period 3 (when the overall pattern of REM periods for all the subjects was considered).

Measures of REM time for the first 3.5 hours of sleep were obtained on 14 out of the total of 16 subjects. In the case of the two remaining subjects (6 and 7) unbroken sleep records were available for only the first 1.5 hours of the night, a time period covering only REM period 1. Both of these subjects fell in group 3 as regards frequency of dreaming in accordance with the suggestion. All records were scored blind. A reliability check between two scorers for agreement on measurement of REM time yielded a correlation of 0.92.

For each subject, mean REM time for all experimental nights and mean REM time for all control nights were determined. Then the difference between the means of each subject's experimental and control nights was calculated. Those differences going in the direction of the "shortening effect" were classified as positive, those going in the other direction, as negative (see Table 2).

The Wilcoxon Signed Rank Test for Paired Observations (Siegel, 1956) was applied to the difference REM time between the experimental and control nights of the seven group 1 subjects—who were expected to show the shortening effect because of their ability to dream in accordance with the suggested topic ($P = 0.05$, two-sided).

It should be noted that for five of the subjects in group 1 the experimental night figures in Table 2 represent pooled data. In the case of these five subjects some of their experimental nights involved the use of multiple element suggestion—as contrasted with the single element dream suggestions already described. When a multiple element suggestion was employed, it meant simply that a subject was instructed to dream about a *series* of several events rather than just a single event. For a detailed breakdown of single versus multiple element nights see Table 3.

3. *Nature of the Underlying Psychological Mechanism.* The aim of this phase of the inquiry was to gain a better understanding of what it was in the trance or in the trance instructions that produced the shortening effect. While avowedly tentative, the main findings can be summarized as follows:

A. The character of the suggested topic, whether pleasant, unpleasant or neutral, did not alter the magnitude of the shortening effect (observations on one subject only).

B. A posthypnotic dream suggestion had to be operating in order

TABLE 3

Comparison of single and multiple element suggestion in reducing REM time
(first 3.5 hours of night)

S	Experimental condition	Number of nights	Range REM times	Mean REM time
2	Control	3	27–41	33.0
	Single element suggestion	1	36	36.0
	Multiple element suggestion	4	17–28	21.3
3	Control	3	43–52	47.3
	Single element suggestion	1	42	42.0
	Multiple element suggestion	5	31–55	40.4
1	Control	4	18–44	32.7
	Single element suggestion	6	17–25	21.4
	Multiple element suggestion	4	12–20	15.5
11	Control	3	14–29	22.3
	Single element suggestion	1	15	15.0
	Multiple element suggestion	3	3–23	11.5
8	Control	3	8–23	16.2
	Single element suggestion	3	2–22	8.7
	Multiple element suggestion	3	15–33	22.8

for the shortening effect to occur. With a trance alone, but no post-hypnotic dream suggestion, there was no reduction in REM time (observations on four subjects).

C. There was some indication that increasing the number of elements in the dream suggestion, i.e., instructing the subject to dream about a *series* of several events rather than just a single event, acted to decrease REM time even further.

Table 3 shows the data for the five subjects in group 1 (71% to 100% recall in accordance with suggestion) with whom the use of multiple element suggestion was examined. Of the five subjects, four showed an even greater reduction in REM time with multiple element suggestion than they had with single element suggestion. The exception was subject 8, who went rather sharply in the other direction.

While the N here was too small to establish any firm conclusions, certainly it can be said that the results of increasing the number of elements in the dream suggestion did not support the provisional hypothesis; namely, that giving the subjects more to dream about would act to increase their REM time. There was clearly no increase in REM time and, with most subjects, there appeared to be an even further decrease.

The above results, while far from comprehensive, have been included in order to indicate the potential fruitfulness of multiple element suggestion. Since this method appeared to be the only experimental variation that made any apparent difference in the magnitude of the shortening effect, it would seem the most promising lead for further inquiry as to the nature of this phenomenon.

COMMENT

1. *Alteration in REM Time*. The current study confirmed the earlier findings of Schroetter (1911), Roffenstein (1924), and Nachmansohn (1925) that subjects could be made to dream on the night following a hypnotic trance about topics suggested by the experimenter during the trance. Moreover, through the use of the REM-EEG approach to the study of dreaming as first described by Aserinsky and Kleitman (1953) it was established that, when instructed to do so, certain subjects will dream about the suggested topic in every REM period of the night. As indicated in the examples given in the results section, the successive reports from the same night were like variations on the basic theme provided by the suggestion. In each dream the influence of the suggestion was clearly visible; yet in each report, the material was embedded in a different context. In other words, the suggestions were incorporated into the dream's structure; i.e., the manifest content. The suggestion did not enter the dream as a separate entity but was contextually related to the nonsuggested dream content.

The present study provided some indication of the extent to which subjects dream in accordance with posthypnotically suggested topics—a point which had not been clarified in any of the earlier investigations. Of 16 Ss who achieved amnesia for a trial trance, seven produced reports in accordance with the suggestion from 71% to 100% of the time. Of the remaining nine Ss, five gave dream reports in accordance with the suggestion from 43% to 57% of the time, and four gave reports in accordance with the suggestion from 0% to 33% of the time.

In the group of seven subjects who dreamed regularly (71% to

100% of the time) in accordance with the suggested topic, it was observed that there was a reduction in the amount of REM time on experimental nights as compared with REM time on control nights when no posthypnotic suggestion had been operating ($P = 0.05$). This reduction in REM time was of interest in that it established that a psychological variable could be used to alter REM duration. In other words, presleep verbal stimulation—in the form of posthypnotic suggestion—influenced not only the content of dreams, but altered the lengths of REM periods as well.

A drawback of the current investigation was that some of the subjects were run much more frequently than others. Partly for esthetic reasons and partly for the sake of simplifying the data analysis, an equalization of the numbers of nights amongst the subjects would have been desirable. However, since the time and facilities for running were limited, the experimenter decided to concentrate on those subjects who regularly dreamed in accordance with the suggested topic (group 1). Throughout the study, it was the surmise of the experimenter that, whatever effects might arise from the use of hypnotic suggestion, they would be most readily apparent in those subjects who reported dreaming in accordance with the suggested topic. Consequently, rather than allotting more nights to Ss in groups 2 and 3, the individuals in group 1 were explored more intensively with a view to learning more about why certain of the subjects showed a reduction in REM time on their experimental nights. The most promising lead resulting from this phase of the study was the observation that giving the subjects more to dream about resulted in an even further reduction in REM time in four out of the five individuals tested.

2. *A Nonverbal Indicator of Hypnotic Hallucinations.* The shortening effect is of some relevance to the current controversy about the essential nature of hypnosis.

Orne (1959) has maintained that he could account for most hypnotic phenomena in terms of role-playing and increased motivation on the part of the subjects to follow the requests of the experimenter. Interestingly enough, the only hypnotic phenomenon which Orne found he could not duplicate through the use of simulating subjects was the hallucinations which could be made to occur in the deep trance state.

In summarizing the results of his investigations, Orne (1959, p. 298) expressed the view that the central and distinctive aspects of hypnosis lie in the individual's subjective experience of the phenomenon, and he concluded that:

. . . in the absence of objective indices of hypnosis the existence of trance may be considered a clinical diagnosis. Until an invariant index of hypnosis can be established, such a diagnosis must be confirmed by the subject's reports of alterations in his experience, since the real focus of hypnosis appears to lie in the subjective experience of the trance.

In the light of the foregoing statement, it would seem that a non-verbal indicator of the occurrence of trance phenomena might be of value for current research on the nature of hypnosis. Reduction in REM time could be useful in providing an observable indicator that hypnotic suggestion exercises some effect. The fact that those Ss who regularly reported dreaming in accordance with the suggested topic showed the reduction in REM time most clearly, lent further credibility to these subjects' reports that they were dreaming in accordance with the suggested topic.

It should be noted that Orne referred to the hallucinations occurring during the deep trance state. But it would seem that if the existence of the shortening effect enables us to accord greater credence to the subjects' reports of posthypnotically suggested dreams, it would be reasonable, also, to accord greater credibility to the reports from these same subjects of hallucinations occurring during the deep trance state.

The shortening effect is also relevant to a recent article by Barber (1962a), in which he raised some doubt as to the validity of posthypnotically suggested dreams. On the basis of postsleep recollections by some of his subjects, Barber contended that reports of posthypnotically suggested dreams may simply be constructions "made up" during periods of spontaneous wakefulness in an effort to comply with the experimenter's instructions. This is an important point. But it is my view that subjects actually do dream in accordance with the suggested topics. Several pieces of evidence from the present study are pertinent: (a) In the current investigation, even though all 16 subjects were chosen by the same criteria of hypnotic "ability," only *some* of these subjects regularly reported dreams in accordance with the suggested topic. (b) It was the latter subjects, group 1, who showed the reduction in REM time. (c) And, in four out of the five group 1 subjects who were tested, the use of multiple element suggestion led to even further reduction in REM time. (d) Moreover, if posthypnotically suggested dreams were actually recall of material "made up" in earlier spontaneous awakenings, then dream reports in accordance with suggested topics could reasonably be expected just as frequently from nonREM as from REM awakenings. However, in a series of nonREM awakenings conducted with four of the group 1 subjects (to be reported as part of a separate follow-up study), the percentage of awakenings yielding reports in accordance with the suggested dream topics dropped sharply. Thus only 47% of the nonREM awakenings yielded reports in accordance with the suggested topic, as compared with 83% for the same four subjects in REM awakenings. These figures on the incidence of REM versus nonREM recall were in general agreement with those of other studies employing similar methodology (Goodenough et al., 1959; Kamiya, 1961; Foulkes, 1962). (*e*) Finally, it should be pointed out that Barber's contention of posthypnotic dream reports simply representing recall from earlier spontaneous awakenings, can be applied just as readily to any type of dream report whatsoever (cf. Kamiya, 1961, p. 170).

3. *Suggested Dreams as a Technique in the Study of the Dream Process.* In the earlier studies of Schroetter (1911) and Roffenstein (1924), hypnosis had been used chiefly to confirm the Freudian theories of dream symbolism. The present study indicated that hypnosis may also be useful when it is desirable to have the subject dream about specific topics. While no analysis of content was carried out in this investigation, the fact that certain subjects would dream about the suggested topic in nearly every REM period of the night indicated the present technique may be useful in exploring questions about dream formation. For example, at what point in the sleep cycle does the subject begin to dream or think about the suggested topic? How is the topic elaborated? Are there any characteristic distortions which take place? Is there greater distortion at the end of a REM period than at the beginning of it? Questions such as these would seem amenable to investigation through the use of suggestion techniques employed in combination with the EEG monitoring of sleep and rapid eye movements.

This paper is based on a dissertation submitted to the University of Chicago in partial fulfillment of the requirements for the Ph.D in Psychology. The writer offers heartiest thanks to Dr. Joe Kamiya who sponsored this dissertation. His many valuable suggestions and his encouragement of the research in all its phases deserve the fullest measure of appreciation. To Dr. Allan Rechtschaffen the writer is indebted both for his reading of the manuscript and for his many valuable suggestions. Grateful acknowledgement is also made to Dr. Austin Riesen for his evaluation of the manuscript.

This study was made possible by funds provided from grant MH-05069-03, National Institute of Mental Health, United States Public Health Service, to Dr. Joe Kamiya, Department of Psychology, University of Chicago.

Bibliography[1]

Adler, G. (1948). *Studies in Analytical Psychology*. London: Routledge and Kegan Paul Ltd.

Amadeo, M., and Shagass, C. (1963). Eye movements, attention, and hypnosis. *J. Nervous Mental Disease*, 136, 139–145.

Andreer, B. V. (1960). *Sleep Therapy in the Neuroses*. New York: Consultants Bureau (International Behavioral Science Series).

Antrobus, J. S. (1963). The effects of varied and repetitive talking on visual vigilance performance under reduced external stimulation. Unpublished PhD. dissertation, Teachers College, Columbia University.

Antrobus, J. S., Antrobus, J. S., and Singer, J. L. (1964). Eye movements accompanying daydreaming, visual imagery and thought suppression. *J. Abnorm. Soc. Psychol.*, 69, 244–252.

Arkin, A. M., and Reiser, M. F. (1964). Experimentally produced sleep talking as a method of sampling sleep ideation. APSS, Palo Alto, Calif.

Arkin, A. M., Hastey, J. M., and Reiser, M. F. (1966). Dialogue between sleep-talkers and the experimenter. APSS, Gainesville, Fla.

Ås, A. (1963). Hypnotizability as a function of nonhypnotic experiences. *J. Abnorm. Soc. Psychol.*, 66, 142–150.

Aserinsky, E., and Kleitman, N. (1953). Regularly occurring periods of eye motility and concomitant phenomena during sleep. *Science*, 118, 273–274.

Aserinsky, E., and Kleitman, N. (1955). Two types of ocular motility occurring in sleep. *J. Appl. Physiol.*, 8, 1–10.

Barber, T. X. (1956). A note on "hypnotizability" and personality traits. *J. Clin. Exp. Hypn.*, 4, 109–114.

Barber, T. X. (1957a). Experiments in hypnosis. *Sci. Am.*, 196, 54–61.

Barber, T. X. (1957b). Hypnosis as perceptual-cognitive restructuring: I. Analysis of concepts. *J. Clin. Exp. Hypn.*, 5, 147–166.

Barber, T. X. (1957c). Hypnosis as perceptual-cognitive restructuring: III. From somnambulism to autohypnosis. *J. Psychol.*, 44, 299–304.

Barber, T. X. (1958a). Hypnosis as perceptual-cognitive restructuring: II. "Post"-hypnotic behavior. *J. Clin. Exp. Hypn.*, 6, 10–20.

Barber, T. X. (1958b). The concept of "hypnosis." *J. Psychol.*, 45, 115–131.

Barber, T. X. (1959a). The "eidetic image" and "hallucinatory" behavior: A suggestion for further research. *Psychol. Bull.*, 56, 236–239.

---

[1] The abbreviation APSS used in this Bibliography designates a paper delivered at the specified annual meeting of the Association for the Psychophysiological Study of Sleep.

Barber, T. X. (1959b). The after-images of "imagined" and "hallucinated" colors. *J. Abnorm. Soc. Psychol.*, 59, 136–139.

Barber, T. X. (1959c). Toward a theory of pain: Relief of chronic pain by prefrontal leucotomy, opiates, placebos, and hypnosis. *Psychol. Bull.*, 56, 430–460.

Barber, T. X. (1960a). The necessary and sufficient conditions for hypnotic behavior. *Am. J. Clin. Hypn.*, 3, 31–42.

Barber, T. X. (1960b). "Hypnosis," analgesia, and the placebo effect. *J. Am. Med. Assoc.*, 172, 680–683.

Barber, T. X. (1961a). Physiological effects of "hypnosis." *Psychol. Bull.*, 58, 390–419.

Barber, T. X. (1961b). Antisocial and criminal acts induced by "hypnosis"; A review of experimental and clinical findings. *Arch. Gen. Psychiat.*, 5, 301–312.

Barber, T. X. (1961c). Experimental evidence for a theory of hypnotic behavior: II. Experimental controls in hypnotic age-regression. *Intern. J. Clin. Exp. Hypn.*, 9, 181–193.

Barber, T. X. (1962a). Toward a theory of "hypnotic" behavior: The "hypnotically induced dream." *J. Nervous Mental Disease*, 135, 206–221.

Barber, T. X. (1962b). Experimental controls and the phenomena of "hypnosis": A critique of hypnotic research methodology. *J. Nervous Mental Disease*, 134, 493–505.

Barber, T. X. (1962c). Toward a theory of hypnosis: Posthypnotic behavior. *Arch. Gen. Psychiat.*, 7, 321–342.

Barber, T. X. (1962d). Hypnotic age-regression: A critical review. *Psychosomat. Med.*, 24, 286–299.

Barber, T. X. (unpubl.). Experimental studies on the symbolic and non-symbolic "hypnotic dream."

Barber, T. X., and Calverley, D. (1962). "Hypnotic behavior" as a function of task motivation. *J. Psychol.*, 54, 363–389.

Barber, T. X., and Calverley, D. (1963). The relative effectiveness of task-motivating instructions and trance-induction procedure in the production of "hypnotic-like" behaviors. *J. Nervous Mental Disease*, 137, 107–116.

Barber, T. X., and Calverley, D. (in press). "Hypnotic behavior" as a function of ego-involvement in a test situation. *J. Psychol.*

Barber, T. X., and Deeley, D. C. (1961). Experimental evidence for a theory of hypnotic behavior: I. "Hypnotic color-blindness without "hypnosis." *Intern. J. Clin. Exp. Hypn.*, 9, 79–86.

Barber, T. X., and Glass, L. B. (1962). Significant factors in hypnotic behavior. *J. Abnorm. Soc. Psychol.*, 64, 222–228.

Barber, T. X., and Hahn K. W., Jr. (1962). Physiological and subjective response to pain under hypnotically-suggested and waking-imagined "analgesia." *J. Abnorm. Soc. Psychol.*, 65, 411–418.

Barker, W., and Burgwin, S. (1948). Brain wave patterns accompanying changes in sleep and wakefulness during hypnosis. *Psychosomat. Med.*, 10, 317–326.

Barker, W., and Burgwin, S. (1949). Brain wave patterns during hypnosis, hypnotic sleep and normal sleep. *Arch. Neurol. Psychiat.*, **62**, 412–420.

Beigel, H. G. (1959). Mental processes during the production of dreams. *J. Psychol.*, **47**, 171–187.

Benussi, V. (1927). Zur experimentellen Grundlegung Hypnosuggestiner Methoden psychischer Analyse. *Psychologische Forschung*, **9**, 197–274.

Berger, R. J. (1963). Experimental modification of dream content by meaningful verbal stimuli. *Brit. J. Psychiat.*, **109**, 722–740.

Berger, R., and Oswald I. (1962). Eye movement during active and passive dreams. *Science*, **137**, 601.

Bernheim, H. (1947). Spontaneous dreams under hypnosis. In *World of Dreams* (Ed. R. L. Woods). New York Random House, pp. 426–430.

Bernstein, M. (1956). *The Search for Bridey Murphy*. New York: Doubleday.

Bolcert, E. (1965). The effects of thirst and a related auditory stimulation on dream reports. APSS, Washington, D.C.

Borlone, M., Dittborn, J., and Palestini, M. (1960). Correlaciones electroencefalograficas dentro de una definicion operacional de hipnosis sonambulica: Communicacion preliminar. *Acta hipnologica latinoamer.*, **2**, 9–19.

Brenman, M., Gill, Merton, and Hacker, F. J. (1947). Alterations in state of the ego in hypnosis. *Bull. of Menninger Clinic*, No. 11, 60–65.

Brenman, M. (1949). Dreams and hypnosis. *Psychoanal. Quart.*, **13**, 455–465.

Breuer, J., and Freud, S. (1895). *Studies in Hysteria*. Boston: Beacon Press, 1960.

Brownfield, C. A., (1965), *Isolation: Clinical and Experimental Approaches*. New York: Random House.

Brožek, J. (1962). Current status of psychology in the USSR. *Ann. Rev. Psychol.*, **13**, 515–566.

Burch, N., and Greiner, T. (1960). A bioelectric scale of human alertness: Concurrent recordings of the EEG and GSR. *Psychiat. Res. Reports*, **12**, 183–192.

Chertok, L., and Kramarz, P. (1959). Hypnosis, sleep, and electroencephalography. *J. Nervous Mental Disease*, **128**, 227–238.

Cobb, J., Evans, F. J., Gustafson, L. A., O'Connell, D. N., Orne, M. T., and Shor, R. E. (1965). Specific motor response during sleep to sleep-administered meaningful suggestion. *Percept. Mtr. Skills*, **20**, 629–636.

Cohen, S. I., Silverman, A. J., Bressler, B., and Shmavonian, B. M. (1958). Practical and theoretic difficulties in "isolation" studies. *Off. Nav. Res. Symposium on Sensory Deprivation*, Boston, Mass., June.

Craselneck, H. B., and Hall, J. A. (1959). Physiological changes associated with hypnosis: A review of the literature since 1948. *Intern. J. Clin. Exp. Hypn.*, **7**, 9–50.

Cubberly, A. (1947). How the normal dream is effected by tension on the body surface. In *The World of Dreams* (Ed. Ralph Woods). New York: Random House, pp. 819–827.

Davison, L., Breger, L., and Fahrion, S. (1966). The effects of exposure to one's own dreams, as revealed in subsequent dreams, GSR and heart rate. *Western Psychol. Assoc. Mtgs.*, Long Beach, Calif.

Directory of American Psychological Association (1965). Washington: Amer. Psychol. Assoc., p. 978.

Deckert, G. H. (1964). Pursuit eye movements in the absence of a moving visual stimulus. *Science*, 143, 1192–1193.

Deckert, G. H., and West, L. J. (1963). Hypnosis and experimental psychopathology. *Amer. J. Clin. Hypn.*, 5, 256–276.

Deikman, A. J. (1963). Experimental meditation. *J. Nervous Mental Disease*, 136, 329–343.

Dement, W. (1955). Dream recall and eye movements during sleep in schizophrenics and normals. *J. Nervous Mental Disease*, 122, 263–269.

Dement, W. (1960). The effect of dream deprivation. *Science*, 131, 1705–1707.

Dement, W. (1964). Experimental dream studies, in *Science and Psychoanalysis* (Ed. J. Masserman), New York: Grune & Stratton, Vol. 7, 129–184.

Dement, W. (1965). An essay on dreams: The role of physiology in understanding their nature, *New Directions in Psychology II*. New York: Holt, Rinehart, and Winston, 135–257.

Dement, W. C., Kahn, E., and Roffwarg, H. P. (1965). The influence of the laboratory situation on the dreams of the experimental subject. *J. Nervous Mental Disease*, 140, 119–131.

Dement, W., and Kleitman, N. (1955). Incidence of eye motility during sleep in relation to varying EEG patterns. *Fed. Proc.*, 14, 216.

Dement, W., and Kleitman, N. (1957a). Cyclic variations in EEG during sleep and their relation to eye movements, body motility, and dreaming. *EEG Clin. Neurophysiol.*, 9, 673–690.

Dement, W., and Kleitman, N. (1957b). The relation of eye movement during sleep to dream activity: An objective method for the study of dreaming. *J. Exp. Psychol.*, 53, 339–346.

Dement, W., and Wolpert, E. (1958). The relation of eye movements, body motility and external stimuli to dream content. *J. Exp. Psychol.*, 55, 543–553.

de Saussure, R. (1943). Transference and animal magnetism. *Psychoanal. Quart.* 12, 194–201.

Desoille, R. (1945). *Le Rêve Éveillé en Psychothérapie*, Presses Universitaires de France, Paris, Epuisé.

Desoille, R. (1961). *Théorie et pratique du rêve éveillé dirigé*, Genève (Suisse) Editions du Mont-Blanc SA.

Diamont, J., Dufek, M., Hoskovec, J., Kristof, M., Pekarek, V., Roth, B., and Velek, M. (1960). An electroencephalographic study of the waking state and hypnosis with particular reference to subclinical manifestations of sleep activity. *Intern. J. Clin. Exp. Hypn.*, 8, 199–212.

Domhoff, W. (1964). Night dreams and hypnotic dreams: Is there evidence that they are different? *Intern. J. Clin. Exp. Hypn.*, 12, 159–168.

Domhoff, B., and Kamiya, J. (1964a). Problems in dream content study with objective indicators: I. A comparison of home and laboratory dream reports. *Arch. Gen. Psychiat.*, 11, 519–524.

Domhoff, B., and Kamiya, J. (1964*b*). Problems in dream content study with objective indicators. II. Appearance of experimental situation in laboratory dream narratives. *Arch. Gen. Psychiat.*, 11, 525–528.

Domhoff, B., and Kamiya, J. (1964*c*). Problems in dream content studies with objective indicators. III. Changes in dream content throughout the night. *Arch. Gen. Psychiat.*, 11, 529–532.

Downing, J. J. (1964). Zihuatanejo: An experiment in transpersonative living. In *Utopiates: The Use and Users of LSD 25* (Ed. R. Blum). New York: Atherton Press, pp. 142–177.

Earl, C. J. (1941). A note on the validity of certain Rorschach symbols. *Rorschach Res. Exch.*, 5, 51–61.

Eiduson, B. (1959). Structural analysis of dreams: Clues to perceptual style. *J. Abnorm. Soc. Psychol.*, 58, 335–339.

Eisenbud, J. (1937). Psychology of headache: Case studied experimentally. *Psychiat. Quart.*, 11, 592–619.

Eisenbud, J. (1939). Method for investigating effect of repression on somatic expression of emotions in vegetative function: Preliminary report. *Psychosom. Med.*, 1, 376–387.

Erickson, M. H. (1935). A study of an experimental neurosis hypnotically induced in a case of ejaculatio praecox. *Brit. J. Med. Psychol.*, 15, 34–50.

Erickson, M. H. (1939*a*). Experimental demonstration of the psychopathology of everyday life. *Psychoanal. Quart.*, 8, 338–353.

Erickson, M. H. (1939*b*). An experimental investigation of the possible anti-social use of hypnosis. *Psychiatry*, 2, 391–414.

Erickson, M. H. (1944). The method employed to formulate a complex story for the induction of an experimental neurosis in a hypnotic subject. *J. Gen. Psychol.*, 31, 67–84.

Erickson, M. H. (1965). A special inquiry with Aldous Huxley into the nature and character of various states of consciousness. *Am. J. Clin. Hypn.*, 8, 14–33.

Erickson, M. H., and Erickson, E. M. (1941). Concerning the nature and character of posthypnotic behavior. *J. Gen. Psychol.*, 24, 95–133.

Erickson, M. H., and Kubie, L. S. (1938). The use of automatic drawing in the interpretation and relief of a state of acute obsessional depression. *Psychoanal. Quart.*, 7, 443–466.

Erickson, M. H., and Kubie, L. S. (1939). The permanent relief of an obsessional phobia by means of communications with an unsuspected dual personality. *Psychoanal. Quart.*, 8, 471–509.

Erickson, M. H., and Kubie, L. S. (1940). The translation of the cryptic automatic writing of one hypnotic subject by another in a trance-like dissociated state. *Psychoanal. Quart.*, 9, 51–63.

Erikson, E. H. (1954). The dream specimen of psychoanalysis. *J. Amer. Psychoanal. Assoc.*, 2, 5–56.

Erle, R. A. (1958). The representation of temporal features of events in hypnotically induced dreams: An exploratory study. Unpublished MA thesis, Clark Univ., Worcester, Mass.

Evans, F. J., and Schmeidler, D. (1964). Reliability of two observers scoring the Stanford Hypnotic Susceptibility Scale, Form C. *Intern. J. Clin. Exp. Hypn.*, **12**, 239–251.

Evans, F. T., Gustafson, L. A., O'Connell, D. N., Orne, M. T., and Shor, R. E. (1966). Specific motor response during sleep to sleep-administered meaningful suggestion: Further explorations. APSS, Gainesville, Fla.

Farber, L. H., and Fisher, C. (1943). An experimental approach to dream psychology through the use of hypnosis. *Psychoanal. Quart.*, **12**, 202–216.

Fenichel, O. (1945). *The Psychoanalytic Theory of Neuroses*. New York: W. W. Norton and Co.

Ferenczi, S. (1926). On forced fantasies. In *Further Contributions to the Theory and Technique of Psychoanalysis* (Chap. 4). London: Hogarth Press.

Field, M. G. (1961). Psychotherapy in Soviet society. *J. Contemp. Psychol.*, **6**, 12–13.

Fisher, C. (1953a). Studies on the nature of suggestion: Part I. Experimental induction of dreams by direct suggestion. *J. Am. Psychoanal. Assoc.*, **1**, 222–255.

Fisher, C. (1953b). Studies on the nature of suggestion: Part II. The transference meaning of giving suggestions. *J. Am. Psychoanal. Assoc.*, **1**, 406–437.

Fisher, C. (1954a). Constructions of dreams and images. *J. Am. Psychoanal. Assoc.*, **2**, 5–60.

Fisher, C. (1954b). Dreams and perception: The role of preconscious and primary modes of perception in dream formation. *J. Am. Psychoanal. Assoc.*, **2**, 389–445.

Fisher, C. (1957). A study of the preliminary stages of the construction of dreams and images. *J. Am. Psychoanal. Assoc.*, **5**, 5–60.

Fisher, C. (1960). Subliminal and supraliminal influences on dreams. *Am. J. Psychiat.*, **116**, 1009–1017.

Fisher, C. (1965). Psychoanalytic implications of recent research on sleep and dreaming. *J. Am. Psychoanal. Assoc.*, **13**, 197–303.

Fisher, C., and Dement, W. (1963). Studies on the psychopathology of sleep and dreams. *Am. J. Psychiat.*, **119**, 1160–1178.

Fisher, C., Gross, J., and Zuch, J. (1965). A cycle of penile erections synchronous with dreaming (REM) sleep. *Arch. Gen. Psychiat.*, **12**, 29–45.

Fisher, C., and Paul, I. H. (1959). The effect of subliminal visual stimulation on images and dreams: A validation study. *J. Am. Psychoanal. Assoc.*, **7**, 58–83.

Fiss, H., Klein, G. S., and Bokert, E. (1966). Waking fantasies following interruption of two types of sleep. *Arch. Gen. Psychiat.*, **14**, 543–551.

Fogel, S., and Hoffer, A. (1962). The use of hypnosis to interrupt and reproduce an LSD-25 experience. *J. Clin. Exp. Psychopath.*, **23,** 11–16.

Forer, B. R., Rabin, A. I., Goldstein, F. J., and Lesser, G. S. (1961). Custom-built projective methods: A symposium. *J. Proj. Tech.*, **25,** 3–31.

Foulkes, D. (1962). Dream reports from different stages of sleep. *J. Abnorm. Soc. Psychol.*, **65,** 14–25.

Foulkes, D. (1964). Theories of dream formation and recent studies of sleep consciousness. *Psychol. Bull.*, **62,** 236–247.

Foulkes, D., and Rechtschaffen, A. (1964). Presleep determinants of dream content: Effects of two films. *Percept. Mtr. Skills,* **19,** 983–1005.

Foulkes, D., and Vogel, G. (1965). Mental activity at sleep onset. *J. Abnorm. Psychol.*, **70,** 231–243.

Freud, S. (1920). *A General Introduction to Psychoanalysis.* New York: Permabooks, Doubleday, 1953.

Freud, S. (1931*a*). *The Interpretation of Dreams* (translated by J. Strachey). New York: Basic Books, Inc., 1960.

Freud, S. (1931*b*). Revision of the theory of dreams. In *New Introductory Lectures on Psychoanalysis.* New York: W. W. Norton and Co.

Freud, S. (1935). *An Autobiographical Study* (translated by J. Strachey). New York: W. W. Norton and Co., 1963.

Freud, S. (1938). The interpretation of dreams. In *Basic Writings of Sigmund Freud,* New York: The Modern Library.

Freud, S. (1959). Dreams and telepathy. In *Sigmund Freud: Collected Papers,* Vol. 4. (Ed. E. Jones). New York: Basic Books, 408–435.

Friedlander, J. W., and Sarbin, T. (1938). The depth of hypnosis. *J. Abnorm. Soc. Psychol.*, **33,** 281–294.

Fromm, E. (1951). *The Forgotten Language.* New York: Rineland and Co.

Fujisawa, K., and Obonai, T. (1960). The psychophysiological studies of hypnotic sleep. *Jap. J. Psychol.*, **31,** 94–101.

Gill, M. M., and Brenman, M. (1959). *Hypnosis and Related States: Psychoanalytic Studies in Regression.* New York: Intern. Univ. Press.

Glass, L. B., and Barber, T. X. (1961). A note on hypnotic behavior, the definition of the situation and the placebo effect. *J. Nervous Mental Disease,* **132,** 539–541.

Goodenough, D. R., Shapiro, A., Holden, M., and Steinschriber, L. (1959). A comparison of "dreamers" and "nondreamers": Eye movements, electroencephalograms, and the recall of dreams. *J. Abnorm. Soc. Psychol.*, **59,** 295–302.

Goodenough, D. R., Lewis, H. B., Shapiro, A., Jaret, L., and Sleser, I. (1965). Dream reporting following abrupt and gradual awakenings from different types of sleep. *J. Pers. Soc. Psychol.*, **2,** 170–179.

Goodenough, D. R., Lewis, H. B., Shapiro, A., and Sleser, I. (1965). Some correlates of dream reporting following laboratory awakenings. *J. Nervous Mental Disease,* **140,** 365–373.

Gorton, B. E. (1949). The physiology of hypnosis. *Psychiat. Quart.*, **23**, 317–343, 457–485.

Gorton, B. E. (1962). Current problems of physiologic research in hypnosis. In *Hypnosis: Current Problems* (Ed. G. H. Estabrooks). New York: Harper and Row, pp. 30–53.

Green, W. J. (1965). The effect of LSD on the sleep-dream cycle. *J. Nervous Mental Disease*, **140**, 417–426.

Gross, J., Feldman, M., and Fisher, C. (1965). Eye movements during emergent stage 1 EEG in subjects with life long blindness. APSS, Washington, D.C.

Gubel, I. (1962). Hallucinogenic drugs and hypnosis in psychotherapy. *Am. J. Clin. Hypn.*, **1**, 169 173.

Hacker, F. J. (1965). Psychology and psychopathology of symbolism. In *Psychology and the Symbol* (Ed. J. R. Royce). New York: Random House, 73–87.

Hall, C. S. (1948). Frequencies in certain categories of manifest content and their stability in a long dream series. *Am. Psychologist*, **3**, 274 (abstract).

Hall, C. S. (1951). What people dream about. *Sci. Am.*, **184**, 60–63.

Hall, C. S. (1953a). A cognitive theory of dream symbols. *J. Gen. Psychol.*, **48**, 169–185.

Hall, C. S. (1953b). *The Meaning of Dreams*. New York: Harper.

Hall, C. S. (1956). Current trends in research on dreams. In *Progress in Clinical Psychology*, Vol. II (Eds. D. Brower and L. E. Abt), New York: Grune and Stratton, 239–257.

Hall, C. S. (1962a). *A Manual for Classifying Aggressions, Misfortunes, Friendly Acts, and Good Fortune in Dreams*. Miami, Fla.: Inst. Dream Research.

Hall, C. S. (1962b). *A Manual for Classifying Characters in Dreams*. Miami, Fla.: Inst. Dream Research.

Hall, C. S. (1962c). *A Manual for Classifying Settings and Objects in Dreams*. Miami, Fla.: Inst. Dream Research.

Hall, C. S. (1962d). *A Manual for Classifying Emotions in Dreams*. Miami, Fla.: Inst. Dream Research.

Hall, C. S. (1963). Strangers in dreams. *J. Pers.*, **31**, 336–345.

Hall, C. S., and Domhoff, B. (1962). Content analysis of reported dreams. APSS, Chicago, Ill.

Hall, C. S., and Domhoff, B. (1963a). Aggression in dreams. *Intern. J. Soc. Psychiat.*, **9**, 259–267.

Hall, C. S., and Domhoff, B. (1963b). A ubiquitous sex difference in dreams. *J. Abnorm. Soc. Psychol.*, **66**, 278–280.

Hall, C. S., and Domhoff, B., Friendliness in dreams. *J. Soc. Psychol.*, in press.

Hall, C. S., and Van de Castle, R. L. (1966). *The Content Analysis of Dreams*. New York: Appleton-Century-Crofts.

Halpern, S. (1961). On the similarity between hypnotic and mescaline hallucinations. *Intern. J. Clin. Exp. Hypn.*, 9, 139–149.

Happich, C. (1932). Das Bildbewusstsein als Ansatzstelle psychischer Behandlung, *Zentr. Psychotherapie*, 5.

Happich, C. (1939). Bildbewusstsein und Schopferische Situation, *Deut. Med. Wochschr.*, No. 2.

Hartmann, E. L. (1965). The D-state: A review and discussion of studies on the physiologic state concomitant with dreaming. *New Engl. J. Med.*, 273, 30–35, 87–92.

Hathaway, S. R., and McKinley, J. C. (1943). *Manual for the Minnesota Multiphasic Personality Inventory*. New York: Psychological Corporation.

Hawkins, D., Puryear, H., Wallace, C., Deal, W., and Thomas, E. (1962). Basal skin resistance during sleep and "dreaming." *Science*, 136, 321–322.

Hilgard, E. R. (1963). Profiles of hypnotizability. Meetings, *Am. Soc. Clin. Hypn.*, San Francisco.

Hilgard, E. R. (1965). *Hypnotic Susceptibility*. New York: Harcourt, Brace and World.

Hilgard, E. R., and Tart, C. T. (1966). Responsiveness to suggestions following waking and imagination instructions and following induction of hypnosis. *J. Abnorm. Psychol.* (in press).

Horowitz, M. J., and Rashid, K. (1965). The use of captured dreams in psychotherapy and teaching. APSS, Washington, D.C.

Hoskovec, J. (1966a). A review of some major works in Soviet hypnotherapy. Unpublished manuscript.

Hoskovec, J. (1966b). Hypnopedia in the Soviet Union: Critical review of some recent major experiments. *Intern. J. Clin. Exp. Hypn.*, 14, 308–315.

Hoskovec, J., and Svorad, D. (1966). Recent literature on hypnosis from the European socialist countries. *Am. J. Clin. Hypn.*, 8, 210–225.

Howarth, E. (1962). Extroversion and dream symbolism: An empirical study. *Psychol. Rep.*, 10, 211–214.

Hunt, J. McV., and Confer, C. N. (1944). Psychological deficit. In *Personality and The Behavior Disorders* (Ed. J. McV. Hunt). New York: Ronald, 971–1032.

Huston, P. E., Shakow, D., and Erickson, M. H. (1934). Study of hypnotically induced complexes by means of the Luria technique. *J. Gen. Psychol.*, 11, 65–97.

Huxley, A. (1961). Freeing the mind. *Conference* (Sci. Info. Bureau), 2, No. 4, 2–6.

Imm, C. R. (1965). An exploration of repression through hypnotically implanted conflicts. Unpublished PhD. dissertation, Stanford Univ.

Jenness, A. (1965). Somnabulism, imagery and hypnotizability. Meeting, *Am. Psychol. Assoc.*, Chicago.

Jones, E. (1912). *Papers on Psychoanalysis* (Fourth Edition). London: Bailliere, Tindall and Cox, 1948.

Jones, R. M. (1962). *Ego Synthesis in Dreams. Cambridge*, Mass.: Schenkman Publ. Co.

Jouvet, M., Dechaume, J., and Michel, F. (1960). Étude des mécanismes du sommeil physiologique. *Lyon Med.*, **38**.

Kahn, E., Dement, W., Fisher, C., and Barmack, J. (1962). Incidence of color in immediately recalled dreams. *Science*, **137**, 1054–1055.

Kamiya, J. (1961). Behavioral, subjective, and physiological aspects of drowsiness and sleep. In *Functions of Varied Experience* (Eds. D. W. Fiske and S. R. Maddi). Homewood, Ill.: The Dorsey Press, Inc., pp. 145–174.

Kamiya, J. (1962). Conditioned discrimination of the EEG alpha rhythm in humans. Paper, *Western Psychol. Assoc.*

Kanzer, M. G. (1945). The therapeutic use of dreams induced by hypnotic suggestion. *Psychoanal. Quart.*, **14**, 313–335.

Kanzer, M. G. (1953). The metapsychology of the hypnotic dream. *Intern. J. Psychoanal.*, **34**, 228–231.

Kaplan, S. M., Gottschalk, L. A., Magliocco, E. G., Rohovit, D. D., and Ross, W. D. (1961). Hostility in verbal productions and hypnotic dreams in hypertensive patients. *J. Psychosom. Med.*, **23**, 311–322.

Klein, D. B. (1930). The experimental production of dreams during hypnosis. *U. Texas Bull.*, No. 3009, 5–71.

Kleitman, N. (1960). Patterns of dreaming. *Sci. Am.*, **203**, 82–88.

Kleitman, N. (1963). *Sleep and Wakefulness*. Chicago: Univ. Chicago Press.

Klemperer, E. (1961). Shortest distance therapy in hypnoanalysis. *Intern. J. Clin. Exp. Hypn.*, **9**, 63–77.

Krakora, B. (1953). Elektorencephalogram pri usiaani, spanku a hypnose. *Neurologie a Psychiatrie Ceskoslovenska*, **16**, 141–154.

Kremen, I. (1962). Subject expectations as a biasing variable in the study of dreaming. Paper, *Amer. Psychol. Assoc.*, St. Louis, Mo.

Krojanker, R. J. (1962). Training of the unconscious by hypnodramatic reenactment of dreams. *Group Psychother.*, **15**, 134–143.

Kubie, L. S. (1934). Body symbolization and development of language. *Psychoanal. Quart.*, **3**, 430–444.

Kubie, L. S., and Margolin, S. (1944). The process of hypnotism and the nature of the hypnotic state. *Am. J. Psychiat.*, **100**, 611–622.

Le Cron, L. (Ed.) (1956). *Experimental Hypnosis*. New York: Macmillan.

Lesser, R. M. (1961). The effects of subliminal stimuli upon images and dreams in the normal and hypnotic condition. Unpublished PhD. dissertation, New York Univ.

Levine, J., and Ludwig, A. M. (1965a). The hypnodelic treatment technique. *Conference on the use of LSD in psychotherapy*, Amityville, N.Y.

Levine, J., and Ludwig, A. M. (1965b). Alterations in consciousness produced by combinations of LSD, hypnosis and psychotherapy. *Psychopharmacologia*, 7, 123–137.

Lewis, J. A. (1965). Electrosleep: A review. APSS, Washington, D.C.

Lindquist, E. E. (1940). *Statistical analysis in educational research*. Boston: Houghton Mifflin.

Linton, H., and Langs, R. (1964). Retrospective alterations of the LSD-25 experience. *J. Nervous Mental Disease*, 138, 409–423.

Loomis, A. L., Harvey, E. N., and Hobart, G. A. (1936). Electrical potentials of the human brain. *J. Exp. Psychol.*, 19, 249–279.

Luria, P. A. (1932). *The Nature of Human Conflicts on Emotion, Conflict and Will: An Objective Study of Disorganization and Control of Human Behavior*. Philadelphia: J. B. Lippincott Co.

McCord, F. (1946). Report of hypnotically induced dreams and conflicts. *J. Pers.*, 14, 268–280.

McDowell, M. (1948). An abrupt cessation of major neurotic symptoms following an hypnotically induced artificial conflict. *Bull. Menninger Clinic*, 12, 168–177.

McKellar, P. (1957). *Imagination and Thinking*. New York: Basic Books.

Malmo, R. (1959). Activation: A neuropsychological dimension. *Psychol. Rev.*, 66, 367–386.

Mandell, M. P., Mandell, A. J., and Jacobson, A. (1965). Biochemical and neurophysiological studies of paradoxical sleep. *Recent Advan. Biol. Psychiat.* (New York) (Ed. J. Wortis), 7, 115–124.

Marcinowski, J. (1911–12). Gezeichnete Träume. *Zentr. Psychiat.*, 11, 490–518.

Maslow, A. H., Hirsch, E., Stein, M., and Honigham, I. (1945). A clinically derived test for measuring psychological security-insecurity. *J. Gen. Psychol.*, 33, 21–41.

Mazer, M. (1951). An experimental study of the hypnotic dream. *Psychiatry*, 14, 265–277.

Mixer, B. (1961). A comparison of hypnotic and nocturnal dreams. Unpublished MS thesis, Univ. Missouri.

Montagu, J. D., and Coles, E. M. (1966). Mechanism and measurement of the Galvanic Skin Response. *Psychol. Bull.*, 65, 261–279.

Moreno, J. L., and Enneis, J. (1948). *Hypnodrama and Psychodrama*. New York: Beacon House.

Moss, C. S. (1957a). A note on the use of the schizophrenic in Rorschach content analysis. *J. Proj. Tech.*, 21, 384–390.

Moss, C. S. (1957b). Dream symbols as disguises. *Etc.: J. Gen. Semantics*, 14, 267–273.

Moss, C. S. (1957c). A forced hypnoprojective fantasy used in the resolution of pseudoepileptic seizures. *J. Clin. Exp. Hypn.*, 5, 59–66.

Moss, C. S. (1958). Therapeutic suggestion and autosuggestion. *J. Clin. Exp. Hypn.*, 6, 109–115.

Moss, C. S. (1960a). Dream symbols as disguises: A further investigation. *Etc.: J. Gen. Semantics*, 17, 217–226.

Moss, C. S. (1960*b*). Current and projected status of semantic differential research. *Psychol. Record*, 10, 47–54.

Moss, C. S. (1961). Experimental paradigms for the hypnotic investigation of dream symbolism. *Intern. J. Clin. Exp. Hypn.*, 9, 105–117.

Moss, C. S. (1962). A mediation theory of symbolism as an aide to the experimental investigation of symbolic behavior. *Psychol. Record*, 12, 75–84.

Moss, C. S. (1965). *Hypnosis in Perspective.* New York: Macmillan Co.

Moss, C. S., Logan, J. C., and Lynch, D. (1962). Present status of psychological research and training in hypnosis: A developing professional problem. *Amer. Psychologist*, 17, 542–549.

Moss, C. S., and Stachowiak, J. G. (1963). The ability of hypnotic subjects to interpret symbols. *J. Proj. Tech.*, 27, 92–97.

Moss, C. S., Thompson, M. M., and Nolte, J. (1962). An additional study in hysteria: The case of Alice M. *Intern. J. Clin. Exp. Hypn.*, 10, 59–74.

Munroe, R. L. (1955). *Schools of Psychoanalytic Thought.* New York: Dryden Press.

Muzio, J., Roffwarg, H., and Kaufman, R. (1964). Alteration in the young adult human sleep EEG configuration resulting from d-LSD-25. APSS, Palo Alto, Calif.

Muzio, J., Roffwarg, H., and Kaufman, E. Alterations in the sleep EEG configuration resulting from LSD. *EEG. Clin. Neurophysiol.* (in press).

Nachmansohn, M. (1925). Ueber experimentell erzeugte Traeume nebst kirtischen Bemerkungen ueber die psychoanalytische Methodik. *Z. Neurol. Psychiat.*, 98, 556–586. In *Organization and Pathology of Thought* (translated by D. Rapaport). New York: Columbia Univ. Press, 1951, pp. 257–287.

Naruse, G. (1960). The abstract image in the post-hypnotic state. *Intern. J. Clin. Exp. Hypn.*, 8, 213–229.

Naruse, G. (1962*a*). A contribution to systematic understanding of modification in post-hypnotic and hypnotic hallucination. *Jap. J. Educ. Soc. Psychol.*, 3, 1–14.

Naruse, G. (1962*b*). Hypnosis as a state of meditative concentration and its relationship to the perceptual process. In *The Nature of Hypnosis* (Ed. M. V. Kline). Baltimore: Waverly Press, 37–72.

Naruse, G. (1965*a*). A genetic consideration of hypnotic hallucination. *Jap. J. Educ. Soc. Psychol.*, 5, 15–19.

Naruse, G. (1965*b*). Hypnosis in Japan. In *Hypnosis Throughout the World* (Ed. F. L. Marcuse). Springfield, Ill.: C. C Thomas, 191–204.

Naruse, G., and Obonai, T. (1952). Decomposition and fusion of mental images in drowsy and post-hypnotic hallucinatory state. *Jap. J. Psychol.*, 22, 175–188.

Naruse, G., and Obonai, T. (1953). Decomposition and fusion of mental images in the post-hypnotic hallucinatory state (II): Mechanism of image composing activity. *Jap. J. Psychol.*, 24, 203–217.

Naruse, G., and Obonai, T. (1954). Decomposition and fusion of mental images in the post-hypnotic hallucinatory state: The influence of perception on mental image. *Jap. J. Psychol.*, 25, 21–34.

Naruse, G., and Obonai, T. (1956). Figure-ground image reversal in the posthypnotic hallucinatory state. *Jap. Psychol. Res.*, 4, 1–10.

Newman, R., Katz, J., and Rubenstein, R. (1960). The experimental situation as a determinant of hypnotic dreams. *Psychiatry*, 2, 63–73.

O'Connell, D. N., Gustafson, L. A., Evans, F. J., Orne, M. T., and Shor, R. E. (1965). Can waking and stage 1 sleep always be told apart by EEG criteria alone ? APSS, Washington, D.C.

Offenkrantz, W., and Rechtschaffen, A. (1963). Clinical studies of sequential dreams. *Arch. Gen. Psychiat.*, 8, 497–508.

Orlinsky, D. (1962). Psychodynamic and cognitive correlates of dream recall. Unpublished PhD. dissertation, Univ. Chicago.

Orne, M. T. (1959). The nature of hypnosis: Artifact and essence. *J. Abnorm. Soc. Psychol.*, 58, 277–299.

Orne, M. T. (1961). The potential uses of hypnosis in interrogation. In *The Manipulation of Human Behavior* (Eds. Biderman and Zimmer). New York: John Wiley and Sons, Inc., 169–215.

Orne, M. (1962). On the social psychology of the psychological experiment. With particular reference to the demand characteristics and their implications. *Am. Psychologist*, 17, 776–783.

Osgood, C. E., Suci, G. J., and Tannenbaum, P. H. (1957). *The Measurement of Meaning*. Urbana: Univ. Ill. Press.

Oswald, I. (1962). *Sleeping and waking: Physiology and psychology*. Amsterdam, The Netherlands: Elsevier.

Oswald, I., Taylor, A. M., and Treisman, M. (1960). Discriminative responses to stimulation during human sleep. *Brain*, 82, 440–453.

Oswald, I., Taylor, A. M., and Treisman, M. (1961). Cortical function during human sleep. In *The Nature of Sleep*. Boston: Little, Brown, 343–348.

Peña, F. (1963). Perceptual isolation and hypnotic susceptibility. Unpublished PhD. Dissertation, Washington State Univ.

Pierce, H. W. (1957). Womb regression symbolism in hypnotically induced dreams. Unpublished MS Thesis, Montana State Univ.

Platonov, K. I. (1959). *The Word as a Physiological and Therapeutic Factor: The Theory and Practice of Psychotherapy According to I. P. Pavlov*. Moscow: Foreign Languages Publ. House.

Poetzl, O. (1917). Experimentell erregte Traumbilder in ihren Beziehungen zum indirekten Sehen. *Z. Neurol. und Psychiat.*, 37, 278–349.

Polster, E. (1950). An investigation of ego functioning in dreams. Unpublished PhD. dissertation, Western Reserve Univ., Cleveland, Ohio.

Public Health Service, Publ. No. 1389 (1965). *Current Research on Sleep and Dreams*. U.S. Govt. Print. Off.

Puryear, H. (1962). Personality characteristics of reporters and nonreporters of dreams. Unpublished PhD. dissertation, Univ. North Carolina.

Quay, H. C. (1952). Emotions in hypnotic dreams: A quantitative investigation. Unpublished MS thesis, Florida State Univ.

Rapoport, A. (1965). Discussant II. In *Psychology and the Symbol*, (Ed. J. R. Royce). New York: Random House, 95–105.

Rapaport, D. (1951). *Organization and Pathology of Thought*. New York: Columbia Univ. Press, 234–287.

Rechtschaffen, A., Verdone, P., and Wheaton, J. (1962). Reports of mental activity during sleep. *Can. Psychiat. Assoc. J.*, 7, 409–414.

Rechtscheffen, A., Wolpert, E., Dement, W., Mitchcll, S., and Fisher, C. (1963). Nocturnal sleep of narcoleptics. *EEG Clin. Neurophysiology*, 15, 599–609.

Regardie, F. I. (1949). Analysis of a homosexual, *Psychiat. Quart.*, 23, 548–566.

Regardie, F. I. (1950). Experimentally induced dreams as psychotherapeutic aids. *Am. J. Psychotherapy*, 4, 643–650.

Reis, W. J. (1951). Comparison of personality variables derived from dream series with and without free associations. Unpublished PhD. dissertation, Western Reserve Univ., Cleveland, Ohio.

Reyher, J. (1962). A paradigm for determining the clinical relevance of hypnotically induced psychopathology. *Psychol. Bull.*, 59, 344–352.

Reyher, J. (1963). Free imagery: An uncovering procedure. *J. Clin. Psychol.*, 19, 454–459.

Roffenstein, G. (1924). Experimentelle Symbol-Traeume: ein Beitrag zur Diskussion ueber Psychoanalyse. *Z. Neurol. Psychiat.*, 87, 362–372. In *Organization and Pathology of Thought*, (translated by D. Rapaport). New York: Columbia Univ. Press, 1951, 249–256.

Roffwarg, H. P., Dement, W. C., Muzio, J. N., and Fisher, C. (1962). Dream imagery: Relationship to rapid eye movements in sleep. *Arch. Gen. Psychiat.*, 7, 235–258.

Roffwarg, H. P., and Muzio, J. N. (1965). Sleep onset stage 1: A reevaluation. APSS, Washington, D.C.

Rokhlin, L. (1963). *Sleep, Hypnosis, Dreams*. Moscow: Foreign Languages Publ. House.

Rosen, J. N. (1953). *Direct Analysis*. New York: Grune and Stratton.

Rosenthal, R. (1963). On the social psychology of the psychological experiment: The experimenter's hypothesis as unintended determinant of experimental results. *Am. Scientist*, 51, 268–283.

Rosenthal, R. (1964). Experimenter outcome-orientation and the results of the psychological experiment. *Psychol. Bul.*, 61, 405–412.

Rosenzwerg, S. (1934). Types of reaction to frustration. *J. Abnorm. Soc. Psychol.*, 29, 298–300.

Rowland, L. (1932). The relation of judgments of excitement value to certain bodily changes shown during hypnotic dreams. *Proc. Okla. Acad. Sci.*, 12, 9.

Rowland, L. (1936). The somatic effects of stimuli graded in respect to their exciting character. *J. Exp. Psychol.*, 19, 547–560.

Rubenstein, R., Katz, J., and Newman, R. (1957). On the source and determinants of hypnotic dreams. *J. Can. Psychiat. Assoc.*, 2, 154–161.

Rubenstein, R., and Newman, R. (1954). The living out of "future" experiences under hypnosis. *Science*, 119, 472–473.

Rychlack, J. (1960). Recalled dream themes and personality. *J. Abnorm. Soc. Psychol.*, 60, 140–143.

Sabot, T. (1965). Sleep therapy—an exhausting review. APSS, Washington, D.C.

Sampson, H. (1965). The laboratory dream. APSS, Washington, D.C.

Scantlebury, R. E., Frick, H. L., and Patterson, T. L. (1942). The effect of normal and hypnotically induced dreams on the gastric hunger movements of man. *J. Appl. Psychol.*, 26, 682.

Schafer, R. (1954). *Psychoanalytic Interpretation in Rorschach Testing*. New York: Grune and Stratton.

Schiff, S. K., Bunney, W. E., and Freedman, D. X. (1961). A study of ocular movements in hypnotically induced dreams. *J. Nervous Mental Disease*, 133, 59–68.

Schjelderup, H. K. (1960). Time relations in dreams. *Scand. J. Psychol.*, 1, 62–64.

Schneck, J. M. (1947). The role of a dream in treatment with hypnosis. *Psychoanal. Rev.*, 34, 485–491.

Schneck, J. M. (1952). An experimental investigation of dual hypnotic dreams. *Brit. J. Med. Hypn.*, 3, 21–27.

Schneck, J. M. (1953a). Self-hypnotic dreams in hypnoanalysis. *J. Clin. Exp. Hypn.*, 1, 44–53.

Schneck, J. M. (1953b). The therapeutic use of self-hypnotic dreams. *J. Clin. Exp. Hypn.*, 1, 28–31.

Schneck, J. M. (1954). Dreams in self-hypnosis. *Psychoanal. Rev.*, 41, 1–8.

Schneck, J. M. (1963). *Hypnosis in Modern Medicine* (Third Edition). Springfield, Ill.: C. C Thomas.

Schonbar, R. (1961). Temporal and emotional factors in the selective recall of dreams. *J. Consult. Psychol.*, 25, 67–73.

Schroetter, K. (1911). Experimentelle Traueme. *Zentr. Psychoanal.*, 2, 638–648. In *Organization and Pathology of Thought* (translated by D. Rapaport). New York: Columbia Univ. Press, 1951, 234–248.

Schultz, J. H. (1964). *Das autogene Training*. Stuttgart: Geo. Thieme Verlag, 11th German Edition.

Shapiro, A. (1966). REM time, dream time, and amount of dreaming: A critical review and a reformulation of theoretical concepts. APSS, Gainesville, Fla.

Shapiro, A., Goodenough, D. R., Biederman, I., and Sleser, I. (1964). Dream recall and the physiology of sleep. *J. Appl. Physiol.*, 19, 778–782.

Shapiro, A., Goodenough, D. R., Lewis, H. B., and Sleser, I. (1965). Gradual arousal from sleep: A determinant of thinking reports. *Psychosom. Med.*, 27, 342–349.

Shor, R. E., Orne, M. T., and O'Connell, D. N. (1962). Validation and cross-validation of a scale of self-reported personal experiences which predicts hypnotizability. *J. Psychol.*, **53**, 55–75.

Siebert, K. (1934). Die Gestaltbildung im Traum. *Arch. Ges. Psychologie*, **90**, 357–372.

Siegel, S. (1956). *Nonparametric Statistics for Behavioral Sciences.* New York: McGraw-Hill Book Co.

Silberer, H. (1909). Bericht ueber eine Methode, gewisse symbolische Hallucinations-Erscheinungen hervorzurufen und zu beobachten. *Z. Psychoanal. Psychopath. Forsch.*, **1**, 513–525. In *Organization and Pathology of Thought* (translated by D. Rapaport). New York: Columbia Univ. Press, 1951, 195–207.

Simon, C., and Emmons, W. (1956). EEG, consciousness, and sleep. *Science*, **124**, 1066–1069.

Singer, J. L. (1966). *Daydreaming: An introduction to the experimental study of inner experience.* New York: Random House.

Singer, J. L., and Antrobus, J. S. (1965). Eye movements during fantasies. *Arch. Gen. Psychiat.*, **12**, 71–76.

Sirna, A. J. (1945). An Electroencephalographic study of the hypnotic dream. *J. Psychol.*, **20**, 109–113.

Snyder, F. (1963). The new biology of dreaming. *Arch. Gen. Psychiat.*, **8**, 381–391.

Snyder, F. (1965). Progress in the new biology of dreaming. *Am. J. Psychiat.*, **122**, 377–391.

Solovey, C., and Milechnin, A. (1960). Hypnotic phenomena, suggestion and oneiric activity. *Am. J. Clin. Hypn.*, **2**, 122–137.

Sperling, O. E. (1961). Variety and analyzability of hypnagogic hallucinations and dreams. *Intern. J. Psychoanal.*, **42**, 216–223.

Spiegel, H., Shor, J., and Fishman, S. (1945). An hypnotic ablation technique for the study of personality development. *Psychosom. Med.*, **7**, 273–278.

Stachowiak, J. G., and Moss, C. S. (1965). Hypnotic alteration of social attitudes. *J. Pers. Soc. Psychol.*, **2**, 77–83.

Stoyva, J. M. (1961). The effect of suggested dreams on the length of rapid eye movement periods. Unpublished PhD. dissertation, Univ. Chicago.

Stoyva, J. M. (1965). Posthypnotically suggested dreams and the sleep cycle. *Arch. Gen. Psychiat.*, **12**, 287–294.

Sutcliffe, J. P. (1960). "Credulous" and "skeptical" view of hypnotic phenomena. *Intern. J. Clin. Exp. Hypn.*, **8**, 73–101.

Sutcliffe, J. P. (1966). The relation of imagery and fantasy to hypnosis. Unpublished studies.

Svorad, D., and Hoskovec, J. (1961). Experimental and clinical study of hypnosis in the Soviet Union and the European Socialist countries: Bibliography. *Am. J. Clin. Hypn.*, **4**, 36–46.

Swartley, W. (1965). Initiated symbol projection. In *Psychosynthesis:*

A Manual of Principles and Techniques (R. Assagioli). New York: Hobbs, Dorman and Co., 287–303.

Sweetland, A., and Quay, H. (1952). An experimental investigation of the hypnotic dream. *J. Abnorm. Soc. Psychol.*, 47, 678–682.

Sweetland, A., and Quay, H. (1953). A note on the K scale of the Minnesota Multiphasic Personality Inventory. *J. Consult. Psychol.*, 17, 314–316.

Tart, C. (1962). Frequency of dream recall and some personality measures. *J. Consult. Psychol.*, 26, 467–470.

Tart, C. (1963). Effects of posthypnotic suggestion on the process of dreaming. Unpublished PhD. dissertation, Univ. North Carolina.

Tart, C. T. (1964a). A comparison of suggested dreams occurring in hypnosis and sleep. *Intern. J. Clin. Exp. Hypn.*, 12, 263–289.

Tart, C. T. (1964b). The influence of the experimental situation in hypnosis and dream research: A case report. *Am. J. Clin. Hypn.*, 7, 163–170.

Tart, C. T. (1965). The hypnotic dream: Methodological problems and a review of the literature. *Psychol. Bull.*, 63, 87–99.

Tart, C. T. (1966a). Types of hypnotic dreams and their relation to hypnotic depth. *J. Abnorm. Psychol.* (in press).

Tart, C. T. (1966b). Influencing the content of hypnotic dreams: Hypnotic dreams about "anything" versus "the meaning of hypnosis." APSS, Gainesville, Florida.

Tart, C. T. (1966c). Some effects of posthypnotic suggestion on the process of dreaming. *Intern. J. Clin. Exp. Hypn.*, 14, 30–46.

Toyoda, J. (1964). The effects of chlorpromazine and imipramine on the human nocturnal sleep electroencephalogram. *Folia Psychiat. Neurol. Japan.*, 18, 198–221.

Trillin, C. (1965). A third state of existence. *The New Yorker*, 58–125.

Troffer, S., and Tart, C. (1964). Experimenter bias in hypnotist performance. *Science*, 145, 1330–1331.

Trosman, H., Rechtschaffen, A., Offenkrantz, W., and Wolpert, E. (1960). Studies in psychophysiology of dreams: IV. Relations among dreams in sequence. *Arch. Gen. Psychiat.*, 3, 602–607.

Van Den Berg, J. H. (1962). An existential explanation of the guided daydream in psychotherapy. *Rev. Exist. Psychol. Psychiat.*, 2, 5–35.

Vogel, G., Foulkes, D., and Trosam, H. (1965). Ego states and dreams during sleep onset. APSS, Washington, D.C.

Volpert, E. A. (1966). *Dreams in natural sleep and hypnosis*. Leningrad (USSR): Med. Publ. Hse.

Watkins, J. G. (1946). The hypno-analytic location of a lost object. *J. Clin. Psychol.*, 2, 390–394.

Watkins, J. G. (1956). Projective hypnoanalysis. In *Experimental Hypnosis* Ed. L. M. LeCron). New York: Macmillan Co., 442–462.

Weiss, S. W. (1962). Hypnosis and dream production in a patient having migraine headache. *Med. Times.*, 90, 395–399.

Weitzenhoffer, A. M. (1957). *General Techniques of Hypnotism*. New York: Grune and Stratton.

Weitzenhoffer, A. M., and Sjoberg, B. M. (1961). Suggestibility with and without "induction of hypnosis." *J. Nervous Mental Disease*, **132**, 204–220.

Welch, L. (1936). The space and time of induced hypnotic dreams. *J. Psychol.*, **1**, 171–178.

Werner, H., and Kaplan, B. (1963). *Symbol formation: An organismic-developmental approach to language and the expression of thought*. New York: John Wiley and Sons.

Whitman, R. M., Pierce, C. M., Mass, J. W., and Baldridge, B. J. (1962). The dreams of the experimental subject. *J. Nervous Mental Disease*, **134**, 431–439.

Williams, H. L., Hammack, J. T., Daly, R. L., Dement, W., and Lubin, A. (1964). Responses to auditory stimulation, sleep loss and the EEG stages of sleep. *EEG Clin. Neurophysiol.*, **16**, 269–279.

Williams, H. L., Morlock, H. C., and Morlock, J. V. (1963). Behavior during sleep: Performance and EEG stages. Paper, *Amer. Psychol. Assoc.*, Philadelphia, Pa.

Winn, R. B. (Ed.) (1961). *Psychotherapy in the Soviet Union*. New York: Philosophical Library (Grove Press).

Wiseman, R. J. (1962). The Rorschach as a stimulus for hypnotic dreams: A study of unconscious processes. Unpublished PhD. thesis, Michigan State Univ.

Wiseman, R. J., and Reyher, J. (1962). A procedure utilizing dreams for deepening the hypnotic trance. *Am. J. Clin. Hypn.*, **5**, 105–110.

Witkin, H. A., and Lewis, H. B. (1965). The relation of experimentally induced presleep experiences to dreams: A report on method and preliminary findings. *J. Am. Psychoanal. Asoc.*, **13**, 819–849.

Wolberg, L. R. (1945). *Hypnoanalysis*. New York: Grune and Stratton, p. 184.

Wolberg, L. R. (1948). *Medical Hypnosis*, Vol. 1 and 2. New York: Grune and Stratton.

Wolpert, E., and Trosman, H. (1958). Studies in the psychophysiology of dreams: I. Experimental evocation of sequential dream episodes. *Arch. Neurol. Psychiat.*, **79**, 603–606.

Ziferstein, I. (1965). Direct observations of psychotherapy in the USSR. In *Selected Lectures: 6th Int. Congress of Psychotherapy, London, 1964*. New York: S. Karger, pp. 150–160.

Zubin, J. (1964). Criteria for the evaluation of the results of psychotherapy. *Am. J. Psychother.*, **18**, 138.

Index